This book is for my sister, Christine Vick, and grandpa,
Harry Davey, two inspirational writers who
I wish were alive to receive autographed copies.

Contents

Part II
Catching the Fish 49

Part III
Having Fun on Hardwater 231

Acknowledgments

Ice fishing can be lonesome. Images of distant solitary fishermen on windswept lakes are characteristic. But despite how individual the sport itself can be, amassing the data for this publication was surely a team effort.

The team's roots are deeply embedded at the home front. From my strong headed endeavor to produce a fishing and hunting magazine right through recent winters of ice fishing research (research is a euphemism for road trip), Leslie, my wife juggled responsibilities and continued to maintain a museum-quality homestead. Thanks to Carly, Amelia, and new arrival, Calvin, whom we like to call the urchins, for understanding that when dad leaves in the middle of the night he's heading to work.

Gratitude to my parents, Paul and Marilyn Vick, for exposing me to the outdoors at a tender age, and subsequently putting up with frogs in the garage and fish guts in the kitchen sink; to my brother Andy, for biking with me to Shingle Creek, and continuing to fend off my sharp tongue when we head out angling.

From an angling standpoint, special thanks to celebrated ice fishing icon, Dave Genz, who candidly volunteered his wisdom; to great friend Brian "Bro" Brosdahl for introducing me to winter angling and remaining an impeccable source for hot spots; to Dick "the Griz" Gryzwinski, whose decades of fishing wisdom transcends time; to Karl Kleman, who seems to always carry a horseshoe on the ice and photographs so well; to Tim Contreras, for drive and ice time companionship on countless expeditions.

Additional thanks to Tom Wilson, Chip Leer, Tom Gruenwald, Ward Julien, Greg Clusiau, and Jim Hansen, whose ice fishing knowledge was generously extended.

Hats off to Zippel Bay Resort (Lake of the Woods), Cyrus Resort (Lake of the Woods), Woodland Resort (Devils Lake, ND), Advenure

North (Leech Lake), and Moonlight Bay Resort (Leech Lake) for providing winter lodging and hands-on fishing advice.

Assembling the newest and best ice fishing equipment in one season is an expensive endeavor. So, special thanks to the following manufacturers who provided me with the right stuff: Ivan's Glo Tackle, Gopher Tackle Mfg. Co., Shearwater Fishing Tackle, Lindy Little Joe/System Tackle, Northland Tackle, Normark Corp., Bay de Noc Lure Co., Jig-A-Whopper, Inc., Alpha Omega Tackle Corp., JB Lures, Inc., Lake Country Lures, Sumner Bros., Gapen Company, Luhr-Jensen & Sons, Inc., Outdoor Creations, Inc., Gamakatsu, VMC, Inc., Feldmann Engineering & Mfg., StrikeMaster Corp., Zercom Marine/Humminbird, Vexilar, Inc., Sportsman's Connection, Fishing Hot Spots, Arctic Fishermen, HT Enterprises, South Bend, Glacier Glove, Straasburg Mfg., Thorne Bros., Red Barn Rods, Hansen's No-Match, Gemini Sport Products, USL Products, Polar Sled, Otter Sales, Canvas Craft, and King Crow Co.

Introduction

"FISHING IS NOT A HOBBY, IT IS A PASSION." I cannot credit this quote to any celebrated naturalist such as Henry David Thoreau or Ralph Waldo Emerson. Instead, this brief but profound statement is a mantra I live by. What distinguishes a hobby from a passion is the manner and intensity with which you approach an activity, and to what degree that activity consumes your mind and body. For example, a fishing hobbyist looks forward to an upcoming outing but does not allow it to interfere with his or her work, social schedule, and family life. In contrast, I, a passionate and nearly obsessed angler, cannot function normally during the days preceding a fishing trip. Thoughts of lunker walleyes and slab crappies eclipse personal responsibility. How can I remember to take out the garbage while I'm consumed with decisions such as, "Should we bring two- or three-dozen minnows?" or "I wonder if four-pound test line will be strong enough?" Is it fair to expect me to pick up baby formula and a gallon of milk when the grocery store is in the opposite direction of the bait shop? In reality, yes, but I think you catch the drift. Fishing is an important part of my life.

In the Midwest, where I live, freshwater angling has essentially two seasons: open water and hardwater (ice fishing). Up here, open-water season typically runs from mid-April through late November. Without question, most licensed anglers pursue their quarry when the air is warm, skies are blue, and summer breezes gently rock aluminum boats. Most fishing-related books, articles, radio broadcasts, and television shows pertain to open-water fishing, but the ice is shifting. Each season, more and more enthusiasts are lured in by the sport of ice fishing. In fact, ice fishing, along with fly-fishing, is the fastest growing segment of freshwater angling in North America's upper reaches.

Winter angling is unequivocally my favorite form of freshwater fishing, and I am not alone. Truth be known, countless anglers now prefer frozen water to open water. The sport is no longer regarded as a necessary evil for summer anglers who cannot endure an entire off-season without wetting a line.

What gives ice fishing its special allure? From the moment you travel onto an icy surface, you are ordained a degree of power and immersed in mystery. The power stems from having the ability to walk or drive, ice conditions permitting, across the surface of your favorite water. No need to own a fancy boat powered by a mammoth outboard motor. The best points, bars, and reefs are accessible by winter anglers of all socioeconomic classes. This power also enables you to pinpoint a location and reach the underwater world by simply popping a hole through the ice. The gateway is open. Empowerment derives from the ability to stand over your quarry. Mystery takes over the moment you forge a corridor to the underwater world. A single hole is your only means of accessing what was formerly approachable via every square inch of surface water. What lies beneath? A tug on the line, what is it? What will rise through your "aquatic" window? Power and mystery are eternal components of ice fishing, regardless of how often you embark; these elements keep me going.

Most anglers living in regions where lakes, rivers, and reservoirs freeze have at least dabbled in winter fishing. The scanty group of anglers who haven't ice fished, or have gone once or twice and don't intend to go again, either have utter disdain for cold weather or they never ice fished with adequate information and equipment. The content of this book is geared toward ice fishermen of all experience and knowledge levels. Casual winter anglers who are ready to get serious about this exploding winter sport, intermediate ice anglers desiring to increase their understanding of hard water, and advanced ice anglers who crave continuing technique and equipment information will benefit from the resource at hand.

First, this book gives winter anglers a detailed look at the equipment that has revolutionized an industry. We cover everything from time-proven equipment to the latest innovations to hit the market. Numerous pages are devoted to photos, detailed descriptions, and the functional uses of everything ice anglers employ. We put tools to the test. Trust me, this is the good stuff. I invite you to read along as our distinguished crew uses and examines portable fish houses, permanent fish houses, sleds, gas-powered and hand augers, electronics, rods, reels, line, tackle, heaters, lights, warm-weather clothing, snowmobiles, ATVs, and many related articles.

Introduction

Along with intense coverage of ice-fishing equipment, the book focuses on specific fishing methods for targeted species. In essence, if you are fishing for walleyes on a shallow rock pile during early ice, we're specific in guiding you with lure, line, rod, and reel selection, as well as recommending a precise jigging method. A broad offering of fishing generalizations not only insults readers, but also contributes little to improving your game. Our references are specific and accurate.

Chapters in the specialization by species section (part II) apply ice-fishing gear and methods to the specific species they were intended for. It would have been easier to write a chapter on the general use of tip-ups or a segment touting the merits of jigging spoons. Instead, we apply these methods to a particular species within a chapter devoted to that species. For example, we cover tip-up use in our walleye, northern pike, trout, hardwater exotics, and jumbo perch chapters. Successfully using tip-ups to catch a particular species requires varied techniques and custom rigging. The same is true for jigging. We include jigging methods and specialized lures in each species chapter.

Another trait that makes this book a must read for ice anglers is our use of fishing situations. We struck out to create an instructional piece that offered readers real-life ice-fishing illustrations. Educational books become bogged down, and even boring, if they incorporate too many hypothetical scenarios and mythical locations. We fished real lakes, rivers, and reservoirs to create this book.

You have likely noticed my use of the pronouns "we" and "our" during this introduction; there is a good reason. The "I" is myself, Noel Vick the author, but more importantly the "we" and "our" are the expert sources who contributed from beginning to end. I selected highly respected ice anglers to assist with individual chapters. For instance, guidance on the panfish chapter comes from noted experts Dave Genz and Tom Gruenwald, two legendary ice anglers. You may not recognize the names of all my sources, but believe me, these are the masters. Their knowledge stems from years and even decades of ice fishing.

I am confident that you will find this book the most informational, practical, and instructional fishing book you have ever laid hands on. Again, the intent of our publication is to apply ice-fishing theory, fact, and technical data to on-the-ice situations. Within these pages are countless hints, tips, and methods that continually reap fish for North America's best winter anglers, and we are now sharing the knowledge.

Part I

Gearing Up

Chapter 1

Staying Warm and Dry

I'VE ALWAYS MAINTAINED THAT ANYBODY CAN ENJOY FISH-ING IF SOMETHING'S BITING. An excellent example of this theory occurs when I tag along on private fishing charters with my wife and her coworkers. Her employer organizes sum-mertime fishing launches as a reward for meeting company goals. Participants range from serious anglers to folks who would rather be sitting on shore grilling bratwurst. What in-variably unites interest is a good walleye bite. Everybody be-comes attentive when the action is hot.

To expound on this philosophy, let's shift to ice fishing. Merely catching fish isn't always enough to appease the masses when temperatures hit the freezing mark. To enjoy themselves, winter anglers also need to be warm and dry. Before outfit-ting jigging poles, purchasing wax worms, or filling the power auger with fuel, make sure there's plenty of warm and water-proof clothing on hand.

A chapter devoted to warmth, dryness, and outerwear might appear tedious and a waste of reading, because the concept of dressing warm isn't revolutionary. This is true. So, instead we're recommending specific clothing items and layering tips that keep this author and other dedicated winter anglers cozy and warm all winter long.

Hands and Fingers

The Most Important Tools on the Ice.   Anglers and nonanglers alike know that fingers and toes are the first extremities to go when a chill sets in. Anatomically, fingers and toes are the farthest body parts from your heart, and the heart is the body's central boiler. So, to compensate for nature's design, you need to pay special attention to protecting extremities.

You need a good *feel* to detect strikes and nimbleness for tying on itty-bitty ice flies, both of which you lose when your hands go numb. Understanding this premise, there are two methods for keeping hands functioning properly. First, you can cover your hands with beefy mittens, poking your paws out as necessary to land fish, bait a hook, and so on. An alternative is to locate a pair of fitted gloves that are fully functional and waterproof.

Big Mitts and Deep Pockets

A heavy-duty pair of mittens or choppers that slip on and off easily is a must. Numerous manufacturers offer seriously warm and durable mitts. Whether you choose to purchase expensive name brands or less expensive models, make sure they're long (extending well beyond your wrist), loose, and waterproof, or at least water resistant. Long mitts are less susceptible to moisture entering the inner lining when reaching down a hole or pushing slush around. The best models extend up to the midforearm or elbow and feature Velcro or cinches to seal them onto your arm. Looseness is a major factor in maintaining warmth. Tightly fitting mittens and gloves hinder circulation, which in turn causes fingers to freeze.

The final determinant in mitten (or mitt) selection is their ability to repel moisture. Few mittens are 100-percent waterproof, but good ones repel water under most circumstances. Heavy wool and thick leather keep water out for quite a while.

At this point, I'm offering a little trade secret—military surplus gear. When it comes to outerwear, the military's demand for quality directly benefits outdoor enthusiasts. Products meeting stringent military cold-weather specifications certainly satisfy the needs of winter

4

anglers. U.S. Air Force arctic choppers are the live all, be all of hand protection. These heavy-duty mittens are remarkably warm, nearly impermeable, and slide on and off effortlessly.

An alternative to reliable mittens are deep pockets. In this instance, deep pockets doesn't refer to financial status, but to the depth and accessibility of your jacket pockets. Often, simply stuffing cold hands in warm and dry pockets for a minute or two does the trick. Large, accessible outer pockets are traits to look for in a winter jacket.

Neoprene

Ah yes, the rubbery, spongy stuff that keeps my hands comfortable all winter long. Neoprene, basically a layering of thinly sliced rubber and nylon, has been used by scuba divers and surfers for decades, stream trout anglers for 10 to 20 years, and its properties have recently been recognized by cold-weather anglers and hunters.

Neoprene gloves keep hands warm, even when wet, and seldom do they interfere with dexterity. Pictured is an affordably priced South Bend neoprene glove.

5

Neoprene's high insulation factor, flexibility, and resistance to moisture make it an ideal fabric for manufacturing into cold-weather gloves. Even thin, two-millimeter density neoprene gloves provide unmatched warmth. This thinness, combined with an overall elasticity, gives neoprene gloves their dexterity. You can reel, bait a hook, land icy cold fish, strike matches, and even start a gas auger while wearing neoprene gloves. About the only impossible task to perform while wearing them is tying a knot with fishing line.

Neoprene also fends off sporadic contact with water, but even if neoprene gloves become completely saturated, their insulating capabilities maintain a degree of comfort. On numerous occasions, I've dipped neoprene-covered fingers into an icy minnow bucket, jigged, iced a fish, and repeated the process for hours in relative comfort. Why do you think trout anglers who frequent cool streams and late-season duck hunters demand that their waders be made of neoprene?

Neoprene gloves are available in numerous styles and from several manufacturers. I prefer short (not extending too far past the wrist) models with Velcro straps for tightening at the wrist. Another important factor in purchasing neoprene gloves is fit. You want them to be close fitting. Snug, not tight, neoprene gloves improve dexterity, and in my opinion seem to do a better job of keeping fingers toasty. Glacier Glove, Berkley, and South Bend are a few manufacturers whose products I've worn and recommend. Neoprene mittens with fold-back tops and fingerless inserts combine the properties of neoprene with the inherent warmth of a mitten.

Feet and Toes

If These Get Cold, You're Probably Heading In.   Sure enough, if your hands become unbearably cold, it's easy to stuff them in a pocket or hold them beneath your armpits, but once the toes go, it's an entirely different animal. Unless you're parked on the ice and have access to a V-8 powered floor heater or you can seek refuge in a cozy ice shanty, things look bleak. Prevention is the best medicine.

Nothing Wrong With Frankenstein Boots

A quality pair of neoprene gloves goes for $20 or less. Heck, for $20 you can buy a bag of cotton socks or a dandy pair of wool ones, but when it comes to winter footwear, be prepared to drop a little more change. We're all familiar with the adage, "You get what you pay for." Well, in the case of cold-weather boots, the slogan rings true. Before setting a boot budget, you need to establish what characteristics a pair of boots needs to possess. Like hands, feet need to be warm and dry.

In boot building, warmth is a function of design and materials. Modern winter boot design is a complicated matter. You're confronted with Thinsulate, Thermax, ThermoPlus, Thermasorb, Centi-Grade, ComforTemp, and so on. Each passing season introduces a new state-of-the-art fabric or compound created to keep your feet warmer than the year before. Believe me, I'm not taking a jab at technology; instead, I'm saying that boot selection can be confusing if you get bogged down in marketing and terminology. Try to keep it simple. Start by going with time-proven manufacturers. I've had success wearing Sorel, La Crosse, Rocky, and Red Ball. These companies place boot building before secondary product lines such as jackets and gloves.

Your next step is determining which models feature the lowest temperature ratings. In this case, lowest temperature rating means the temperature the manufacturer believes a particular boot is effective down to. Industry leaders offer ratings at or below –100-degrees Fahrenheit. If you're like me, –100-degrees Fahrenheit is a temperature range for sitting beside a campfire and sipping coffee, not being exposed to the wrath of nature. So use budgetary prudence when considering anything rated lower than –100-degrees Fahrenheit.

Winter boots achieve low temperature ratings by incorporating insulating materials with effective sole design. Again, we're not comparing high-tech fabric to high-tech fabric; this is why it's important to be comfortable with a brand name. Insulating fabrics aside, make sure your chosen boots offer a decent tread with plenty of distance between your foot and the sole. It doesn't matter how much insulation surrounds the top and sides of your feet if there's a lack of insulation beneath your feet. The greater the distance between the ice and your feet, the warmer your feet will be! Why do you think most portable fish houses have floors? Try on boots to get a feeling for what models afford the most cushion and produce that peculiar elevated feeling. Boots giving you that strange floating-on-air sensation likely offer the greatest distance between the outer sole (ice) and the bottom of your foot.

Height of boot is another consideration. Numerous calf-high and taller models are now available. Nontraditional boot height combined with tightening devices are designed to keep snow from piling inside while trudging across frozen lakes. The Sorel Glacier and Chieftain, and La Crosse Winter Breaker are a few calf-high models sporting –100-degree Fahrenheit or greater ratings.

Most upper-end winter boots are waterproof, so if you buy top-of-the-line boots, exterior wetness isn't generally a concern. Internal moisture, on the other hand, is of concern. Better models feature insulation materials that wick, or draw moisture, from sweating feet and pull it past insulation contacting your feet and socks. Wet feet are cold feet.

Tough to Beat Bunny and Mickey

Of all the boots I've exposed to subzero temperatures, none have performed like U.S. military issue Mickey and Bunny boots. They're ugly and cumbersome. So what? If your feet are still happy at the end of the day, who cares if you look like the abominable snowman?

Bunny boots are white and Mickey boots are black. Other than color, the primary difference between them is temperature rating. Bunnies are effective to slightly lower temperatures than Mickeys. However, as I've told anyone who inquires about the variance, it's

Military surplus Bunny boots are 100-percent waterproof, amazingly warm, and affordable when available.

like the difference between being really comfortable and really, really comfortable.

The method behind the madness is design. Deep inside their hideous exterior is an ingenious layering of felt liners and rubber that traps heat yet allows moisture to escape. They're so remarkable that even when completely filled with water they retain heat.

Beta, the primary contracting Mickey and Bunny boot manufacturer, built tons of these beauties from the Korean War until the late 1980s. The military then switched to lighter Gore-Tex boots and production of Mickey and Bunny boots ceased, as we knew it. What's left in the marketplace derive from military surplus outlets, both retail and Internet based. Get your paws on a pair of these before they're gone forever!

Boots Don't Matter If the Socks Aren't Right

There are various theories regarding what type of sock or combination of socks is the warmest. You hear about multiple sock-layering methods, single thick wool applications, and even a few that involve women's nylons; yes, they're out there. Regardless of what novel mixture of sock fabrics and thickness you work with, dryness is the key to warmth.

The biggest mistake ice fishermen make, which inevitably leads to numb toes, is starting with wet feet. Imagine this scenario: You're driving 200 miles under cold, dark skies hoping to arrive at a lake access by sunrise. The truck's heater blasts hot air while your thoroughly insulated feet sweat like a tax evader during an IRS audit. You finally arrive, jump out into the chilly night, and, as outside air temperatures reach your moistened socks, things get uncomfortable and, eventually, downright miserable. The moral of this tale is to always begin with dry socks. So, on long road trips, you should either pack a second pair of socks to slip on at arrival or wear light shoes, instead of boots, while driving.

Regarding sock selection, I advocate one good pair of socks rather than layering. A single wool or cotton-wool blend sock inside a quality boot is a formidable team. Multiple socks frequently generate unwanted perspiration, which can lead to frosty feet. Another problem often encountered when layering socks is impeded circulation, and nothing ices feet faster than a lack of blood flow.

The only form of sock layering I support is slipping on a thin pair of neoprene socks and covering them with light wool or cotton socks.

9

The neoprene wicks moisture away from the skin and draws it into the outer wool or cotton sock. As we discussed earlier, neoprene is a tremendous insulator.

Head and Neck

Capping and Wrapping the Body's Smokestack. Experts agree that the human head is the primary suspect of body heat loss in cold weather. Everybody knows that heat rises, right? Body heat also rises and at a rapid rate in chilling conditions. Scientists contend that things do not get cold; instead, cooling is a factor of heat loss. Relating this premise to winter angling, you can minimize heat loss by wearing proper head-gear such as

- stocking caps,
- fleece hoods, and
- helmet liners.

A basic wool stocking cap suffices 9 out of 10 times. Wool caps meet two requirements of effective winter head coverings. For one, wool's insulating ability keeps heat from escaping through your head. Two, a wool stocking cap covers your ears, and ears are among the first extremities to fall victim to frigid air. Inexpensive and extremely warm, a military surplus navy watch cap is my first choice.

The next tier in head wear is for times a simple stocking cap won't do. When outside temperatures hover around zero-degrees Fahrenheit, and the windchill factor makes matters worse, you need serious protection. Weather like this demands that you cover as much of your head, face, and neck as possible. Whipping winds have a way of finding weak spots in your armor, and nothing spawns the chills faster than a wicked draft. Times like these call for pullover hoods, helmet liners, and masks.

Polar Hood from Syndicate Sales and Head Sokz are two pullover hood brands that are popular with skiers, snowboarders, and a few prepared anglers. Now that they're available in subtler colors and camouflage patterns, more sports enthusiasts will be slipping them on in the future. Synthetic fleece, or polar fleece, is the secret to their success. Polar fleece is soft, lightweight, warm, and it wicks moisture away like neoprene.

Adding to polar fleece's effectiveness is the unique design of these hoods. Their long neck fabric, combined with toggles and strings, allows you to wear them in multiple manners. Use them as a neck warmer, full hood, full hood and face mask, neck warmer and face mask, or long stocking cap. They cover the gamut from a simple head covering to extreme cold-weather protection for your head, face, and neck.

Another interesting and effective head covering, once again, comes from military stockpiles. Pilot helmet liners, originally used by armed forces from around the world, are warm and custom fitted. The U.S. Army's extreme cold-weather (ECW) helmet liner is perfect for ice fishing. Numerous military surplus stores carry them in hat sizes ranging from 7 to 7 3/4. These shops should also handle military issue polypropylene hoods. Poly hoods are an inexpensive means for protecting your head and neck.

Speaking of necks, no matter how well covered your head might be, all is for naught if prevailing winds continually contact your neck. Although polar fleece hoods offer neck protection, helmet liners and stocking caps do not. Neck protection should be a function of your thermal undergarments or outer jacket. Wear long johns featuring a turtleneck, or pull a separate turtleneck sweatshirt over a thermal underwear top. High-collared winter jackets, with a hood, provide additional wind defense.

A separate face mask is a final headgear consideration if you're wearing a stocking cap or helmet liner without a built-in mask. Snugly fitting neoprene face masks do a superb job. Look for them in ski and snowmobile shops or larger sporting goods outlets.

Outerwear and Innerwear

Covering the Mainframe.   "A system is as good as the weakest link." This adage pertains to countless situations encountered throughout life. In the case of cold-weather clothing, it means that every article of clothing, from head to foot, needs to do its job or the system fails. So, although you've followed my hand, head, and foot suggestions, if you don't put equal effort into dressing your torso, there will be hell to pay—an icy hell.

One beauty of ice fishing is the lack of beauty. What does this mean? Take a gander at clothing in a ski shop and look for a common theme. This component is evident if you catch a group of hard-core snowmobilers parked and jaw jacking at a trail crossing. What is the tie that binds? Fashion! Vanity is important to those who ski and sled, and

11

narcissism comes at a price. Color-coordinated helmets, jackets, bib overalls, boots, and above all, snowmobiles don't come cheap. Fortunately, style isn't a primary concern for winter anglers. We might be a motley crew, but we'd rather be ugly and toasty than pretty and frozen.

Thermal Underwear and Layering

Whether an ice-fishing experience is pleasant or miserable is often dictated by underwear. Huh? After stepping out of the shower, the first clothing to contact your skin is the most crucial. Start with a quality matched set of thermal underwear tops and bottoms; 100-percent cotton works fine. There's nothing wrong with blended materials, either, but without hesitation, I reach for my polypropylene stuff when outside temperatures are of consequence. The wicking ability of polypropylene is important to maintaining dryness, and as an insulator, this synthetic material has few rivals. I prefer polypropylene tops with built-in turtlenecks. With no surprise, military surplus outlets commonly sell affordably priced polypropylene underwear sets.

Next, cover your polypropylene undergarments with a loose-fitting pair of cotton sweatpants and a sweatshirt. This second layer adds warmth, plus acts as a receiver for moisture wicked through the polypropylene. You might consider adding a cotton or cotton-polyester blend, long-sleeved turtleneck shirt beneath the sweatshirt if your long underwear top does not offer neck coverage.

In the process of putting on long underwear and sweats, you've established layering. Anyone who spends a great deal of time outdoors will tell you multiple layers outperform singular, heavy garments. Formed between clothing layers are pockets of air that accentuate insulation, and you can always remove layers if you get too warm.

The Right Jacket and Pants

There are tons of winter jackets on the market, varying from simple, no-name discount versions to expensive custom-made arctic parkas. What's an ice angler to do? Can you gauge quality based on price? Yes, but not completely, because if you put serious effort into layering undergarments, reliance on a winter jacket's thermal properties somewhat diminishes.

Here's my personal criterion for a satisfactory ice-fishing coat:

1. It needs to be rated for use in cold to extreme conditions.

2. The outer shell must be waterproof, which also means windproof.

3. It has to offer a high insulated collar with a hood.

4. There have to be pockets galore—places for minitackle boxes, matches, and so on.

5. The wrists should have Velcro adjustments to keep the snow out and allow you to slip them inside arctic mitts.

6. I prefer parka-length jackets, but they are not necessary—the extra length keeps your behind warm when sitting on a cold bucket. Waterfowlers who ice fish are fortunate because the prescribed jacket is the same one they use for duck hunting. Of course, camouflage is optional when ice fishing.

Covering your lower half, or legs, is partially accomplished if you followed my earlier recommendations regarding thermal underwear and sweatpants. The criterion for cold-weather pants includes much of what I named in the previous paragraph, such as being waterproof, windproof, and insulated.

In extreme cold situations, insulated bibs, or snowmobile pants, meet the challenge. They're warm, waterproof (in most cases),

Creepers, by Straasburg MFG, effortlessly strap on to winter boots, creating a slip-resistant combination for walking on frozen surfaces.

13

windproof, and overall bibs keep waistlines covered while throwing in an extra layer of insulation over your chest and back. Your friendly neighborhood military surplus store handles awesome extreme cold-weather pants. There are several types of wool-lined pants in the surplus market. The extreme cold-weather navy deck pant is a favorite of mine; opt for an impermeable version if available.

An alternative in milder conditions, or if you spend time in a portable fish house, is to throw a durable pair of rain pants over long johns and sweats. Durable means a woven fabric (waterproof) outer shell, because inexpensive, plastic rain pants will rip and crack in freezing conditions. Manufacturers such as Columbia, Fenwick, and Walls make what I call fishing pants, a cross between rain pants and snowmobile pants. Lightweight, waterproof, insulated, durable, reinforced in critical areas (knees and seat), suspender design—these are fantastic for ice fishing.

A final suggestion comes from my experience wade fishing in cold rivers and late-season duck hunting. Seek a pair of stocking foot (no boot) neoprene chest waders. Next, grab a pair of military surplus Mickey or Bunny boots at least one size larger than you'd typically wear. You need the extra room to accommodate thick neoprene stockings. Slap the two together, and you're wearing the world's warmest and driest lower body coverings. Admittedly, the conglomeration makes one look like a chicken with Frankenstein feet, but it works.

A Final Thought

Staying warm and dry ensures more time on the ice and the opportunity to catch more fish. Remember these basics, and you'll be better suited to endure winter's wrath:

- Protect hands and fingers.
- Invest in quality boots.
- Wear weather-specific socks and keep them dry.
- Cover your head and neck.
- Put on thermal underwear as a foundation.
- Dress in layers to accommodate temperature changes.
- Wear the right jacket and pants to stay warm and dry.

Chapter 2

Choosing a Fish House

THE PREVIOUS CHAPTER DELVED INTO WHAT A WINTER ANGLER REQUIRES TO KEEP WARM ON THE INSIDE, THAT IS INTERNALLY, PHYSICALLY, BY DRESSING WARM ON THE OUTSIDE. What I may have overlooked in describing the perfect outdoor outfit is that educated ice fishermen spend as little time as possible exposed to winter's raw fury. Instead, they prefer burrowing inside a fish house, or ice shanty, as old-timers and cast members of *Grumpy Old Men* affectionately refer to them. In short, it's unnecessary to bundle up and brave outside conditions when there's a cozy fish house awaiting a tenant.

The primary functions of a fish house are similar to that of outerwear. Fish houses, like suitable winter apparel, need to keep their host insulated, dry, and protected from cutting winds. A gamut of designs, ranging from fast-setting portable models to elaborate permanent structures, meet these parameters.

Portable Fish Houses

Comfortable, Mobile, and Changing the Way We Fish. Extensive outerwear isn't critical to those who spend most of their time angling from a shelter. With the passing of each winter season, more hardwater anglers rely on portable fish houses.

Portable, when referring to ice-fishing shelters, speaks to any structure that you can erect, fish in, collapse, and remove from the ice during a single outing. The range of designs is far reaching. Today's market bears a selection of portable fish houses that meet the diverse demands of modern anglers who've crawled out of ice fishing's primordial ooze. The days of enduring bone-chilling temperatures and stinging winds are over. In my estimation, based on the affordability of portable houses, there's no longer a legitimate reason for sitting on a frozen bucket. I would much rather hook, catch, and release fish from the comfortable confines of a portable fish house than painstakingly hunch over an icy hole that requires constant skimming.

Portable fish houses fall into three categories.

1. Suitcase-style houses—old fashioned, but still popular. When fully collapsed, they neatly fold into what looks like an over-sized artist attaché case. Most models offer wood floors, canvas walls, and steel or aluminum internal framing; suitcase-style portables are often built by local canvasing businesses.

2. Second-generation suitcase-type portables. Most have synthetic walls, a composite floor that doubles as an equipment-carrying sled, and steel tube framing.

3. Trap-type portables (coined from Fish Trap) pioneered by ice-fishing legend, Dave Genz. These feature manufactured floors, canvas or synthetic walls, and a unique tubing system that allows users to quickly cover and uncover themselves while seated. Each category has its own place and time on the ice, and many winter anglers own more than one type of portable fish house.

Trap-Type Portables

Let's give credit where credit is due. A couple decades ago, an energetic Minnesota angler named Dave Genz developed the first truly portable fish house. Suitcase-style portables were already in use, but Dave needed a fish house that fished the way he did, which was, "on the move." So one day Dave hunkered down in his workshop, and lo and behold, his brainchild evolved into a revolutionary product. Dave's blood, sweat, and tears manifested themselves into what we know as the Fish Trap. It ice fished like a boat. Meaning, Dave had constructed a portable fish house that could move from location to location on the ice as readily as a boat on open water. It retracted like a caterpillar, offered comfortable seating, had ample storage, and most important, could uproot and move with little effort.

Today's Fish Trap looks slightly different than the original white canvas and plywood models he peddled years ago, but the concept and quality are still there. Dave's influence on ice fishing is evident in numerous facets of the sport, but nowhere is his ingenuity more prevalent than in portable fish house design. Over the past several years, other companies have developed portable fish houses embodied after the original Fish Trap. Believe me, there are some good ones out there. Mobile-minded winter anglers can now choose from several trap-type portable fish houses.

Fish Trap and Fish Trap II (USL Products)

Hard-core anglers like to call it the Trap Attack. That's when a group of fishermen, each sporting their own Fish Trap, assault a body of

Customization is a common practice among portable fish house owners. Here, you can see what professional bass fisherman Mark Fisher has done to his stock Fish Trap. Notice the Coleman back rest; utilities holder for hemostats, clippers, tape measure; brackets to hold frame sections; and hanging baskets for food, gloves, propane canisters, and trash.

water, fan out, and keep moving until they engage active fish. It's an awesome sight when a half dozen or more Fish Traps leapfrog across the ice!

The original Fish Trap, now built and marketed by USL Products in Plymouth, Minnesota, and still under the watchful eye of Dave Genz, has a floor that doubles as an equipment sled with a built-in adjustable bench seat. Once collapsed, the lightweight sled is perfect for dragging your gear across the frozen tundra. The elevated bench seat eliminates the need for a bucket or chair to sit on, hence freeing storage space.

As much as I like the Fish Trap, a one-person portable, rarely do I hit the ice without my Fish Trap II. Considered a two-person portable fish house, I prefer using the Fish Trap II as a roomy one-person vessel. Instead of opening front to back like the Fish Trap, the larger Fish Trap II opens from side to side, creating space for its two adjustable bench seats. I usually sit on the left bench (being right-handed) and spread odds and ends across the open seat. The larger Fish Trap II also provides wider spaces between holes, creating room for heaters, flashers, lanterns, and minimizes line tangling, but don't get me wrong, the Fish Trap II is still big enough to accommodate two anglers, as it was intended.

Otter Skin by Canvas Craft

Entering the trap-type market in the early 1990s was an established Minnesota boat-canvasing outfit named Canvas Craft. They took the basic flip-over portable design and gave it a few twists.

The Otter Skin, as it's dubbed, is a combination of an Otter Sled, a polyethylene sled manufactured by Otter Sales in Maple Lake, Minnesota, and Canvas Craft's original framework and canvasing. The result is a portable fish house featuring a deep and durable sled, sturdy framing, and a canvas shell of the highest quality. The sleds are roomy, offering oodles of storage space, and their elevated bow plows through heavy snow without sacrificing passengers or payload. Another feature of an Otter Skin portable is its coloration, or lack thereof. From inside, the black sled and canvas allow outside light to effectively radiate through the ice, snow, and holes beneath your feet, providing maximum visibility. Otter Skins by Canvas Craft come in four sizes, ranging from an efficient two-person model to their massive four-person extra-large model, which boasts a 6-foot 6-inch ceiling and 11-foot-by-6-foot 8-inch horizontal dimensions when fully opened. Snowmobile and ATV towing kits are optional.

Otter House and Otter Resort by Otter Sales

Otter Sales further expands the flip-over market with a line of superb sled/fish house combos, which are available in green (Packers) and purple (Vikings); it's a marketing thing. All models offer two-way zippered doors, flame retardant 11-ounce canvas, and both back and front windows with flaps. Their rugged polyethylene sleds feature molded runners, and the high sides and raised bow hold loads of gear; snowmobile and ATV trailer hitches are optional.

Polar Sled Flip-Overs

Expanding on the variety of pop-over or flip-over portable fish houses available to consumers is Polar Sled in Buffalo, Minnesota. Company proprietor, Jim Thielen, knows that he's entered a highly competitive marketplace, so he banks on the fact that knowledgeable winter anglers demand quality. Features such as 11-ounce poly/cotton

A roomy and mobile Otter Sales portable shelter attaches to a snowmobile. Most flip-over portables have optional snowmobile and ATV hitches.

The flip-over category of portables has molded synthetic floors that double as carrying sleds and the industry's fastest setup times. The result is a practical and highly mobile fish house. Pictured is a two-person portable by Polar Sled of Buffalo, Minnesota; generous interior space and a deep sled are merits of the Polar Sled line.

canvas (seriously heavy), all-aluminum framing, and rear zip-out ventilation (cross breeze) are standard. Additionally, purchasers can select from yellow, black, or blue houses; all of which feature black roofs. Dark tops retain warmth and promote illumination from below.

Ice Ranger by Frabill

Frabill, a great friend to ice anglers, hailing from Allenton, Wisconsin, comes to the plate with several portable fish house designs, and the Ice Ranger, like their other models, fills a specific need. They build Ice Rangers for organized anglers who tote everything but the kitchen sink, yet don't want to be anchored to a spot.

There are several notable features on the Ice Ranger. For one, its deeply sided sled walls accommodate a five-gallon bucket, locator, auger, tackle, tip-ups, rods, and a built-in seat. The four-position flip-over windbreak, when fully opened, provides outstanding headroom and horizontal space for a fish house of its size—truly a fantastic one-person portable.

Quick Flip and Flip-N-Fish by Sportsmax

The two-person Quick Flip weighs only 23 pounds, and the one-person Flip-N-Fish comes in at just 16 pounds. Their sleds are pullable via the included towrope or optional hitch assembly. High sides also give Quick Flip sleds a generous carrying capacity, and the portables' black shells are made from ripstop denier nylon. Plus, Sportsmax is proud that Quick Flips come fully assembled right out of the box!

First-Generation Suitcase-Style Portables

As noted, the term *suitcase* derives from the look and feel of a portable fish house once it's collapsed. Numerous members in this category maintain a kinship with their designated label, suitcase, based on design, but just as many models have broken from the mold through flooring modifications and the way their frames erect and collapse.

The first couple suitcase-type portables we'll examine stick close to party lines, which means that, other than an improvement here and there, they look and function much like the originals. The beauty of wood-floored portables is that there is no limit to size, number of holes, and hole configuration. Some large models fish and sleep up to six anglers, and feature customized hole placement.

Ice Igloo by Canvas World

Based in White Bear Lake, Minnesota, Canvas World has been manufacturing suitcase-style portable fish houses for years, and their experience is evident in the finished product. Canvas World's entire line of portables offer flame-retardant canvas, half-inch plywood flooring, two air vents, heavy-duty zipper doors, two large windows, and tubular steel framing. Floor sizes range from four feet by four feet to eight feet by eight feet, with four sizes between. Dark-house versions are also available.

Northlander by Canvas Craft

Canvas Craft, another master of traditional suitcase-style portables, puts together five models: four feet by six feet eight inches, four feet by eight feet, five feet by six feet, six feet by eight feet, and eight feet by eight feet. All Northlanders feature 11-ounce canvas, which is considered heavy duty in the fish house industry, in addition to half-inch,

Controlling the Conditions—Heating and Lighting

Ice fishing requires illumination and warmth, but in a portable package. The best units combine the merits of heat and light. Some products to keep in mind are Coleman's Northstar lanterns, which are bright, easily handled, and generate enough BTUs to heat one- and two-person portables. The Dual Fuel Northstar burns both un- leaded gas and canned white gas, and features electronic match- less lighting; a disposable propane canister model is also available. Newer Northstar Powermax lanterns pack a similar punch in a smaller chassis. Pressurized fuel cartridges supply energy, thus eliminating the need for hand pumping. The fuel source is a lead- ing determinant in purchasing a lantern. Lanterns fueled by dis- posable LP canisters are spill free, and spare canisters readily store in a portable shelter.

All Coleman lanterns feature adjustable light levels. Controlling light intensity allows you to react to outside light levels; too much artificial light is sometimes blamed for spooking fish at night.

A waterproof flashlight is an essential piece of ice-fishing gear. Flashlights provide pinpoint illumination for tying knots, baiting hooks, or igniting lanterns in the dark. Night fishermen have popularized miner-style headlamps. These battery-powered lights furnish hands-free illumination, and they're quite affordable.

Fluorescent tube lanterns can sometimes substitute for fueled lanterns. Battery-operated, electric lanterns such as Coleman's Twin Tube model are water resistant. On the downside, electric lanterns produce no heat, only moderate light, and subfreezing temperatures can hinder their performance.

Heat is best generated separately from light when supplying a large area. The Mr. Heater sunflower heater sets the standard. The original and adjustable unit easily attaches to refillable LP tanks, ranging from 5 to 20 pounds. Mr. Heater's three heat ad- justments kick out 8,000, 12,000, and 14,000 BTUs, respectively. Adjustable or thermostatic heat is necessary because winter tem- peratures can be erratic. A favorite modification is to implement Mr. Heater hosing and fittings, allowing the tank to sit outside while the sunflower face and stand remain inside; this method is safer and saves space. The upright Mr. Heater/Cooker also heats food, but it's the electric spark ignition and disposable LP canister fuel that make it appealing. Giant portables and permanent shelters might require the added warmth generated by the Mr. Double Heater and Mr. Triple Heater. The Mr. Double Heater radiates 8,000 to 28,000 BTUs, and the Mr. Triple Heater gives off up to 42,000 BTUs.

Permanent fish house users usually choose fixed copper-lined heating systems. With a large refillable LP tank outside, a thermostatically controlled heater such as the Handi-Heater makes the grade. Heat-shielded Handi-Heater models vary in output from 15,000 to 30,000 BTUs.

Safety is an issue when dealing with heating and lighting. You should always ignite transportable, match-lit heaters and lanterns outside. Store and handle LP tanks, canisters, and pressurized cartridges according to manufacturer's instructions. Unleaded fuel is flammable, and white gas is even more volatile, so reduce spillage by pouring with a funnel and keep flames away from surplus fuel. Combusting heating and lighting sources absorb oxygen and can release harmful carbon monoxide, so adequate ventilation is of concern for permanent and portable shelter users.

Innovations constantly improve the sport of ice fishing. Jim Hansen, of Hansen's Little Bear Bait and Tackle in White Bear Lake, Minnesota, custom fits a Coleman Northstar lantern and sunflower heater face onto a five-pound LP tank. This concise heating and lighting package fits nicely into small portable shelters, yet packs enough power to heat and light larger fish houses.

five-ply, marine-plywood floors (Douglas fir). Also, Northlander fish house purchasers benefit from having two 12-inch-by-18-inch windows, screened ventilation, and steel tube framing (telescoping poles) with sturdy nylon clips (snap together instead of thumbscrews). Floors come uncut, allowing customized hole placement and a dark-house option.

Second-Generation Suitcase-Style Portables

The next wave in suitcase-type portables endeavored to not only reduce the bulk and setup time of traditional models, but also convert the floor into a useful sled. True efficiency is being able to transport gear inside of what will eventually become your shelter! Their synthetic floors, predominantly polyethylene in composition, double as sleds. Once you get past synthetic floors and tubular internal framing, remaining characteristics, including size and setup procedure, vary from manufacturer to manufacturer.

Clam Classic by USL Products

This is USL Product's original, and still wildly popular, suitcase-style portable. The floor of the Clam Classic, which comfortably fishes two to three people, folds neatly in half like a clam. Once closed with equipment inside, begin walking and pulling because the floor has transformed into a sled.

The house is a spacious five feet by six feet with six feet six inches upstairs. You've also got two windows, two doors with bidirectional zippers, and precut holes with covers.

Clam Junior by USL Products

The Clam Junior carries the same characteristics as the Clam Classic but in a smaller package. This one- or two-person portable is four feet by six feet with four feet six inches of headroom. Collapsed, it's the perfect size for carrying in an automobile trunk or back end of a sport utility vehicle; plus, the Clam Junior weighs only 40 pounds.

Clam Sleeper by USL Products

The spacious eight-foot-by-eight-foot (seven feet six inches high) Clam Sleeper is as much a permanent as it is a portable. Amazingly, the four-person fish house, despite its size, still breaks down to a manageable size, and when equipped properly, it provides overnight lodging.

The house features two doors with bidirectional zippers, four windows, and plenty of ventilation. It's the perfect base camp for a wintry afternoon on the ice. Match a Clam Sleeper with a few Fish Traps and, you will not only delight USL Products, but also be outfitted for a true mobile experience.

Trophy Series by Sportsmax

The Sportsmax line of Trophy portable fish houses are lightweight, built to last, and come fully assembled. All three models feature blackout-coated denier nylon shells, which are waterproof and fire retardant; the deep black outside coating absorbs light (heat generation) and promotes illumination through your holes. You'll also find two windows and two doors on every model. Their polyethylene floors fold in half, creating a storage box that doubles as a sled. Sportsmax continually strives to improve their products, and when this book was being published, similar but updated models were on their way.

Deluxe Hideout by Frabill

Frabill's Deluxe Hideout accommodates up to three anglers and comfortably fishes two. The unique frame and sled-floor design allows users to fully erect the house in less than one minute and provides maximum headroom and horizontal space. The entire galvanized steel frame and covering collapse inside a one-piece toboggan-style sled floor. Possibly the Deluxe Hideout's greatest features are its **A**-frame wall extension and tent stretching bar, which when combined, reduce wind flap and provide plenty of jigging space. The ceiling sits at six feet when open, and you also get two doors with bidirectional dual zippers and a sled that carries quite a load.

Speed Shak XL, Speed Shak Club, and Speed Shak Pony by Frabill

The folks at Frabill refer to their Speed Shak series as the condos of portable fish houses. They are spacious, durable, and can be raised in a flash. What is a fast setup time? All three sizes of Speed Shaks can be both erected and collapsed in less than one minute! Their internal galvanized pole framing and outer 11-ounce poly/cotton canvas (black) also make Speed Shaks durable and well insulated.

25

Fish Houses on Wheels

Combining Comfort With Mobility.   Incredibly, we're this far into a chapter about shelters and have given but passing mention of permanent fish houses. You know, those cabin-sized structures winter anglers laboriously push or pull onto frozen waters. The fact is that permanent structures don't fit into a cutting-edge ice-fishing philosophy; these cumbersome entities hinder success because they discourage mobility. That being said, there is no getting around the fact that relaxing in a big, heated shelter is pleasant, even if nothing's biting. So, wasn't it just a matter of time before someone developed a cozy, hard-sided shelter that could relocate like a portable? A handful of manufacturers now design and build what are called fish houses on wheels.

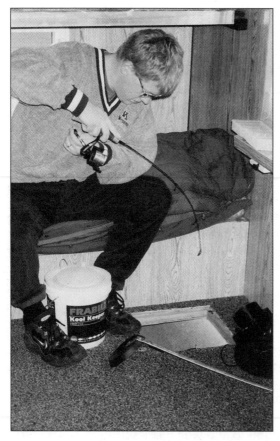

Comfort, luxury, and portability come together in a fish house on wheels. Here, the author battles a fish through a bunk-side hole of a King Crow Co. 8-foot-by-16-foot unit.

Choosing a Fish House

Basically, what you've got is a permanent shelter that rides on a steel-framed trailer, which you can easily raise and lower from the ice. A common scenario involves a pickup truck and fish house on wheels pulling onto a lake. Once they reach a specific location, the driver and passenger get out, unhitch the trailer tongue, and manually or hydraulically lower both sides of the fish house. They step inside the house, flip on lights, kick on the heat, remove hole covers, drill holes, and commence fishing. After a few hours of angling, the pair decides to relocate. They close up shop, crank up the fish house, lock it in place, rehitch the tongue, and drive away. Simple as that.

Fish houses on wheels are available in several sizes and designs. Typical lengths range from 8 to 16 feet and widths from 6 feet 8 inches to 8 feet. In reality, just about any physical request is doable, with the exception of U.S. and state highway width restrictions.

The walls of a fish house on wheels are insulated like a small house and the majority feature sliding-glass windows with screens and insulated doors. Most are aluminum or wood sided. On the exterior, you'll also find propane tanks with a regulator, patio lighting, ventilation ducts, and trailer lights.

Internally, fish houses on wheels are as basic or elaborate as the purchaser requests. Features such as thermostatic propane heat, cookstove, bunks, indoor-outdoor carpeting, hole covers, 12-volt lighting system, cupboards and storage galore, and wood paneling, for the most part, are standard equipment. The next tier of goodies presents amenities such as running water with a sink, indoor toilet, shower, exterior TV antenna, ceiling fans, refrigerator, bench seats, built-in folding table, livewell, and individual lights above the holes. Serious customization requires that you place an order well in advance of delivery, but if it's humanly possible and legal, they'll build it.

The following fish house on wheels manufacturers are the industry's finest:

King Crow Co. 320-275-3776
Frank's RV Service, Inc. 612-323-0099
Performance Engineering 320-864-5389
Al Poach 612-263-0890 or 612-295-5339
The Fish House Store 507-332-4037

One category of gear I've yet to mention is equipment sleds. If you purchased a flip-over fish house, you've already got a carrying sled. In fact, the sleds on Otter, Polar, and similar fish houses are identical to those sold separately. So, the most cost-effective and sensible means to procure a sled is to get a flip-over fish house. Why the photo? The only specific sled I want to show you is the old refrigerator door the Griz, a legendary ice-fishing guide, uses to transport stuff—a resourceful guy.

Permanent Fish Houses

Homelike Accommodations, but Stuck in a Rut. I'll be brief. Permanent fish houses, meaning any hard-sided shelter structure that sits in one place all winter, are fantastic winter retreats, but they're certainly a nonfactor in a mobilized ice-fishing regimen. Treat your permanent fish house like a base camp and warming house.

Rental Fish Houses

Permanent Shelters That Move When the Fish Do. In big lake country, such as Minnesota, Wisconsin, Michigan, and other northern states, resorts, guide services, and lakeside businesses maintain rental shelters. Both sleeper (with bunks) and day (no sleeping accommodations) fish houses are available. Business owners take great care in placing and relocating their rental houses throughout the ice-fishing season. Some outfits even offer packages that include bait, tackle, and meals. Rental fish house sizes vary from units that entertain only a couple hard-core anglers to ones that accommodate a dozen or more people. The cozy environment of a rented, permanent fish house is a great way to expose newcomers to the sport of ice fishing.

A Final Thought

Your home away from home. Fish houses, be they permanent or portable, afford ice anglers the luxury of fishing in a warm and dry environment. A permanent shelter makes an ideal base camp for a group of anglers, while a wealth of different portable designs enable them to crisscross a frozen lake while maintaining total comfort. No comprehensive ice-fishing program goes into effect without some sort of refuge from wintry conditions.

Basically a fish house should:

- *Be mobile.*
- *Keep you and your equipment dry.*
- *Protect you from cutting winds and frigid temperatures.*

Chapter 3

Electronics

"ONE, TWO, OR THREE ARM LENGTHS DOWN?" This used to be a question frequently asked from one fisherman to another. Say a guy attached a clip-on weight to his lure and determined via "arm length estimations" that the water was approximately 18 feet deep. Through a process of trial and error, he then found crappies about halfway down. If five to six feet is an arm length—the typical finger tip to finger tip span of an average-sized man—then halfway down, or nine feet, is roughly one and a half arm lengths, a primitive means for establishing depth.

Electronic equipment has changed the way we fish. The revolution began in 1959 when Carl Lowrance introduced the "Little Green Box." Between 1959 and 1984 Lowrance sold over one million of these amazing portable flashing units, and there are plenty of them still in use as both open water and ice-fishing tools. However, times change, and technology changes with it. Flasher units continue to improve, more and more liquid crystal display (LCD) graphs hit the market, and Global Positioning System (GPS) technology is now available to civilians.

Electronics are no longer a luxury; for the modern ice fishermen they have become a necessity. Increased fishing pressure along with heightened angler expectations demand technological advancements and better equipment, and all this comes at a cost. Fortunately, today's marketplace bears a wealth of brands

There's no turning back. The once-primitive pastime of ice fishing has embraced technology, and nowhere is it more evident than in fishing electronics.

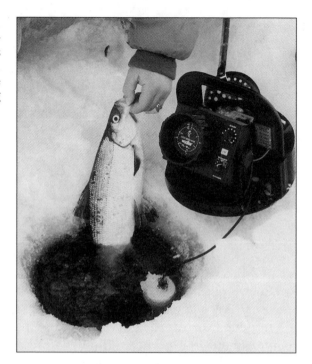

and models that are affordably priced. Complete ice-fishing-specific flasher packages retail for less than $300, portable LCD units and graphs modified for ice fishing go out the door for under $200, underwater camera systems start at around $300, and you can even procure an entry-level handheld GPS unit for a paltry $100.

Price is important but so is size. For instance, all you see of a top-notch graph mounted on a boat's dash is the head unit or screen. But what you don't notice is the system that gives life to the screen. Twisting strands of wire, cumbersome 12-volt marine batteries, and an accompanying charger unit are buried deep within the hull and console. It would be unfeasible to tote such a complex and bulky system onto the ice. Understanding this, manufacturers such as Humminbird, Eagle, and Lowrance developed fully self-contained portable LCDs and flashers. Vexilar and Zercom hit the market with compact and portable high-end flashers designed with the ice fishermen in mind. And every consumer-oriented GPS manufacturer constructs at least one model that'll fit inside a jacket pocket.

The next several pages examine the flashers, portable LCD units, GPS units, and underwater cameras used by winter anglers. I do want to notify readers that my intention is not to offer step-by-step instructions on how to operate each and every unit on the ice. Rather, I aim to expose you to what's available while making a few recommendations along the way.

I have a liberal arts background, so I maintain a school of thought that endeavors to understand fish behavior and location instead of getting bogged down in technology. However, electronics are essential in a comprehensive ice-fishing system, and I never leave the driveway without at least a fully charged portable flasher. But rest assured that your comprehension of underwater structure, predator-prey relationships, and lure selection outweighs the urgency to fully understand the seemingly thousands of ancillary features of today's electronics. Know your electronics, but don't allow their complexities to cut into your fishing time.

Flashers

Rivaling the Importance of Rods, Reels, and Bait. As nontechnical as I profess to be, it seems that every year my boat's console welcomes another newfangled hunk or two of electronics—sometimes new replaces old, and other times one simply squeezes into the mix. Giant-screened LCD graphs, an oversized GPS head unit, and a marine radio give my boat's cockpit the look and feel of the Millenium Falcon—a *Star Wars* allusion for all you sci-fi buffs. But a look across the garage to my ice-fishing gear begs of a simpler time. A basic but substantial piece of fishing electronics stands out—flashers, nothing but portable flashers.

Bar none, portable electronic flashers are the way to go. A circular face and straightforward display make them easy to view and equally easy to understand. And despite a flasher's outward simplicity, a savvy ice angler can distinguish depth, structure, bottom content, and can even mark fish by correctly analyzing the whirling lights or LCD (liquid crystal display).

Another merit of flashers is their ability to display immediate or "real time" results. If your unit shows 14 feet of water and suddenly a bar or mark appears at 10 feet, you know that a fish or other object just entered the transducer cone. Typical LCD graphs are subject to a brief but appreciable time delay from the moment a fish or object enters the cone until it actually appears on the screen. Instantaneous results are necessary when tempting an approaching fish to strike a

The fishing industry offers ice fishermen two choices in portable flashers. You can go with either an LCD (liquid crystal display) or an LED (light-emitting diode) screen. Pictured is Zercom's LCF-40 Ice, which is a popular LCD flasher.

lure while both fish and lure are visible on the screen. But more on jigging with a flasher later.

Portable flasher units are designed to shoot through water as well as ice. A flasher's transducer makes immediate contact with water once a hole has been drilled, thus *sounding* is effortless. But what about researching an area without laboriously cutting dozens of holes? Again, this is not a problem. Powerful flashers easily fire through thin, clear, and obstruction-free ice (four to eight inches). Furthermore, with the assistance of a little puddle of water, a transducer can penetrate nearly any thickness of ice; liquid is required to generate adequate sonar transmissions. Carry a plastic one-gallon jug of water with you for such occasions.

If ever there was an industry standard in ice fishing, Vexilar, Inc., of Minneapolis, has set one in the field of ice-fishing electronics. Their incomparable color LED (light-emitting diode) flasher, the FL-8, sets the bar for hardwater electronics. It's such an important piece of equipment that the majority of depth finder situations cited in this book specifically refer to the Vexilar FL-8, although most of the following flasher wisdom can be transferred to other units.

Vexilar FL-8

The Vexilar FL-8 is a little black box that lights up like a Christmas tree when powered. Standing alone, the head unit can be held in the palm of an adult hand. Attach it to a portable carrying case and battery and you've got the Patriot Missile of ice fishing. Even when fully "accessorized," the package remains lightweight and easy to manage.

Other than its convenient size, the next distinguishing characteristic of a Vexilar FL-8 is the signature three-color display. An LED beams red, orange, and green signals while rotating at high speed in a clockwise direction. Red, which portrays the strongest signal, reveals the bottom and potentially nearby fish. Orange, next in the line of signal strength, indicates weeds, a lure, or maybe fish moving in and out of the transducer cone. And last, green, the weakest signal, shows sparse weeds, small lures, zooplankton, and suggests that fish are either coming or going.

The FL-8 delivers 400 watts on a 12-volt supply, so it carries plenty of power for a portable flasher. Other brands claim to employ greater

Neither snowstorms, freezing rain, nor cold can keep this FL-8 from revealing the underworld. Pictured is an old Si-Tex unit (Vexilar is the modern namesake) paired with Dave Genz's Ice Box from USL Products.

wattage, but the FL-8 quickly dispels the need for increased (and likely wasted) power by teaming its 400-watt output with a highly sensitive receiver. Transducer sensitivity supersedes grandiose wattage statistics.

Working in concert with an FL-8's high sensitivity are six depth settings, which range from 0 to 20, 30, 40, 60, 80, or 120 feet, as well as an adjustable gain, or sensitivity control. Multiple depth settings allow you to focus on a specific range. For instance, imagine that you've spied a few walleyes holding just above the bottom in 26 feet of water. The 0- to 20-foot range won't even show the bottom, the 0- to 40-foot range will display the bottom and the fish but not nearly as well as the 0- to 30-foot setting. So set the maximum range as close to the actual depth as possible.

The adjustable gain allows an angler to intensify or minimize signal strength within a depth setting. Imagine you're bouncing a tiny jig and wad of waxies in 22 feet of water. Your depth setting is switched for 0 to 30 feet, and the gain control is cranked to the 12 o'clock position, a rather intense setting. Both the dancing lure and incoming fish appear red on the screen. Begin lowering the gain setting so the lure fades from red through orange to green. Ultimately, you want the diminutive presentation to be visible as only a mere green sliver. Approaching fish will enter the cone as a green mark, rapidly convert to orange, and ultimately turn red at the moment of truth. This is the vaunted instant where the mark made by a fish (red) seemingly merges with your bait (green), resulting in a pulsing red nebula. The enhanced red blotch indicates that a fish sits nose to nose with your presentation. Famed ice fisherman Dave Genz, a strong proponent of the Vexilar FL-8, recommends setting the hook when a fish (red mark) envelopes what was formerly a green mark (your bait), regardless of whether you feel a strike or not. Dave recognizes that at times fish hit so delicately that only electronics such as the FL-8 will indicate a strike.

The only sweeping criticism of the Vexilar FL-8 is that it's difficult to read in bright sunlight. LCD screens are certainly more distinguishable under light skies than colored displays, but the advantages of using the FL-8 versus all rivals transcends this minor glitch. Plus, a couple of remedies are at hand. Vexilar offers the Sun Hood, which is a low-priced light-blocking cone custom cut for the FL-8. Simply slide the Sun Hood onto the FL-8 face and commence viewing. Cheaper yet, the smallest consumer coffee can, usually 13 ounces (Folgers is my choice), can be resurrected as a makeshift sun visor. Grab an empty can, cut out the bottom, and spray it with black paint inside and out. The budget sun visor slips nicely around the outside of the FL-8 face, and it can easily be removed and reinstalled.

Anything else? Yep. Vexilar recently added SLT technology to their FL-8, creating the FL-8 SLT flasher. This is the only way to go. SLT is interference rejection circuitry that blocks out echoes and cross signals from other depth finders. In fact, two ice anglers can actually sit side by side without interference if SLT technology is in place. Without SLT, it's nearly impossible for two or more anglers to simultaneously use depth finders within a 30- to 50-foot radius of each other. Screens become so cluttered with "trash" signals, they're rendered useless.

FL-8 Accessories

At this point, you should have a decent grasp of the FL-8 unit itself. From here on out, we're dealing with transducers, cone angles, carrying containers, batteries, and chargers. The standard FL-8 transducer works with a 19-degree cone angle, which is the same or within a few degrees of other transducers. Vexilar offers a tighter 9-degree transducer for better accuracy in deep water. And if that's not enough, ice fishermen can even purchase a dual beam 9- and 19-degree transducer with switch box. Table 3.1 demonstrates the coverage areas provided by 9- and 19-degree transducers. Depth is measured in feet, and the degree columns (also in feet) portray diameter measurements.

The ultimate Vexilar transducer is the self-leveling Ice-Ducer. A cylindrical foam sleeve and grommet combine to "float" the transducer inside a fish hole. By adjusting the grommet, you can raise and lower the actual transducer in order to place it as close to the bottom of the hole as possible, regardless of ice thickness. On a traditional adjustable arm and leveling bubble mount, the transducer's effectiveness is hindered if there is thick ice, which can interfere with transmissions since this mount holds the transducer just below the water's surface. Another benefit of using an Ice-Ducer is how effortlessly you can move an entire FL-8 unit from hole to hole without worrying about leveling the transducer.

Integrating the FL-8, or another flasher/depth finder for that matter, into a transportable package is your next task. Vexilar offers the round 10-inch diameter Porta Case that effectively brings together the FL-8, transducer, and battery into a compact system that fits nicely on the bottom of a five-gallon bucket. Ice fishermen universally embrace

Table 3.1 Depth and Degrees

Depth	9 Degrees	19 Degrees
10	1.57	3.35
15	2.36	5.02
20	3.15	6.69
25	3.94	8.37
30	4.72	10.04
35	5.51	11.71
40	6.30	13.39
45	7.08	15.06
50	7.87	16.73
55	8.66	18.41
60	9.44	20.08
65	10.23	21.75
70	11.02	23.43
75	11.81	25.10
80	12.59	26.77
85	13.38	28.45
90	14.17	30.12
95	14.95	31.80
100	15.74	33.47
120	18.89	40.16
130	20.46	43.51
140	22.04	46.86
150	23.61	50.20

Cone angle coverage statistics provided by Vexilar, Inc.

five-gallon buckets because of their fish and gear carrying capacities, as well as their value as a stool. The comprehensive Vexilar FL-8 SLT Pro Pack includes the head unit, Porta Case, Ice-Ducer, battery, charger, and a battery status indicator.

Dave Genz's Ice Box is a specially designed portable box that can accommodate just about any flasher or LCD unit. The molded carrier features a large handle, spacious battery housing, and room for winding up extra transducer cable. From the Ice Box's front side, sprouts an eyehook designed to suspend a dangling Vexilar Ice-Ducer without the foam sleeve. And the Genz brainchild also accommodates an optional adjustable arm and bubble mount for use with any puck-type transducers. Puck transducers aren't balanced, so an adjustable arm and bubble are required for straight shooting.

Powering a flasher can be an undertaking since finding a 12-volt source that's reliable in cold weather, is easily rechargeable, and doesn't harbor the size and weight of a cinderblock isn't easy. Motorcycle starting batteries were the first power sources to gain popularity with ice fishermen. These strong 12-volt batteries produce plenty of power, but they're awkward, heavy, finicky in very cold conditions, and aren't designed for low amperage draws over extended periods of time.

The next line of portable depth finder batteries are also lead acid in design, but they're much smaller and some are even manufactured precisely for fishing applications. Vexilar sells a manageably sized and maintenance-free sealed lead acid battery that comes complete with a charging unit.

The final, and as far as I'm concerned the best, all-around depth finder battery is the sealed gel cell. These compact and inexpensive batteries are rugged, quickly rechargeable, long lasting, and free of gaseous fumes. In general, portable 12-volt batteries, regardless of composition, should be charged fully, never completely drained, and stored at room temperature. But I'll be honest; the very first sealed gel battery I owned was thoroughly abused yet lasted for three entire

The Vexilar FL-8 SLT is the most potent portable flasher system on the market. The pictured unit features an optional light attachment, battery, and carrying case.

ice-fishing seasons! Now I won't guarantee you similar results, but sealed gels are indubitably the finest.

With so much discussion surrounding the Vexilar FL-8, it's a wonder they have time to engineer and build anything else—but they do. The Vexilar LPS-1 is a nifty handheld, flashlight-styled flasher perfect for taking quick depth checks. Simply touch the waterproof unit to relatively thin ice or a splash of water on thicker ice and take a reading. Depth is registered via a digital LCD readout. Strikemaster offers a similar device called the Polar Vision. From the standpoint of function, neither device replaces flashers, but they do afford anglers yet another weapon in the war on fish.

Techsonic Industries' Zercom Marine division is the industry's other serious player in ice-fishing electronics. For a number of years, they've been designing and marketing real time sonar (RTS) products. The bulk of their hardwater sonar products features LCD readouts versus flashing ones, as are found on FL-8's.

The displays on the Zercom LCF-40 Ice and Zercom Pro Ice are rounded like a flasher, but generate liquid crystal readouts with greenish-glow back lighting. The compact 1,000-watt units offer four depth ranges (40', 80', 160', and 400') and exceptional grayscale. RTS is also available on the budget-minded Zercom RTS Ice, which has a vertical display.

Zercom's latest entry is the ColorPoint three-color flasher. Like their other models, it comes packaged with a 7.0 amp battery and charger, carrying case, and self-aligning transducer (S.A.T.). The ColorPoint is simple to operate, provides exceptional target separation, and operates at a frequency that keeps it from "cross talking" with other units.

Global Positioning System

Forget Lining Up the Red Barn With the Green Dock and the A-Frame. Believe me, satellite navigation wasn't developed as a tool for sportsmen. Heck, in Minnesota we have a hard time persuading the state legislature to pony-up the funds necessary to maintain stocking programs. But in an effort to remain instructional versus editorial, I'll bail out on further budgetary discussions. . . .

In the late 1970s, the U.S. Department of Defense unleashed this 24-hour satellite-driven global positioning system (GPS). The federal government exclusively used GPS for military and navigational purposes for the system, but eventually GPS technology was introduced to the civilian market, and that's where we stand today.

Hunters and anglers are some of the greatest beneficiaries of GPS technology. Through a small walkie-talkie-sized or dash-mounted GPS receiver, sportsmen can mark favorite fishing holes, find a deer stand, and even chart their way back home, although GPS manufacturers encourage outdoorsmen to learn and trust traditional compasses. GPS receivers display actual longitude, latitude, and altitude coordinates, which are generated through interfacing a receiver signal with outer-space satellites. The amount of time it takes for a GPS receiver to acquire and retransmit a satellite signal mathematically calculates the user's position. A minimum of three satellites is required to obtain an accurate two-dimensional (longitude and latitude) position, and simultaneous contact with four or more satellites provides a three-dimensional reading (longitude, latitude, and altitude). Most recreational GPS units feature a screen revealing exactly how many satellites are being contacted and the signal strength of each.

Being satellite based, GPS works in both good and bad weather conditions. LORAN-C, the government's maiden navigational system, wasn't nearly as reliable. LORAN-C, also having military roots, works off land-based transmitters versus orbiting satellites. But just like radio transmissions, LORAN-C is affected by foul weather, the curvature of the earth, and physical obstructions. Although significantly more dependable than LORAN-C, GPS receivers operate at peak performance in open spaces because suffocating buildings, trees, and other obstructions can tamper with accuracy.

How accurate is GPS? The U.S. Department of Defense, if they wanted to, could blast this book right out of your hands! But when the federal government, under the Reagan administration, offered GPS to the public, they installed a little margin of error. SA, or *selective availability,* was introduced for national security purposes. With SA in place, a civilian GPS receiver is accurate within 100 meters nearly 100 percent of the time and is usually accurate to 50 meters.

Ice fishermen have been using GPS receivers for some time. The chief application for GPS on the ice is marking favorite spots, especially on large lakes and reservoirs. Landmarks, maps, and depth checks are adequate clues to finding destinations in most situations. But in the case of huge landmarker-free spaces, GPS tracking is potent. Many fishermen store their favorite open-water "waypoints," or spots, in order to revisit them in the winter. Weed beds, bars, and rock piles that are easy to locate electronically from a boat are harder to find through the ice. GPS cuts down on time wasted searching.

GPS receivers are also fantastic tools for finding home base after dark or in the midst of a snowstorm. Again, traditional compasses are a more steadfast means of navigation, but the back lit "compass" and "plotter" features on a GPS receiver make traveling to and from the ice easier and safer.

A number of companies have introduced lake maps complete with popular GPS coordinates. These specialized maps allow fishermen of all skill levels to promptly locate noted reefs, bars, and flats with a GPS receiver. Fishing Hot Spots (FHS) produces an outstanding series of maps that cover major bodies of water throughout ice-fishing country. FHS's detailed and waterproof maps often incorporate a number of worthwhile GPS coordinates with traditional map data. King Tutt's Walleye Whiffer Maps I and II are the real deal in GPS mapping. Orin Tutt's remarkable Mille Lacs Lake maps demonstrate the type of detail that can be achieved at a local level. GPS maps should be available for a number of larger bodies of water in your area.

Choosing a GPS Unit

I'm a long ways from being an egghead or a technogeek, but I have resigned myself to the fact that GPS should be part of every serious fisherman's arsenal, as long as simplicity complements sophistication. The acronym KISS, short for "keep it simple stupid," is trite but accurate. If you're anything like me, you demand a minimal number of buttons and easy-to-read screens. Manufacturers like Garmin, Magellan, Lowrance, and Eagle each offer models meeting these provisions.

In selecting a GPS receiver, the first considerations to make are where and when the unit will be used. Boaters can certainly get by with a permanently fixed dash-mounted unit. But if you intend to take it into the woods or on the ice, consider a portable model. Handheld GPS receivers are the craze. These units are the size of a cellular phone, yet they maintain the strength and features of their bigger brothers. Stick the receiver in your coat pocket or slide it into an optional mounting bracket. Ice fishermen commonly mount GPS brackets to snowmobile and ATV dashboards, in addition to dashes on their boats, so a single GPS receiver can be used year-round.

42

Getting Around the Frozen Tundra

Mobility is a theme that runs throughout this book. From fish house selection to hole-drilling patterns, you cannot escape that successful ice fishermen are mobile ice fishermen. At the foundation of any mobile ice-fishing system, you'll find a means of transportation for getting across the frozen tundra, and I'm not speaking about the hallowed grounds of Lambeau Field in Green Bay, Wisconsin (even a Viking fan such as myself respects history and legend).

Ice thickness and distance are the fundamental circumstances that determine what form of transportation ice fishermen use. Anyone who takes advantage of winter's opening sequence must embark on foot. Published state guidelines offer four inches as the minimum ice thickness to tread on. I chose not to print or identify these sources because they are only suggestions not rules. In fact, safe ice relates to both thickness and quality. Although I don't endorse specific numbers, I've personally felt comfortable walking on less than four inches of ice. In such conditions, I always wear a life jacket, carry handheld ice spikes and a chisel, and fish with at least one partner.

In regions along the fringe of ice-fishing country, anglers seldom encounter ice strong enough to support anything beyond the weight of a human. A short winter with erratic temperatures maintains ice for only a short duration, sometimes just a couple weeks.

Snowshoes and cross-country skis accelerate travel time during the period when the only means of accessing a lake is by foot. The wide profile of snowshoes further distributes body weight across the ice (ice thickness reference), and snowshoes make traversing through deep snow much easier. Skiing is the fastest method of nonmotorized travel. Ice anglers who enjoy winter camping and portaging into remote locations regularly strap on cross-country skis.

In a continuing effort not to drag this discussion into the realm of technical overload, I'm not going to walk you through the features and operation of any specific unit. But I will present a list of traits to look for while shopping for a GPS receiver.

In a handheld model, it's okay to go small, but opt for as large a screen as possible. Larger screens are much easier to read, particularly while zooming about on an ATV or snowmobile. Speaking of transportation, I already endorsed choosing a unit with a matching bracket and holder.

I endorse excess when it comes to logging waypoints, which are the actual spots you want to relocate at a later time. You don't want to run out of waypoint storage! Look for a receiver with a memory that holds at least 200 waypoints, and it doesn't hurt to go up to 500 if you fish on a lot of different lakes. Working in conjunction with waypoints is the *plotter*, which permits you to see your actual position in relation to the intended destination or waypoint. An Etch-A-Sketch-type line even tracks movement as you approach a waypoint.

Battery life is also crucial. Twelve hours of continuous use is a respectable rating, and some of the better units claim to operate for 24 hours off a single juicing. Also ensure that the intended GPS receiver has a lithium battery backing up its memory in the event the main power does fail.

A final item to consider is the capability of expanding the receiver's powers through uploading and downloading information. Mapping software is already available, and it's safe to assume that more and more prewritten GPS lake data will be available in the future.

Underwater Cameras

Validating Blips and Bars.   Imagine harnessing your fishing buddy, stuffing him down a hole, and demanding that he return with a detailed report of what lies below. Or better yet, send him down with a diving camera so he actually documents life beneath the ice. Fortunately for contemporary ice fishermen, the underwater world, which was formerly reserved for Jacques Cousteau, can now be viewed live and without getting wet. Enter underwater camera systems. . . .

Used for years by freshwater and saltwater divers alike, underwater camera systems have finally gained popularity in fishing circles. A basic underwater camera system consists of a high-resolution and watertight optical lens; connecting cable; some type of monitor; car-

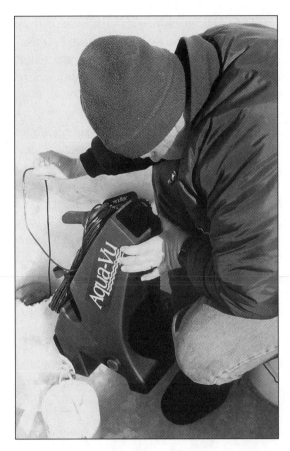

Underwater viewing systems have found a niche with the ice-fishing crowd. Simply lower the watertight lens to a desired depth and watch your lure, incoming fish, and aquatic environments. Pictured is an Aqua-Vu II by Nature Vision camera from the company that pioneered underwater camera use in fishing.

rying case; and possibly a *boom,* or long pole, to lower and direct the lens underwater. Telescoping "painters" booms do a fine job.

The ability of the lens to distinguish objects in a dark underwater environment is amazing. What shows up as benign bumps and bars on a flasher or LCD unit reveals their true identities on the monitor of an underwater camera system. To many, a mark on a flasher is an obvious fish, but what species? Submerse an underwater camera and it's possible to determine if you're sitting over a school of crappies or gigantic shiner minnows.

Exploring bottom composition is equally fascinating. What you believed to be a very hard and flat bottom is actually hundreds if not thousands of boulders barely protruding from the lake floor. Underwater cameras can expose minor structures (a few rocks or a small brush pile) over seemingly featureless areas. Transition zones where sand greets rubble or gravel fades to muck are as visible as if they occurred in your driveway. And what about weeds? Poking the camera lens along an outside weedline discloses otherwise concealed caverns and pockets, which potentially hold fish. And think about being able to distinguish between cabbage and coontail without ever hooking a weed.

Once a site has been established, it's time to pop a second hole about 18 inches to two feet from your primary hole. Drop the camera lens down to the same level as your lure and get ready for some serious entertainment—a true "fish-eye" view. Watch how fish react to your presentation. Do they immediately smack it, or does it apparently disinterest them? Jig hard then soft with long pauses and short pauses; you can observe every reaction a fish makes. Lackluster interest might tip you to the fact that it's time to change lures and/or bait.

The preceeding paragraphs afford a pretty good picture of how an underwater camera system clarifies the underwater environment. But what about using the camera as a fishing tool? The topic of underwater cameras cannot enter and exit a conversation without contro-

The Vista Cam is a popular, affordable, and high-quality underwater viewing system. It was the first complete package to hit the market under $400.

versy swelling. There are strong proponents and opponents for the use of underwater cameras as fishing instruments. Opponents argue that underwater cameras provide fishermen with an unfair advantage over their quarry. They go on further to claim that use of such cameras extinguishes any sense of sport in fishing and that underwater cameras aid and abet poachers.

Camera supporters combat the unfair advantage claim by arguing that existing electronics reveal the whereabouts of fish as readily as cameras; underwater cameras simply afford a clearer peek. As for the sporting aspect, any serious fisherman will assert that the mere fact of knowing a fish exists has little to no bearing on whether they can be caught. Underwater camera champions also understand that poachers are poachers, and regardless if said technology is legal or not they'll continue using it or go on poaching without it. If existing game and fish laws were better enforced and fish stocking budgets were never trimmed, there would be less fear of technology.

Before purchasing an underwater camera system, you'd best check state or provincial rules and regulations and be assured their use is legal where you want to fish. Once past that hurdle, the next step is to choose a make. My ice-fishing experiences have been with the Aqua-Vu and Aqua-Vu II by Nature Vision and the Vista Cam Underwater Video system. Watch for more manufacturers to enter this market over the next few years.

A Final Thought

Electronics enable fishermen to outsmart fish in new and better ways. Prices vary, and several manufacturers have good equipment. Some key considerations when planning a purchase are

- Size
- Features
- Portability
- State rules and regulations regarding use

Part II

Catching the Fish

Chapter 4

Walleye

THE 1980S WERE THE COMING OUT YEARS FOR LARGE-MOUTH BASS, PARTICULARLY IN THE NORTHERN STATES. These warm-water, big-mouthed predators went from inciden-tal status to their current elevation, in which tournaments are common and catch and release practices are expected. The popularity of walleye fishing took a similar turn during the 1990s, but instead of a northward surge, interest in walleyes ranged east, west, and south from its roots in the north-cen-tral states and Canada. Walleyes are to the late '90s and new millennium what largemouth bass were to the '80s, and don't expect the tide to change anytime soon.

What makes walleyes so alluring? The hunter and gatherer in all of us points to the meat. It's rare to encounter someone at a dinner table that'll challenge a statement touting fresh walleye as the most delectable of all freshwater catches. Sim-ply stated, whether they're baked, grilled, or panfried, wall-eyes are fit for kings.

Others are attracted to the curious behavior walleyes en-gage in. Walleyes are predominately nocturnal, bottom-dwelling, carnivorous, structure-relating, schooling predators that are challenging to stalk. Their conduct is engaging, but still others are mesmerized by the physical attributes of these highly evolved creations. The telltale jeweled lens pieces of a walleye are physiologically designed for effectiveness in

Throughout much of their range, walleyes are the most sought-after wintertime species. Their outer beauty and inner tastiness are celebrated far and wide.

low-light conditions. Shades of gold, green, and black mingle to create an impressive silhouette, yet one that goes virtually undetected beneath the surface.

Every body of water bears walleyes exhibiting unique shades, each matching its environment. A visible midstripe, or lateral line, runs along both sides from tail to gill; the bar acts as an acute sensory agent that detects distressful tremors of injured minnows or the presence of larger predatory fish. Wickedly sharp teeth line their bony jaws, every one of them able to shred baitfish or puncture the finger of a careless angler. Who can forget the ghostly white-tipped tail—other than their marbled eyes, a walleye's tail coloration is its most distinguishing characteristic. Nothing's more stirring than seeing a dark shadow come into view of an ice hole, when suddenly its identity is revealed through a flash of white. Combine these walleye characteristics with ice fishing's special appeal, and you've got an attractive proposition.

Winter Walleye Behavior

A Species That Doesn't Shut Down for Winter.　There are temperate species, such as large- and smallmouth bass, that although they do feed beneath the ice, the winter months aren't their finest hours. On the opposite end of the spectrum, freshwater inhabitants such as lake trout and eelpout (burbot) are at the top of their game when water temperatures plummet and surfaces harden. Walleyes fit some- where in between. They feed throughout the calendar year. The total volume eaten and frequency of meals varies from season to season, but rest assured, walleyes feed 12 months a year—wintertime is no exception.

Walleye movement during the hardwater season is chiefly a reac- tion to the availability of forage, primarily baitfish, which are native minnows and immature game fish species such as yellow perch. The winter months mark the end of a body of water's annual biological cycle, and by the end of this cycle, food sources have waned to their lowest levels. Aquatic prey of all types have been pursued and con- sumed for months, and not until springtime's renaissance will they repopulate. So walleyes and other predatory fish species must con- tend for a dwindling forage base.

That which challenges walleyes benefits winter anglers. A depleted food source means that there's less forage and in fewer locations. Anglers hope this occurrence results in more walleyes vying for baitfish in select and targetable locations.

Winter Walleye Location

Culmination of Many Factors.　Authors are forever attempting to avoid cliches. Trite expressions effectively get points across to readers, but overuse is taboo. Well, it's time to use one of few cliches I'll allow myself: When buying a home or business what are the three most important factors to consider? Location, location, and loca- tion! Guess what? The same is true for successfully tracking winter- time walleyes.

As they do during open-water season, which includes spring, sum- mer, and fall, winter walleyes continuously migrate from spot to spot. Their preferred grounds change according to cold-water periods that include early winter, midwinter, and late winter (more on this in a moment).

Built into any winter walleye game plan is a consideration for light and how it affects walleyes. The highly sensitized, light-absorbing eyeball of a walleye is a critical tool for nighttime and deep-water feeding, but what gives walleyes an advantage in the dark leaves them vulnerable under bright skies. Light level or light intensity is a significant factor in wintertime walleye location. Bright skies combined with snow-free ice drive walleyes deep. Conversely, factors such as a light-blocking snow cover and cloudy skies permit walleyes to frequent shallower terrain.

A walleye's aversion to light concentrates feeding to low-light periods. Historically, the best times to attack winter walleyes are at dawn, dusk, and sometimes overnight. The morning bite commonly transpires from an hour before sunup to an hour or two afterward. Because dawn is preceded by several hours of darkness (extended feeding period), morning walleye activity may not be concentrated.

Sundown is preceded by a long afternoon of daylight, which walleyes find less conducive to feeding. The intense dusk bite is therefore the result of having not fed for numerous hours. Overcast skies sometimes diffuse walleye activity throughout the day, but you can still count on a little push at dawn and dusk.

Pure nighttime walleye feeding varies from lake to lake more than dawn and dusk activity does. Shallow and stained-water lakes offer either zero nighttime bite or an unpredictable pattern. Also, walleyes on these lakes have a tendency to forage in short bursts throughout the day. However, large, clear, deep lakes commonly produce catches of walleyes under dark skies. If you fish a particular body of water often enough, it's possible to establish specific peaks in nighttime activity.

When is the best time to fish walleyes? Any chance you can! We'd all like to fish in ideal light conditions with a customized weather pattern, but perfection is seldom possible. Weather is something to deal with, not something that determines if you fish or don't fish—dangerously cold temperatures and blizzards being the only exceptions. Optimum conditions for walleye fishing consist of stable to dropping barometric pressure with a mild air temperature. High pressure, which usually accompanies cold temperatures and bright skies, reduces walleye activity. A drop in barometric pressure, which commonly coincides with increased cloud cover, snow, and rising temperatures, triggers walleye feeding. Stable conditions

A walleye's ability to see in near-total darkness and feel what it cannot see makes them formidable nighttime predators.

are also favorable, preferably stable with low pressure. I pay more attention to what meteorologists say about barometric pressure than air temperature.

As stated earlier, there are many factors that determine where walleyes reside beneath the ice. If you combine these physical factors with seasonal changes, it's possible to pattern their whereabouts.

Early Winter

Winter's Best Bite.   Winter walleye zealots live for first ice. Many of the season's fastest bites and biggest fish materialize during winter's first few weeks. Walleyes are active, accessible, and angler pressure hasn't yet driven fish to quieter and more remote places. Walleyes feed aggressively and regularly during the early ice period. They smack large forage such as shiner minnows and perch with reckless abandon. This hostility encourages early winter anglers to offer brawny

Late Autumn Clues Lead to Wintertime Success

Most northern lakes undergo turnover in spring and fall. Fall turnover is when plummeting lake surface temperatures equal deeper, cooler temperatures; chilling surface waters descend and mix with deeper layers. Eventually, temperatures balance to a uniform temperature (39-degrees Fahrenheit is the water temperature that starts fall turnover). Not every lake undergoes a true turnover, but some degree of water temperature equalization occurs whether a lake is young and deep (oligotrophic), old and shallow (eurotrophic), or somewhere in between (mesotrophic).

What's the benefit of understanding turnover and temperature balance? *Fish location!* Fish move to different depths due to temperature preference and oxygenation concerns. For instance, spring weather warms shoreline areas, and heat-seeking fish arrive. Conversely, late summer's heat drives fish into cooler, deeper climes. However, when water temperatures equalize throughout a fish's range (turnover periods), they're free to roam.

During fall turnover, lakes become clear; organic particles, which give lakes much of their color, settle to the bottom, and algae die off. The result is increased light penetration, which drives fish deeper and limits their activity to low-light periods (think breaks and morning and evening action).

Fish seek shelter provided by remaining vegetation. In open-water season, weeds emerge, grow, and die. Late fall is when the most weed types and volumes perish. The result is decreased oxygen production and diminished cover and vegetated feeding stations. Look for flourishing green areas—weeds are good.

Late fall is when anglers take a hiatus from their sport, but those who venture out are rewarded. Knowing where fish are during late fall is key to relocating them at first ice. Water temperature, light levels, sunlight angle, and overall underwater conditions remain stable from late fall through early winter, so there's a strong chance that fish located during late fall will still be in the vicinity at first ice. On a prewinter scouting trip, look for rock piles, underwater bars, and remaining green vegetation. Mark them on a map and reference shoreline objects (cabins, points, bridges, etc.) so you can return to these locations following ice up.

lures tipped with big baits, and a walleye's predictable timetable accompanies a walleye's propensity to feed. Early morning and evening hours see the greatest concentration of scavenging walleyes.

Combine characteristic early winter feeding behavior with the presence of classic walleye structure and you've got an exciting situation. Structures such as shoreline points and bars, breaks, outside weededges, and rock humps are magnets for early ice walleyes. Structure within structure (i.e., a weed bed on a rock hump) or structure adjacent to structure (i.e., a rock pile sitting off the tip of a point) are even more powerful.

Shoreline Points and Bars Provide Fundamental Walleye Habitat

It's important to understand the differences and similarities between a point and a bar. Points, whether they be shoreline or contours of an island, are the visible, physical landmasses that jettison into a body of water. Points vary dramatically in size, shape, and how their banks descend and figure once beneath the surface. Think of a bar as an underwater point. Typically, bars are elongated, submerged shoreline extensions that protrude beyond points. Just as often, though, bars occur randomly from shorelines that offer no tangible clues revealing their presence. Many bodies of water feature bars that rise and twist at midlake. What simplifies any confusion over identification is that walleyes frequent countless variations of points and bars.

Major shoreline points and bars are fantastic venues for opening the ice-fishing season. They are not only easier to find and fish than offshore structure, but also host swarms of fish.

Points provide a natural holding area for both forage and predatory fish like walleyes. In general, fish gravitate toward structure, or in other words, fish relate to material changes or objects within their range. Points provide this commodity, or environment.

As for points, bigger is usually better—more structure equals more fish. Smaller points with less submerged structure surely hold fish, but just a few anglers can tap them out quickly. So begin by identifying the dominant shoreline point or points on your chosen lake.

The next objective is determining how a point breaks. Break refers to the slope of the bottom as it descends. Some points feature gradual breaks, others steep breaks, and still others a combination of the two—these are the finest. An example of a steep or sharp break is one that drops from 10 to 20 feet in just a few paces. An angler might have to cover 50 yards to encounter a similar depth change across a gradual break.

The steepest break on a point is the first place to inspect. Walleyes tend to slide up sharp breaks during low-light periods to feed over the shallows of a point or an adjacent bar. Locate the juncture where the steep slope plateaus, or levels off, and commence drilling holes.

Going hand in hand with a sharp break is deep water. Another characteristic I did not discuss earlier is that points, particularly lengthy ones, generally probe into deeper water than run-of-the-mill shoreline stretches. Access to deep midlake water is always a bonus, regardless of what species you're after. Deep water provides a safe haven and midday walleye lounge. Plus, deep water and basin areas play a greater role as winter ensues (more on that later).

Better yet if your point has both a steep side and a tapering side. This combination allows the luxury of exploring a steep break, top of the break, and gradual glide down the backside. You can effectively address this situation by drilling a series of holes across the entire depth spectrum. Cut a couple holes at the base of the steep break (deepest point); a series heading up the break; several at the apex; a couple more over the flat; and, if inside a workable distance, a few heading down the lazy break.

Your first set of deep holes provides access to daytime fish, or ones just preparing to invade. Holes across the break are to engage incoming walleyes or ones that stay to feed over steps and ledges on the break. Walleyes cruise along breaks to pin baitfish against the vertical wall, giving them a predatory advantage not available in the open water. Holes popped along the top of the break will likely provide the hottest action. Here, you'll confront incoming fish as well as those crisscrossing the flat under blackened skies. Holes popped over the slow, tapering break are there just in case walleyes don't arrive via the deep side.

Adding to the innate attractiveness of a shoreline point is the presence of mixed bottom content or remaining green weeds. Most walleye-friendly points and bars in the North Country offer a sand bottom, gravel bottom, or a mixture of the two; patches of rocks and weeds are a bonus. Rocks often occur as an adjacent pile or nearby hump lying off the tip of a point. In the case of an adjacent rock pile, look for steep and gradually breaking sides, just as you would on a shoreline point.

Rock piles that are close by but not attached to a shoreline point are a treat. The rock pile presents a top, various breaks, and access to deep water, but the real prize in this situation is the gap or saddle lying between the rock pile and point. In fishing terms, a saddle is a deep gap between two shallower structures. An example of a prime saddle would be where a shoreline point breaks to depths of 20 feet, flattens for 50 yards, then rises up the edge of a rock hump. The saddle itself potentially yields walleyes all winter . On your map, highlight facing breaks on the point and rock pile, which form the upper lips of the saddle; these are bread and butter spots!

The presence of weeds, the other contributing factor mentioned a moment ago, augments a point's ability to produce early winter walleyes. We recognize remaining green vegetation for its capacity to attract and hold aquatic insects, baitfish, and subsequently, freshwater fish species. Healthy cabbage, coontail, milfoil, or other species often form the outside weededge over a point. Outside weedlines along a point form a perfect route for foraging walleyes to travel. This is a prime example of favorable features combining to create outstanding fish habitat.

A little elaboration on bars is in order. You should fish shoreline bars that do not originate from a point just as you would a point, because a bar is essentially an underwater point. Bars are similar to points in that they typically offer sand or gravel bottoms. Bars may also feature both steep and gradual breaks, and rocks and weed growth are as common to bars as they are to shoreline points.

Maps reveal that underwater bars frequently have a more irregular shape than points. Irregularities appear in the form of fingers and inside turns, both of which draw walleyes. Narrow and nebulous extensions, or fingers, protruding from a bar behave like miniature points. Walleyes and their prey follow and relate to these tentacles, because, as described earlier, fish gravitate toward oddities in an otherwise regular structure. The juncture where a finger curls and greets the bar's main body is an inside turn. Here, fish corral and linger longer than they do anywhere else on the bar. An inside turn grants walleyes access to the finger, the bar's main body, as well as deeper water—location, location, location! Offshore bars, which typically occur in large basin lakes, take precedence later in the season (more on them later).

Shoreline Breaks and Flats Offer
Subtle Clues in Big Places

From the moment a shoreline disappears beneath the surface, it evolves into an erratic staircase leading downward, eventually meeting the basin. Some staircases are steep and others slope progressively. Along these slopes, you'll encounter breaks as well as shelves. Shelves are flat areas where depth remains constant between breaks. A small shelf might only cover a few yards, and a giant shelf, sometimes referred to as a flat, can ramble on for 100 yards or so.

Walleyes find shoreline breaks and shelves particularly attractive during early winter. On average, northern lakes with sand or gravel shorelines feature three distinct breaks from top to bottom. Obviously this is an average, because many lakes have only one or two breaks, and others offer multiple breaks, but a three-break scenario is a good illustration. Early ice walleyes usually relate to the first and second breaks. The first break occurs between 4 and 10 feet of water, following a gradual drop to that range. Then after another controlled descent, you'll encounter a second break in the 12- to 18-foot range. The third break, again following a gradual slope, snaps off somewhere between 20 to 40 feet deep and ultimately greets the main basin. The deeper third break enters the fray later in the winter.

The key to tracking early winter walleyes on the first and second breaks is pinpointing depths. For instance, let's say that the first shoreline break is an abrupt drop from 5 to 8 feet deep, and the second break occurs at 12 feet. This means that the top of the first shelf, which is at 8 feet, is the transition you're looking for. Walleyes cruise along this edge like remote-control cars on an electric track.

The second break in our model is a sheer plunge from 12 to 18 feet, followed by another modest shelf. Our second hot transition zone is right at 18 feet, or where the break greets a second shelf. Again, expect to find walleyes zipping along the seam.

Adding to the allure of first and second shoreline breaks are features like weeds, rocks, and contour irregularities. Weededges corresponding with shoreline depth breaks create a doubly good scenario. In shallow, stained-water lakes, the first break might occur right at or just beyond the outside weededge. Shoreline depths of 10 feet and less harbor most walleyes on these lakes.

Clear lakes featuring deep outside weededges potentially hold shoreline-relating walleyes off both the first and second breaks. The shal-

A deep break outside Zippel Bay (Lake of the Woods) was responsible for this impressive walleye. *Fish & Game Finder* field editor and fishing guide, Tom Wilson, brought her up with a traditional lead-head jig and local run emerald shiner.

low first break might only yield fish for brief periods at dawn and dusk though. First breaks on such lakes frequently occur in conjunction with weed flats or an inside weededge. The more interesting second break, commingled with an established outside weededge, is surely worth investigating.

Expansive shoreline breaks are particularly substantial on gigantic basins. In my region, hot spots such as Lake of the Woods, Mille Lacs Lake, Lake Winnibigoshish, and Leech Lake produce loads of early ice walleyes over shoreline breaks. Remember that breaks are common shoreline occurrences, but not universal ones. Numerous bowl-shaped lakes present only one or two breaks and sometimes none at all.

What makes a shoreline flat attractive is its unification with a break. If you're confronted with a mammoth shoreline flat that bounces between 8 and 9 feet for 100 yards or so, then suddenly drops to 14 feet, where do you set up? You could randomly blast holes across the flat, but your odds are dramatically improved by hitting the edge of the flat, the break, and the base of the drop.

Weeds Are Gaining Status
As Classic Walleye Structure

On many lakes, submerged vegetation dramatically influences the whereabouts of walleyes, and remaining green weeds are particularly significant during the early ice period.

Aquatic plants, through a complex process known as photosynthesis, produce the oxygen necessary to maintain an underwater ecosystem. Other than oxygenating a body of water, weeds also host a throng of aquatic critters. Insects, zooplankton, baitfish, and immature game fish species thrive amid the cover. Entire food chains exist within the borders of a single weed bed.

For decades fishermen have scoured weedy areas for species such as northern pike, largemouth bass, and sunfish, but only recently have walleye hunters recognized the merits of aquatic vegetation. The label classic walleye structure is traditionally reserved for formations such as rocky reefs and sand breaks. True, these are proven structures, but it's time to add aquatic vegetation to the list. Weeds, chiefly referred to as cover, become structure when they are thick and offer distinct edges, or when they sprout in places otherwise void of structure.

Thick weeds are favorite lairs of shallow-water walleyes. They dig in and use weeds for protective cover, wait in pockets to ambush unsuspecting prey, slither up and down channels within a weed mat, and patrol outer edges looking for schools of baitfish. As cover, walleyes seek dense vegetation sprouting in the deepest available water. Towering stalks of cabbage or clumps of coontail create choice resting places for inactive walleyes. The light-blocking and nearly predator-proof foliage offer nighttime-like conditions.

Weed beds also provide walleyes access to forage. Open pockets commonly appear throughout the body of a weed mat. Clearings give walleyes access to careless crayfish and unwary minnows. Also looming below the canopy of most weed beds is a matrix of piscatorial corridors, which walleyes will travel during morning and evening hours.

Pockets and corridors deserve consideration on lakes with extensive weed mats, but what about situations where weeds are less dominant? Should you ignore weeds in places where rocks and humps rule the roost? Not a chance! Often the hottest "spot on the spot" is where a random weed clump sprouts on or just off traditional structure. For example, let's say you're working a shallow sand break that runs parallel to shore for a couple hundred yards. If you were to identify a 4-foot-by-10-foot batch of coontail sitting along the break, you'd be in business! This is another example of structure within structure.

The final and most predominant circumstance to address about weeds is when they form a deep and tangible outer wall. Summertime bass and bluegills especially like outside weededges, but what about wintertime walleyes? On many fertile small to midsize lakes, hearty outside weededges are the primary venues for tracking early ice walleyes.

Outside weededges create a lane for walleyes to travel while feeding. During the early ice period, walleyes regularly advance to the outside edge from surrounding depths. Morning and evening hours provide the best access to what is usually an intense, but short-lived walleye bite.

Figure 4.1 shows weed bars and weed-covered sand/gravel bars. These are frequented by winter walleyes during the early ice period, or until vegetation begins to perish. Pockets inside the greenery also host ambushing walleyes, and breaks beyond the weedy structure warrant attention all winter long.

The finest spots on an outside weededge, like points and bars, are where it twists into a finger, or there's a bald spot, leaving a lane or cut into the weed bed itself. Many times identifiable bars are vegetation-covered fingers protruding from a shoreline weed bed. Weedy underwater bars or fingers that offer a measurable outside weededge have a knack for holding early ice walleyes. Cuts or clear lanes originating from the outside weededge provide walleyes access to various depths and circumstances within a weed bed. The pair of outside weedline corners leading into a clearing requires serious attention!

Midwinter Walleyes

Staying on Fish During the Migration. Walleyes are not sedentary creatures. Oh sure, it's difficult for walleyes to live up to the standard they set during early winter, but a slowdown does not constitute a shutdown. Just because your ace in the hole weedline has laid down and died, or that reliable rocky point dried up, don't be

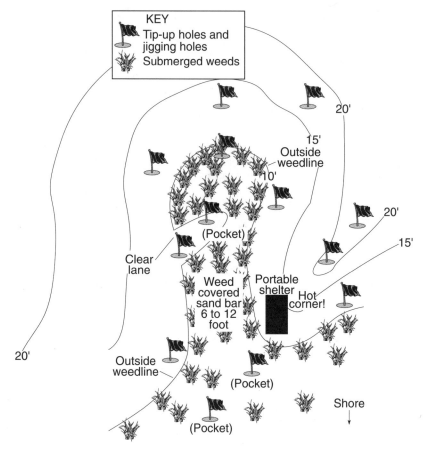

Figure 4.1 Locations where walleye may be found.

coerced into believing that walleyes have dipped into cold-weather hibernation. No, instead it's time to explore deeper, farther, and quieter haunts.

Midwinter is characterized by increased snow cover, dead and dying vegetation, a further depleted forage base, lowered oxygen levels, uncomfortably cooled shallows, and an ever-expanding angler base traversing shoreline areas. Other than an escalating snow cover, which cuts unwanted sunlight penetration, everything else regarding midwinter changes leads walleyes away from the shallows.

The first major criterion to consider at midwinter is depth. Once early ice spots shut down, assume that the fish moved to the nearest available deeper water or attractive offshore structure.

Walleye

Walleyes vacate their shallow haunts as shoreline water temperature approaches freezing. The colder water is uncomfortable, and oxygen levels continue to plummet as weeds perish. Baitfish have left for the same reasons, thus making shoreline shallows uninhabitable, except for an occasional nighttime walleye run.

The term *deep* is relative. In a prairie-type dishpan lake, deep might mean only 10 or 15 feet. Whereas deep might constitute 40, 50, or even 60 feet on a large, clear body of water. Regardless, what walleyes look for at midwinter is a warm (relative to the colder shallows), oxygenated environment, complete with a food source.

Figure 4.2 shows the following:

1. Steep shoreline breaks act as natural corridors for foraging walleyes. Scattered rocks and weeds add to the break's attractiveness.

2. Walleyes will hold on various breaks skirting a major sand or gravel bar. Search for abrupt three, four, and five-foot drops to either side of the gradually tapering structure.

3. A sandbar's deep edges and tip offer ideal cruising lanes. Sections with bottom-content transitions and faster breaks yield the most fish.

4. Some of the hottest first ice action occurs along outside weedlines within a bay. Pay special attention to lanes and cuts, isolated patches, and pockets within the weed bed. Deep weedlines will continue to yield walleyes until the greenery dies off or fishing traffic drives them from shallow cover.

5. Unmapped oases sprouting from within an otherwise ordinary formation, such as a rock pile sitting in a weed flat, always deserve exploration.

6. The convergence of structure with structure, or cover with structure creates a spot with heightened interest. A lush weedline running into a rocky jettison or a rock pile contacting a weed bar is a great example of this phenomenon.

7. What's better than a distinct outside weedline? How about a weedline shaped like a bar, which covers a range of depths. Remember, bars and points have a universal tendency to corral walleyes.

8. Subtly rising weed humps or sunken islands are of special interest if they occur beyond the shoreline's outside weededge.

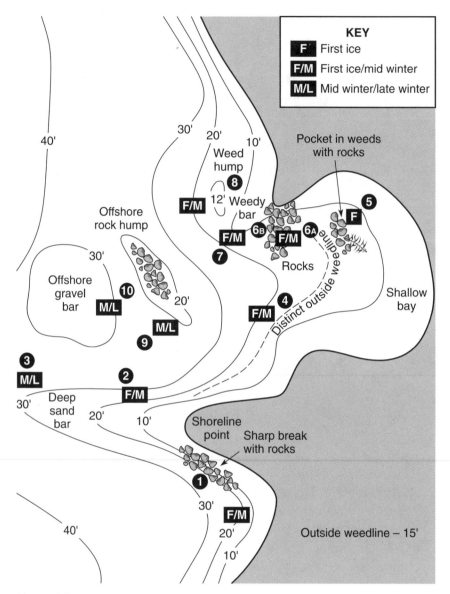

KEY

F	First ice
F/M	First ice/mid winter
M/L	Mid winter/late winter

Figure 4.2 Walleye look for structure in a habitat.

Why? Because now you have a weed-free gap lying between two edges—the shoreline weededge and the hump's weededge. The ultimate feeding lane.

9. Offshore rock piles are a no-brainer. Such structures are magnets for roaming walleyes, baitfish, and various other species.

The reef tops typically activate during low-light periods, while the breaks and surrounding basin host fish throughout the day.

10. Giant offshore gravel bars and mud flats offer walleyes desirable bottom content transitions as well as depth breaks. On a number of large lakes such deep and seemingly featureless sections produce tons of fish.

Deep Breaks and Bars Are Where the Action Continues

Previously, in the section covering early winter walleye location, I detailed the standard three-break shoreline. A lake's first and second breaks get the nod during ice fishing's opening sequence. As winter ensues, the arena switches to deep shoreline breaks.

Deep breaks on a typical northern tier lake occur somewhere between 20 and 40 feet of water. Once walleyes migrate to deep breaks, their conventional evening and morning feeding binge can filter into

Sauger, a close relative to the walleye, are distinguishable by dark spots on their dorsal fin and lack of white trimmings on their lower fins. Sauger and walleye coexist on numerous waters, particularly large lakes, reservoirs, and river systems.

daytime hours. Building snow cover and deep water combine to decrease light penetration. This improves your chances of hooking a fish or two during off-peak periods.

Deep offshore bars are synonymous with big, open-basin lakes, and they're also synonymous with producing walleyes through the heart of winter. What differentiates deep bars from ones described earlier is their entire scope of depth and how high they elevate. Typical midlake bars might rise from depths of 20 to 40 feet, but they peak somewhere in the 5 to 10 foot range. Whereas true, deep bars rise to a lesser degree, and they usually cover a far greater surface area. An example of an ideal deep bar would be one that lifts from 35 feet, plateaus at 20 feet, and rambles for a couple hundred yards.

Bottom-content transitions are something else to look for when considering deep offshore bars. The basins of numerous lakes feature areas where hardpan or silt greets sand, gravel, or rocks. A good example of this occurs on Minnesota's Mille Lacs Lake where the Gravel Bar, an enormous structure, rises to 28 to 30 feet from surrounding depths of around 35 feet. Here, the hardpan main basin gives way to an elevated gravel platform. Adding to its allure are several reefs sprinkled across the top of this popular deep bar, again, structure within structure.

At this time, it's prudent to bring shoreline points back into the mix because many yield walleyes all winter long. Large points with steep breaks and immediate access to deep water are alluring to walleyes throughout the hardwater period. The difference between early ice and midwinter location on a given point is depth. Early in the season, walleyes move up breaks and on top of flats to forage, but as winter wears on and the shallow-water food base vanishes, so do the walleyes. They no longer have reason to invade shallow reaches. Instead, low-light feeding frenzies commence over deep breaks off points, and saddles between points and other nearby structure.

Offshore Reefs and Mudflats Are Isolated but Productive Midlake Structures

Fishing's terminology gets downright confusing when discussing structure. Take a hump for instance. A hump, an abrupt bottom elevation, also goes by the names sunken island, rock pile, reef, bar, and pushup.

In my world, sunken islands are vegetation-covered platforms rising from various depths. Rock piles are just that, piles of rocks, typically small and integrated into other structure. Reefs are large hard-bottom formations, which occur offshore and near shore. Bars, as described earlier, are expansive, flat-topped sand or gravel structures appearing at midlake or adjacent to a shoreline. Last, a pushup is just another word for a hump. Whew.

Having said that, what you're looking for during midwinter are offshore reefs—big, boulder-infested, steep-breaking reefs. Offshore reefs give walleyes what they need during winter's wickedest period: immediate access to deep-water safety, a preferred temperature zone, a variety of depths within a finite range, and a perfect backdrop in which to pursue baitfish.

Key elements to look for on an offshore reef are large rocks, irregular fingers or arms, a deep crown, sheer breaks, and where the reef's footings meet the main basin, we hope in conjunction with a

Offshore rock structure consistently produces walleyes (as shown) during midwinter. Identify the top, break, and transition to the basin or midlake flat. Walleyes will use everything a hump has to offer, and their specific location depends on light levels (time of day) and availability of forage.

bottom-content change. Whether you should fish the reef top depends on how shallow the structure gets. By midwinter, you can usually ignore the apexes of reefs that peak at less than 6 or 8 feet of water. Conversely, do not ignore a reef top that crests anywhere from 12 to 40 feet.

More winter anglers are tapping what I call a "no-man's-land" walleye bite. This definition is misleading because it implies that you can randomly track walleyes over open water, which is only partially true. The whole picture reveals packs of walleyes roaming the main basin, while maintaining some reference to offshore structure. Midwinter commonly finds walleyes hanging 50, 75, or 100 yards and more from offshore reefs and bars. Midday hours put walleyes in a neutral to inactive mode outside structure before their evening invasion. Savvy fishermen can locate and coax them into snapping when conventional wisdom tells us they won't.

As prosperous as deep reefs are mudflats. Mudflats, like gravel bars, are plateau-shaped formations that rise from the basin, but instead of having a solid composition, mudflats are a suspended mass of silt. The hovering sediment is home to countless invertebrates (aquatic worms, etc.) and immature insects (mayfly larvae, etc.). To a degree, walleyes are attracted to these morsels, but they're far more interested in baitfish and perch, which rely on the goodies nestled inside the mud. Mille Lacs Lake, named a moment ago for its gravel bars, is even more famous for its mudflats. The 130,000-acre lake's upper half is littered with amoebic-shaped mudflats that entertain walleyes and perch all winter. As with other offshore structure, such as reefs and bars, a mudflat's best features are fingers, inside turns, breaks, and saddles between mudflats.

Rivers and Backwaters As Alternative Venues

Unstable ice conditions make rivers unattractive venues for early ice walleye fishing, with the exception of backwaters. However, as air temperatures drop and ice conditions improve, certain river systems produce loads of wintertime walleyes and sauger.

Generally, adequate ice forms only over stagnant and light-flowing sections of river. River backwaters best represent stagnant locales. These out-of-the-current channels, bays, and sometimes entire lakes produce well at first ice. Their shallow waters freeze early and myriad species invade to feast. Key conditions to look for are outside edges of submerged timber, deep holes within a backwater, rare patches of remaining vegetation, and structure near the main channel entry or current break.

Midwinter river anglers seek deep holes on slow-flowing portions of the main channel. You can see a good example of this on the St. Croix River near the towns of Hudson, Wisconsin, and Stillwater, Minnesota. Here, long 30- to 40-foot main channel troughs host walleyes and sauger, among other species. Ice fishermen work from the base of the trough on up opposing breaks. They usually engage sauger in the 30- to 40-foot gully and find walleyes on various points leading up the slope.

Late Ice Walleyes

Fattened Up and Preparing to Spawn. Midwinter walleye locations and techniques usually hold until the end of the season in most places. In Minnesota and Wisconsin, there's a month or more of ice fishing left when walleye season closes, granted locations such as Lake of the Woods offer extended seasons. Most fishermen switch gears and pursue perch, crappies, sunfish, and whitefish after walleye season closes.

If local regulations permit walleye hunting into March and April, turn your attention to spring spawning areas. Walleyes start migrating to favored spawning grounds, shallow sand and gravel shoals, about the time melted snow begins funneling down old holes.

Prespawn walleyes stage, or hold, just off points and breaks beyond shallow spawning terrain. Return to some of the honey holes that produced during early ice, and you can upsize lures and live bait because prespawn feeding is voracious.

How to Ice Winter Walleyes

The Tools and Techniques. The stage has been set. Research and experience have fused together to identify a probable walleye haunt, and if you're sitting on fish, well over half the work is done. Because it doesn't matter how fancy your spoons are or how much your ATV cost, if you're not on fish, all will be for naught. Again, location, location, location! Having said that, there are several tools and techniques necessary to complete the perfect outing. Integrating the right equipment and tackle with proven methods is the challenge. Read on!

Jigging

Movement gets things killed. What? That's right, the trigger, which induces walleyes to inhale shiner minnows and crush fleeing perch, is movement. Their eyes are designed to distinguish the subtlest gesture in blackened water. A thin stripe running horizontally along their sides detects the flickering fins of tiny baitfish. An aerodynamically assembled physique allows walleyes to strike with incredible speed and accuracy, and a nasty set of piercing and shredding teeth render captured prey motionless, then dead. Movement impels this violent sequence.

The act of jigging creates a motion that induces fish to strike. Every day, every species, and every lure require a different jigging action. In the case of walleyes, jigging aims to duplicate the motion of injured or fleeing baitfish.

Jigging is the definitive means for catching walleyes and sauger through the ice. A Nils Master swimming jig coaxed this late winter sauger to strike.

When is jigging suitable? Every time you embark! Moments when jigging is not the preferred method are few and far between. And when a winter angler commences jigging, there's a good chance it's with a spoon. The lexicon of jigging spoons covers a gamut of sizes and patterns manufactured by a horde of companies, each model geared toward a special circumstance.

A recent trend in ice fishing is the manufacturing of meticulously painted jigs with finishes rivaling German automobiles. The impetus behind these museum-quality jigs is realism. Cold-water walleyes are innately more lethargic than during the summer months; therefore metabolism is down, and when they do feed, walleyes verge upon forage at a slower pace. This laid-back approach gives them greater opportunity to examine quarry. Improved water clarity during the winter months increases the demand on your presentation. Interesting and realistically painted lures have a better chance of getting inhaled in a cold-water environment. Certain lures seem to work better on certain lakes, while jigged in a particular fashion, but before we enter into jigging methods, let's classify jigging spoons.

Wide-Flash Spoons

Earlier you read about the combination of early ice, shallow structure, and hostile walleyes. Well, there's a group of jigging spoons specifically built to meet the task. I call them wide-flash jigging spoons.

These gaudy, wide-bodied lures perform admirably in water 12 feet and shallower. Wide-flash spoons are remarkably light for their size, causing them to flutter when dropped. The trembling generates intense vibrations, which make this category of jigging spoons effective in dingy water. Often coupled with their obtuse shapes are vivid paint jobs, again, boding well for use on aggressive fish or in stained water. Examples include Northland's Flash'n Fire-Eye Minnow and the willow spoon series by Bad Dog Lures and Ivan's Glo Tackle.

Pounding Spoons

This broad category covers 90 percent of today's jigging spoons. In general, pounding spoons are torpedo shaped, lead bodied, minnow looking, and come in sizes ranging from 1/16th ounce to 1 ounce. And the right size and weight combination is effective in 5 to 50 feet of water.

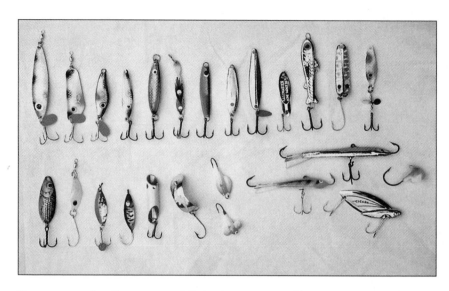

The top row of walleye spoons falls in the category of heavy pounding. They are Ivan's Glo Tackle's Smasher, 3-D Crusher, 3-D Slammer, and 3-D Jigging Spoon, Northland Tackle Buckshot Rattle Spoon, Bad Dog Lures Lazer Twin Minnow, Jig-A-Whopper Rocker Minnow, Shearwater Fishing Tackle Thumper, Bay de Noc Swedish Pimple, Acme Kastmaster, System Tackle by Lindy Little Joe Deadly Dart, Jig-A-Whopper Hawger Spoon, and JB Lures Pro Varmit. The first six lures in the second row are wide-flashing spoons. They are the Northland Tackle Fire-Eye Minnow, Ivan's Glo Tackle Willow Leaf, Bad Dog Lures Jeweled Willow and Crippled Minnow, Outdoor Creations Torpedo Lure, and Shearwater Fishing Tackle's Helgamite. Two excellent lead swimming jigs are the Northland Tackle Mini Air-Plane Jig and System Tackle by Lindy Little Joe Flyer. Next come swimming jigs by Nils Master and Rapala. Reef Runner's Cicada is a phenomenal blade bait, and rounding things off, you've got a quintessential lead-head jig, the Northland Tackle Fireball.

No other category of jigging spoons gives anglers a more diverse field of lures to choose from. Tackle producers such as Ivan's Glo Tackle offer fishermen the Crusher (heavy), Smasher (minnow imitating), Slammer (great action), among others, each fitting into the pounding classification. Other examples of pounding spoons are Thumper by Shearwater Fishing Tackle, Rocker Minnow by Jig-A-Whopper, and Swedish Pimple by Bay de Noc Lure Co.

Low-Profile Spoons

Use these demure lures when you're looking for just enough hardware to place bait in front of lethargic fish. A small minnow or min-

Occasionally, you need smaller panfish-size jigs to invoke hits from sluggish walleyes. Arrive prepared for any circumstance by carrying a wide assortment of lure sizes.

now head is often teamed with these slender, drab jigging spoons. The Pin Minnow series from Bad Dog Lures are perfect illustrations of low-profile spoons.

Ultradeep Situations

If your lure looks and acts like a minnow, you're in good shape. Nothing behaves more like a real minnow than a properly worked swimming jig. These horizontal jigs come in shapes and colors that rival actual minnows and immature game fish, and their darting and slashing motions exemplify nature at its best.

Swimming Jigs

Too often in today's world we get caught up in the race to have the newest and coolest—basically, keeping up with the Jones. Ice fishing is no different. In an effort to pluck the wildest pattern from a store shelf, we often neglect time-proven lures. Traditional lead-head jigs account for as many winter walleyes as do any other style of ice-fishing lure. This is partially because some anglers elect to not expand their arsenal beyond jig heads. Another reason is that conventional lead-head jigs are awfully tough to beat in deep water.

They drop fast and provide good feel. A jig's heavy and condensed composition causes it to drop fast and send strong messages (nibbles, hits, etc.) back to the sender. A forged single hook makes unhooking fish and rebaiting efficient. Northland FireBall Jigs are the finest examples of hardwater jigs.

Swimming jigs meet specific criteria. First, they're perfect for a search-and-destroy approach while hopping from hole to hole. Second, their furious action works wonders on hostile walleyes, but a note of caution. Swimming jigs require that their users employ control and confidence. Control is necessary to make use of their tapered fins and water-slicing shapes; confidence factors in because true advocates of swimming jigs do not use live bait complements. The hottest swimming jigs come from Normark/Rapala, Nils Master, and Bad Dog Lures. Traditional lead-head swimming jigs by Northland

Lead swimming jigs are an underrated weapon for icing hardwater walleyes. Swimming jigs generate hopping and circling motions that habitually entice foraging walleyes, northern pike, perch, and trout.

and System Tackle by Lindy Little Joe also produce circling and darting action, but they're designed for use with a minnow dressing, whole or partial, live or dead.

Color Selection

Color choice is as localized a component of winter fishing as is live bait selection. Certain colors are hot on certain lakes, and even these situations can change over the course of a hardwater season or even an afternoon.

Historically, lures painted in chartreuse, florescent orange, bright green, or combinations of these colors gain interest from walleyes. Traditional metallic silver, bronze, gold, and copper catch their fair share of fish, too. Many spoons now incorporate bright finishes over a metallic backdrop. There's no damage done by working in a little glow-in-the-dark (phosphorescent) paint while fishing in stained water, deep water, or at night.

Live Bait Tipping

We've covered a lot on jigging spoons with only scant mention of live bait. Truth be known, 9.9 times out of 10, when a jigging spoon disappears beneath the ice, it is coupled with live bait. Consider the jigging spoon your attractant and live bait the stimulus to strike.

Live bait selection for walleye jigging comes from the minnow genre. A walleye's primary food source is baitfish, so there's little reason to use anything else. Bait store minnow options vary from region to region, generally coinciding with native species. You'll want to purchase whatever minnow species are native to your area and endorsed by bait store owners. Like trout anglers say, "Match the hatch!"

With a spoon in hand and a bucket of bait, the next step is rigging. Your options are to hook either a whole or a partial minnow—a couple factors will influence your decision. Whole live minnows work best when walleyes are aggressive and you need minimal jigging to generate hits. Upgrade and downgrade minnow size based on how walleyes react to your offering. For instance, short strikes and disinterest call for using smaller bait, whereas, you can fend off pesky perch and tiny walleyes by increasing minnow size. Another thing to consider is that live minnows swim freer and appear more natural on single-hook jigging spoons than those with treble hooks.

Overall, partial minnows work better on jigging spoons. Pinch or cut off the front half of a chub or fathead, and thread it onto one or two barbs of a treble hook. A minnow's head is the natural bull's eye of foraging walleyes, and consequently there's little need for the remainder of the body. The smaller target ensures better hook setting. Upgrade spoon size if you're concerned about the total package being too petite.

Speaking of hooks, keep them sharp and replace worn out ones. Ultrasharp Mustad Triple Grip and VMC Barbarian treble hooks make ideal replacements. Bad Dog Lures sells a line of replacement hooks (Jeweled Trebles) that feature a molded-colored attractant at the base of the shank—not a bad idea either.

Jigging Methodology

A quality tool is rendered useless in the hands of a novice. Don't fret, because I'm not going to make this fully analogous to jigging spoons, but it's enough to say that a seasoned ice angler dances spoons better than a rookie.

Typically, walleyes are creatures of the lake floor, meaning they spend most of their time within a few feet of the bottom. Your job is to master that range. Jigging is a combination of speed, height, drop, and pattern. Speed is how fast you pump a spoon up and down. Height is the maximum point a spoon reaches on the lift. Drop refers to whether a lure free falls or descends with a taunt line. Pattern denotes the simple or complicated details making up a jigging sequence.

A basic walleye jigging sequence consists of three to five one-foot lifts off the bottom. Each deliberate lift is followed by a limp-line descent, with the final jig concluding in a three- to five- second pause or gentle quiver above the bottom. In essence, every jigging pattern is a variation of this basic method.

Snapping is an effective modification, particularly when using wide-flash spoons in shallow water. Instead of lifting, snap the spoon upward with a one- to two-foot crack of the rod tip. Follow each snap with an unabated free fall. Wide-flashing spoons flutter and circle when falling without resistance. End a series of snaps with a brief motionless stint just off the bottom. You can use snapping at any depth and with any type of jigging spoon. The game plan is to stimulate uninterested walleyes, give aggressive fish what they want, or to drag fish in from a distance.

78

Walleye

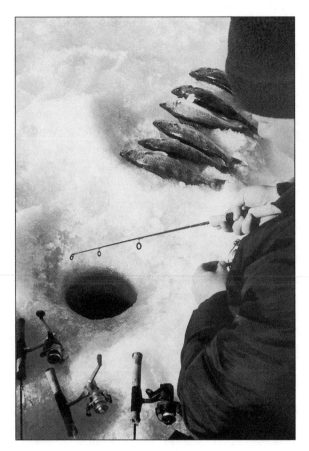

A good spot; active jigging methods; and an arsenal of prerigged rod, reel, and lure packages result in a fine mixed bag of walleyes and sauger.

Snapping heavier spoons over silt, sand, or mud bottoms affords the opportunity to introduce what I call desert storming, named for the sandy surface cloud created. The billow results from bottom contents rising after a heavy jigging spoon smacks the lake floor. The disturbance often attracts walleyes and nearby baitfish. You can work desert storming into various walleye jigging sequences.

A way to bolster a desert storming technique is by making your jigging spoon imitate an injured minnow struggling on the lake floor. Drop a minnow-tipped spoon to the bottom, and raise and lower your rod tip just enough for the lure's main body to elevate, but the hook and live bait portion remain on the bottom. Pump and quiver the bait for a few seconds, then pause. Game fish species such as walleyes and perch routinely inhale chow right off the bottom. We can hope they'll embrace yours.

At the opposite end of the spectrum emerges the lazy lift and lower approach anglers often use with jig heads in deep water. A single-hooked live minnow sweeping up and down in deep water is tempting. Reverse tip a live minnow by facing the head away as you run the hook point through the belly and up and out the back behind the dorsal fin. Gently raise and lower the combo off the bottom with one- to two-foot margins; follow every few moves with a respite. If nothing happens, gingerly quiver your rod tip, and let it sit once more. Still nothing, it's probably time to move.

You just read about quivering, a technique used with a lead-head jig and live minnow. Well, you can incorporate quivering into just about any approach. Quivering is best factored into a jigging sequence when a bait traditionally sits still. So try a jig-fall, jig-fall, jig-fall, jig-fall, rest, and if nothing happens, quiver the bait for a few seconds, then freeze again. If there is still no action, continue quivering, freezing, and starting over. More often than not, quivering outproduces total stillness.

One of my favorite quivering variations for walleyes is to delicately pump a long glass rod at the butt rather than the tip. The action on my Thorne Bros. solid glass spinning rod is so smooth that I can pump the reel and butt up and down in one- to two-inch bursts, and the energy transfers directly to the rod tip and lure. The line never jumps, so the spoon glides up and down temptingly.

Factored into these jigging presentations is the assumption that you're watching a flasher all the while. I can't imagine jigging without seeing my lure frolic about as prospective fish enter the strike zone. Tweaks and modifications in a jigging sequence directly result from observing fish as they react to a presentation. You can implement elements such as quivering when a flasher reveals available fish aren't responding. A flasher will also tell you whether to jig right along the bottom or several feet up, based on fish location. A fishless flasher should tell you that it's time to mosey along.

In summary, there is no quintessential jigging method that's sure to catch walleyes every time out. Instead, ice fishermen need to customize a jigging sequence that best fits their environment. Walleye mood, their relative distance to the bottom, lure type, and total depth are all factors that you need to build into a tailored jigging approach. Experiment, watch what other anglers do, and ask around local bait shops. In time you'll develop a feel for jigging, and this experience will assist in germinating customized techniques for other waters.

Tip-Ups and Setlines

Stationary lines provide ideal support to aggressive jigging. In Minnesota, winter anglers are permitted two lines per person; in Wisconsin this number jumps to three; and in North Dakota you can spread the field with four lines a person. There are times when one line is plenty, but there are other moments when volume and variety put fish on the ice.

Treat tip-ups as an experiment. Jig deep and lay a tip-up shallow or vice versa. Use different and bigger bait on your tip-up. For example, if you're jigging with cut fatheads on a break in 15 feet of water, set a tip-up and live shiner minnow either shallower, on top of the flat, or deeper, beyond the break. The remote presentation is effective for discovering walleyes that might be funneling away from your primary holes. Also, the larger minnow is equipped to challenge bigger, badder fish.

There are several tip-up variations available to winter anglers. Each type purports to alleviate common ice-fishing foibles, such as line freezing, hole freezing, and inability to signal strikes at great distances. Guess what folks? I carry two models of tip-ups regardless of what Old Man Winter whips up. I never leave home without at least a couple HT Enterprises Polar Tip-Ups or Arctic Fisherman Beaver Dams.

Setlines or deadsticks are another way to approach the multiple-line issue. Tip-ups offer superior access to distant realms, but setlines

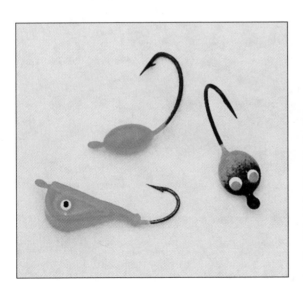

Anglers often use weighted hooks with tip-ups; they combine the properties of a plain hook and sinker while tossing in a little color. Pictured clockwise from the lower left corner is a Sumner Bros. Flirty Girty, Gopher Tackle weighed kahle hook, and a Shearwater Fishing Tackle flathead jig.

The standard for all other tip-ups is the Arctic Fisherman. Notice the hallmark sturdy wood craftsmanship and submerged brass spool. The author wraps a spongy waterproof tape around one end of the wood to safely embed hooks while transporting.

The Polar Tip-Up from HT Enterprises is the only other traditional remote line you'll need. You can easily detect a strike on this lightweight and inexpensive device when its blaze orange flag unfurls.

A clip-on weight and line marker make tip-up fishing easier. Line markers, such as this System Tackle by Lindy Little Joe product, keep permanent tabs on how much line to let out when resetting a tip-up. You can use clip-on weights to rapidly reach the bottom while adjusting line markers.

are a viable option when you're keeping the arsenal within the confines of a shelter or if outside temperatures are balmy and holes aren't freezing over. A setline rigged inside a fish house usually consists of a plain hook, colored bead (attractor), sinker, float (bobber), and an undulating minnow. As with a tip-up, an oversized minnow beneath a float has the power to lure big walleyes and those that demonstrate little interest in lively spoons.

Rigging a setline is elementary, but choosing the components requires some forethought. Start with top-of-the-line hooks. Advancements in manufacturing and sharpening have brought about a bold new class of fishing hooks. VMC, Owner, and Gamakatsu are a few companies currently building cutting-edge hooks—no pun intended. My favorites are the VMC cone cut octopus hooks and Gamakatsu's shiner hooks. Match hook size to minnow, so it pays to carry a variety of sizes.

Colored beads can bolster the attraction. Slide a chartreuse, blaze orange, metallic, or glow-in-the-dark bead on the line before tying up. Experiment with colors. Quality colored hooks by VMC, Gamakatsu, and Owner give you some dazzle without using a bead attractant.

Floats or bobbers are another category that's expanded over the past decade. The advent of slip bobbers revolutionized the way we still fish in deep water, and now winter anglers have a wealth of slip floats to choose from. Thill and Gapen's manufacture the industry's finest balsa wood bobbers. Both companies offer models and sizes geared for specific situations.

The key to using any type of bobber is setting buoyancy. Even a properly selected float is useless if weight isn't adjusted accordingly. For instance, imagine that your golden shiner offering has been tugged on a couple of times by light biters. The bobber pops up and down, but there's no opportunity for a hook set. Try making the minnow easier to grab by lowering resistance. Add an additional split-shot sinker or two so your float barely rides above surface under its own power. This way, if a walleye takes a whack at it, there will be little to no opposition, hence increasing your odds by allowing the fish to run.

A deadstick is like a setline in that it presents walleyes a lethargic live bait offering, but deadsticks are float free. Instead of suspending bait above the bottom via a float, as on a setline, the rod tip of a deadstick handles the load.

Drop your bait to the bottom, bring it up a couple cranks, and place the rod tip over the center of the hole. There are several ways to position your rod during the waiting period, the best of which are the many rod holders now in stores, available in freestanding, bucket-mounted, or portable fish-house mounted varieties.

Regarding rod selection for a deadstick, the finest ones feature a sensitive colored tip for visually detecting strikes, as well as extra length (32 inches plus) for smooth hook sets. Thorne Bros. designs a custom deadstick rod that was requested by The In-Fisherman's Doug Stange. The durable 32-inch pole features a limber tip that reveals even the slightest taps.

Rods, Reels, and Fishing Line

For decades ice-fishing equipment wallowed in the dark ages, despite the fact that the open-water industry was advancing at a rabbit's pace. Fortunately, we now live in an era when winter anglers demand improved gear and manufacturers are willing to churn it out. Say good-bye to spiked jiggle sticks teamed with offensively thick line!

Some asked, "Why can't I put a regular reel on a short summer fishing rod?" Well, you can. Dozens of rods are now constructed specifically with ice fishing in mind, and your existing open-water reels, as well as a handful of cold-weather models, pair well with these poles. Factored into the rod and reel equation is fishing line. Many of today's high-tech lines now meet the stringent demands of winter use.

The criteria for selecting a winter walleye reel is slightly different from choosing one for summer fishing. For one, casting distance isn't a concern. Another variance is size, because rarely will you use as large a reel for ice fishing as you do in open water—balancing a large reel with a short ice rod is difficult. What you do need is a smooth-turning, well-lubricated, open-face reel with a reliable drag system and adequate line capacity. The fewer bells and whistles the better, because frivolous extremities are vulnerable to cold weather. Abu Garcia, Mitchell, Shimano, and South Bend fabricate the reels affixed to my ice-fishing rods.

Maybe more important than reel selection is choosing rods. Rods detect and transmit strikes and ultimately exert the lethal blow that hooks a fish—all highly critical elements in ice fishing. The first choice to make is deciding between graphite and fiberglass, both of which compounds have inherent benefits. Most rods on the market are manufactured from graphite blanks, both hollow and solid. Graphite's leading qualities are sensitivity and lightness. Fiberglass rods are known for their durability, uniform curvature under stress, and smooth hook sets. Again, both hollow and solid blank models are available.

In a graphite or fiberglass walleye rod, look for something 28 to 42 inches long, preferably with a cork handle. Length is important for a sweeping hook set; shorter poles tend to rip lures from fish mouths. Cork is the perfect handle material because it doesn't get slippery when wet, warms quickly in your hand, and forwards action from rod blank to hand with minimal loss of feel.

Guides (eyes) are also important. Some manufacturers put on too few guides and use inferior materials. A respectable 36- or 42-inch walleye jigging rod should feature four or five guides including the tip. More guides typically mean flatter line transit, because the line can closely follow rod movement. Multiple well-placed guides also transfer the load to the rod's butt, which puts power and control in your hand. As far as guide design, your better rods feature ceramic guides such as those made by Fuji.

On the upper end of the rod-building spectrum sits Thorne Bros. and Red Barn Rods, two respected Minnesota manufacturers. There are probably local builders in your area that put out custom poles, too. Shimano, Mitchell, Berkley, HT Enterprises, and South Bend offer quality commercial models. Another thing to look for are hot buys on ice-fishing rods constructed from broken, but premium open-water blanks. The remaining tips are fitted with cork handles, and an ice-fishing rod is born!

Completing the rod and reel equation is properly matched fishing line. This is a juncture at which opinion and personal preference run rampant. The modern age of ice fishing turned attention to monofilament or nylon lines, most of which were the same ones open-water anglers already used. Then came a sampling of lines specifically geared for winter use. We next saw the advent of superlines, which are a variety of high-tech braids and fuses developed to give unmatched strength and sensitivity. In response to the onslaught of superlines, arrived an improved batch of monofilament products. Hardwater anglers are unquestionably beneficiaries of this evolution.

To keep line selection as simple as possible, let's begin with nylon options and line strength. The overwhelming majority of winter fishermen use nylon lines and will continue to do so. Strength, sensitivity, and low diameter are properties a cold-weather line requires. For jigging walleyes, line test strengths ranging from 6 to 10 pound will suffice. Narrower diameter 6- and 8-pound test lines are less visible, therefore preferred. You might consider going to 10-pound test in shallow water, dingy water, or if northern pike invasions are of concern.

Ice cold water changes some intrinsic properties of nylon line. Stiff, low-stretch, abrasion-resistant lines such as Berkley XL, which perform well in a boat, or on a baitcast reel, become too rigid for spinning use. They tend to uncoil easily and corkscrew uncontrollably down a hole. Better equipped for ice fishing are soft, supple, low-memory lines such as longtime favorite Berkley XL. Once submerged into an icy environment, supple lines seem to firm up to a point at

More winter fishermen are releasing large walleyes, realizing that the quality of fishing depends on the return of breeding females. Plus, small 15- to 19-inch walleyes make much better table fare. This beefy Lake of the Woods walleye was quickly returned to the water.

which they take on heightened sensitivity, but without the stiffness dilemma. There are a number of limp, low-diameter nylon lines from Berkley, Stren, Fenwick, Cortland, Silver Thread, and Maxima on the market. Every season a few new models, each claiming to introduce different characteristics, hit the stores. Buy a couple different kinds, spool them on various outfits, and compare their performances. While writing this book, my preferences for jigging walleyes were Berkley SensiThin, tried and true Berkley XL, and Stren Easy Cast.

Regarding line color, it's another case of matching your environment. In stained or green water, go to a colored line such as Berkley XL in green. Otherwise, clear nylon makes the grade. Lower test strengths and narrowed line diameter are the best medicines for making line as transparent as possible. Compare relative line diameters while shopping for line; manufacturers, especially those with new and improved products, print line diameter statistics on the outer packaging. If you're still confused, simply ask someone. Veteran ice fishermen and sporting goods store personnel will surely offer a suggestion or two.

Superlines have some, but limited, use on the ice. Their unmatched strength and sensitivity lend superlines highly effective for open-water situations, but their potency can be a detriment in supercold water. You need some stretch while fighting a walleye beneath the ice, and superlines were developed to yield as little as possible. A situation in which superline strength and sensitivity matches beautifully for winter walleyes is when using a long fiberglass pole, which has limberness built in. I'll sometimes use fused superlines such as Berkley Fireline and SpiderWire Fusion on warmer winter days or while cooped up in a fish house. Superlines collect water and subsequently freeze in cold weather.

A Final Thought

Being the nocturnal, bottom-dwelling, carnivorous, structure-relating, schooling, predators that walleyes are, it's no surprise they are so popular with winter anglers. And when the right tools, techniques, and structure come together in concert, the mysterious walleye enters the realm of the predictable and catchable.

The following structures are magnets for walleyes:

- Shoreline points
- Bars
- Breaks
- Outside weededges
- Rock humps
- Structure within structure (i.e., a weed bed on a rock hump)
- Structure adjacent to structure (i.e., a rock pile sitting off the tip of a point)

Chapter 5

Northern Pike

AS A FISH, BEING ON TOP OF THE ROCK IS A GOOD THING. Think about it, lesser species such as crappies, sunfish, and perch have two primary concerns in their day-to-day lives. Number one, they're perpetually challenged to locate food. Second, subservient species are forever on the lookout for opportunistic predators. Northern pike also vex about where their next meal is coming from, but being what they are, pike seldom stress about becoming a meal—except cannibalistic encounters in which big pike prey on small pike.

Often referred to as freshwater wolves, northern pike rule the waterways. Throughout most of their range, northern pike are the largest and fiercest fish beneath the ice. This lofty position on the food chain is earned through a pike's ability to track down, capture, and kill forage. A pike's hunting capabilities stem from its keen sense of smell and knack for recognizing movement. Sheer muscular power permits pike to lash out and clutch fleeing baitfish; rows of surgically sharp teeth, encased within a crushing jaw, ensure that nothing escapes. Pike regularly prowl during the daytime hours, but activity tends to peak in the morning, with a secondary blip just before dusk.

These characteristics translate into one fantastic fight for winter anglers! Striking, thrashing, attacking, and smacking are all terms associated with battling icy northern pike. Seemingly pesky, pound-and-a-half and two-pound pike skirmish

Northern pike rarely permit winter's wrath to curb their appetites. These unofficial kings of freshwater fishes are widely distributed and frequent visitors at the holes of ice anglers.

with a fervor beyond their size. Few scenarios in ice fishing's lexicon compare to a knock-down-drag-out war with a trophy-caliber northern. These are remarkable fish!

Pike keep their environment in check. A healthy northern pike population holds panfish numbers at a manageable level and even grants an elite contingency to grow to slab status. The act of pike feeding on pike reduces the number of snakes and advances the cause for huge northerns.

We've established that northern pike are ferocious aquatic watchdogs. Another interesting behavioral aspect is their solitary nature. Unlike panfish and perch, and even walleyes to a degree, northern pike rarely travel in schools. Instead, pike reside in loose groups when relating to favorable habitat. Small to midsize pike often congregate inside a confined range, but the big boys prefer isolation.

Northern pike are generously distributed across the northern states and throughout Canada. These adaptable creatures make a comfortable living in elevated reservoirs to the west; the prairie pothole region; diverse and fertile waters in Minnesota, Wisconsin, Michigan, and Northern Illinois; lakes ranging east to Maine; and Canada's infinite glacially forged tracts of water.

Lakes to Look For

Pike Waters Are Not Created Equal. Northern pike are nearly as prolific as panfish. Few pieces of water within the northern pike's range are free of these carnivores, but lakes maintaining specific characteristics produce more and bigger fish. Once you've secured a lake for winter pike fishing, identifying specific locations is the task at hand.

All Shapes and Sizes

Northern pike rarely discriminate against the size of a body of water. I've hooked northerns in waters ranging from scanty farm ponds all the way up to lakes having more surface acres than I'd care to count. However, when you factor in the solitary and territorial nature of larger pike, it's safe to assume that bigger is better. Realistically, a 100-acre hole in the woods can only maintain so many large pike, if any. Inversely, a structure-ridden 10,000-acre lake potentially hosts hundreds if not thousands of midsize to huge pike.

Working in association with overall size is physical shape. Big, round featureless lakes certainly contain pike, but a little contour goes a long way. Bays, points, channels, narrows, inlets, outlets, and islands are physical attributes pike find appealing (more on their specific roles later).

Deep Forage Base

All the space and structure in the universe is meaningless without food. You could appropriate this passage to human populations in third world nations, but for this discussion, I'll reserve it for northern pike. Pike eat all year, therefore requiring a plenteous food base, and to cultivate hefty pike, a body of water must contain big, juicy foodstuffs.

Northern pike are carnivores. Their meat-eating diet runs the gamut from immature game fish species to naturally occurring baitfish. Staple food sources vary greatly from lake to lake, but a common thread among bodies of water known for producing giant pike is the presence of big bait.

Pike certainly dine on panfish, but they favor hefty minnows. Just look at a sunfish or crappie and imagine how difficult it must be to digest such a spiny, plate-shaped morsel, but pike will concede in a crunch. They much prefer luscious shiner minnows, chubs, fatheads, and shad.

Giant pike are often the payoff for fishing a big piece of water with a rich forage base. Aggressive jigging with a Bay de Noc Coho-Laker Taker scored this prespawn pike in only five feet of water.

Further aiding and abetting pike growth are larger baitfish types like smelt, ciscoes (tullibee), whitefish, and suckers. These species develop to larger sizes, hence fulfilling the needs of bigger northern pike. Perch, unnamed to this point, provide another abundant food source that also grows to sizes meeting the requirements of trophy-caliber pike.

Varied Structure and Depth

A moment ago, I emphasized the importance of a lake's shape and size—shape being irregular or full of features and size being large. Specific structures, features, and depths provide favored surroundings at different times throughout the winter. For instance, shallow weeds host activity early in the winter, whereas deep basin areas near offshore structure play a greater role later in the season. The perfect body of water offers a mixture of rocks, bars, breaks, humps, flats, and weed zones.

A couple final cogs in the structural wheel are tributaries and spawning grounds, which can be the same. Pike love to loom around current areas such as creek and river mouths. Why? First, baitfish flock to inlets and outlets throughout the hardwater season. Second, tributaries often double as runways leading to chosen breeding areas. Spawning areas certainly aren't limited to tributaries, though. Shallow backwater bays and sloughs, adjacent to the main lake, also host springtime rituals.

Winter Northern Pike Location

Attacking the Attacker. Most winter pike enthusiasts are stationary creatures. You've seen them; they pop a couple holes, throw out some flags, retire to lawn chairs or the front seat of a truck, and crack open cold ones. Not to say you can't take pike employing such passive means, but a proactive or mobile approach ensures greater success.

If the fellows in the previous drama happened to toss a dart that remarkably landed on pike-infested waters, more power to them. However, in all likelihood, unless they put careful consideration to use, they've hammered holes over marginal terrain. Times like these call for mobility.

Potential pike haunts often encompass great expanses. Clinging to a solitary location might produce a fish or two, but seldom can you hook fish after fish. Occasionally, a picture-perfect northern pike spot puts out consistently when fish are active, but a more reliable approach is to diversify. Explore various, but adjacent, depths and structures; then, if you don't encounter pike, relocate to a different area. Mobile ice-fishing techniques are as applicable to pursuing northern pike as they are to any other hardwater species.

Early Winter

Ice fishermen of all ranks and motivations laud the first ice period. Whether you fancy walleyes, perch, trout, or panfish, the season's initial coating of ice heightens expectations, but if I had to isolate a single species warranting the greatest attention, it would be northern pike. For a few short weeks succeeding ice up, the most notorious and feared pike invade the shallows.

The migration to shallow zones relates to our discussion on the correlation between late fall and first ice, which was a sidebar in the walleye chapter (see page 56). Briefly, for a stint beginning a week or two before ice up and ceasing a few weeks into ice-fishing season, the shallows come alive. Some weeds remain intact, oxygen is plentiful, water temperature is tolerable, and there's enough food to go around. Pike like what they see.

Shallow Weeds and Weedlines

Panfish use weeds. Walleyes sometimes favor weeds. Perch, in a pinch, will rally around greenery, but pike are completely lost without them. If you take nothing else away from this chapter, remember that northern pike are weed fish. Any mat of green vegetation remaining below the ice potentially yields pike, regardless of depth.

Look for vegetation while creeping onto the season's first coating of ice. Four to six inches of fresh ice is relatively transparent, and without a brushing of snow, weed beds should be clearly visible, the greener and thicker the better.

Shoreline weed flats often consist of several types of weeds; cabbage, coontail, and milfoil are the dominant species in most pike waters. Expect to find tall stalks of cabbage comprising middepth weeds as well as the outside edge; their looming broad-leafed canopies provide protective cover and ambush points. Coontail, a feathery-looking and rootless aquatic plant, usually forms dense clumps in depths up to about 10 feet. Milfoil, both Eurasian and Northern (domestic), appear in elevated mats sprouting as deep as 15 feet of water; exotic Eurasian milfoil has rapidly become a pike mainstay. A typical milfoil bed extends to or near the surface, and stringy stems root in the lake floor. Pike settle in the gaps formed between the lake bottom and underside of the foliage.

A characteristic shoreline weed zone features both an inside and an outside weededge. An inside edge is the breach between shore and where weeds begin showing up, an extremely shallow section of water. The outside edge is the point at which weeds cease to exist. The depth of an outside weededge is chiefly dictated by water clarity. Murky water retards growth and might cause the outside edge to establish in 10 feet of water or less. Conversely, the outside weededge in clearer conditions can manifest in 15 feet, 20 feet, or deeper water.

Weededges, both inside and outside, form natural cruising lanes and should be high on your list of prospects. An inside edge isn't worth exploring if it establishes in only a foot or so of water, but if

Rarely is it wise to pass on healthy green weeds. Pike use inside edges, outside edges, and emergent edges as long as oxygen levels and food supplies hold up.

there's a distinct brim in three, four, or five feet of water, you'll want holes along that edge. The deeper outside edge is a far better candidate, though. Regardless of what winter period is underway, as long as deep outside weeds subsist, pike will be present. Never, and I mean never, pass on a well-defined outside weededge!

Speaking of definition, 9 out of 10 times, the thickest, tallest, and most defined outside weededge attracts the most pike. If you can combine irregularities with the aforementioned attributes, you've really stumbled onto something. In this instance, irregularity denotes fingers and cuts. A weedy finger, as established in the walleye chapter, is an extension from the primary weededge. A cut is the opposite, a juncture where the outside edge slices into the main weed bed leaving a bare spot. Northern pike find both deviations suitable for ambushing and pursuing forage.

Within a weed flat, the main body between inside and outside edges, pockets (clearings) are key. Early winter sees pike milling about shallow and middepth weeds, hunting baitfish, immature game fish, and panfish. Pockets afford anglers weedless access and provide pike ambush points.

Bulrushes, Reeds, and Cattails

Anglers overlook some lucrative early ice spots. The overt signs of bulrushes, reeds, or cattails popping through the ice beg for attention, but anglers commonly pass by. Don't fall into the same trap!

Bulrushes and reeds occur as freestanding islands or shoreline condiments. Offshore bulrush islands attract foraging pike throughout the winter months. Edible perch and various baitfish species regularly take up residence among such islands. Look for northerns cruising the perimeter and making occasional forays into the frozen rushes. The deeper the rushes the better, for example, a bulrush island that tops out at five or six feet will entice more pike than one cresting at only two or three feet.

What makes shoreline bulrushes and reeds interesting to pike is overall size and relative depth. Again, a gigantic patch of bulrushes or reeds will hold more fish than a smaller one. The depth reference is germane to the premise that deeper is superior. An exemplary shoreline bulrush or reed bed ends with a steep break or slopes significantly throughout; pike delight in cruising deep water along a bed.

Want to further narrow your options? A large bed capping off a shoreline point is the crème de la crème. Bulrushes or reeds adjacent to a point present a three-faceted edge, along with the inherent qualities of a shoreline point. Still more? Beds that fade into submerged vegetation (i.e., cabbage or coontail) are desirable in any circumstance.

Cattails, on the other hand, propagate in murkier and more secluded reaches. Back bays on prolific pike waters often contain vast cattail bogs. Such bogs feature distinct edges that drop steeply. Northern pike patrol the perimeter searching for forage; panfish and baitfish commonly reside along the edge or beneath the floating canopy.

Shallow Bays and Coves

Rarely is a bay or cove too shallow when contemplating pike fishing at first ice. Backwaters, which are rendered helplessly weed choked all summer, host throngs of northerns during winter's opening few weeks. This confined environment contains everything a pike requires. Oxygen is plentiful, some weeds will still be up, baitfish and panfish are present, and water temperatures haven't reached the intolerable range.

Inside a bay, it pays to seek classic pike structure. Thriving weed beds, weededges, bulrushes, cattail bogs, rocks, inlets, and outlets concentrate activity within a shallow bay. Pike also wander broad flats, which are common inside shallow bays; you should certainly address shallow weedy flats. Coves and harbors also lure pike at first ice. These closed environments tend to be highly fertile and filthy with baitfish, but their hardwater lifespan is brief.

Narrows and Channels

By definition, a narrows is an area where two distinct sections of a lake join in a bow tie fashion. A channel is similar, but it constricts or closes for a longer distance before opening up. Either way, both venues are northern pike thoroughfares.

Pike understand that bottleneck areas naturally funnel traveling baitfish and panfish. Early winter finds northern pike lingering inside and just outside narrows and channels waiting to ambush gullible prey. Additionally, such tracts are first to freeze over, providing ice fishermen a stage for a maiden outing.

Inlets, Outlets, and Springs

I touched on the attraction of inlets and outlets earlier, so I'll refrain from duplicating established ground. Just keep in mind that northern pike are opportunistic creatures that prefer to ambush quarry rather than hunting and gathering. Inlet and outlet areas extend a prime situation for northern pike to crouch and wait for passing baitfish.

The current and oxygenation that springs generate attract all sorts of finned critters, pike included. A word of caution—ice conditions over and around inlets, outlets, and springs can be unstable, so please exercise caution.

Shallow Rocks

Although rocks aren't my leading choice at first ice, they do warrant recognition. Shoreline rocks, rocky points, and rock piles near shore hold baitfish, perch, and subsequently roving northern pike. Rocky places intermixed with greenery are of special interest.

One specific circumstance when shallow rocks do take precedence is on lakes harboring tullibee or whitefish populations. These shiny, overgrown baitfish are one of few species that spawn in the fall, and often their breeding season overlaps first ice. Pike simply cannot resist interfering with breeding whitefish.

Midwinter

Northern pike, not unlike other freshwater species, vacate shallow surroundings as winter wears on. A scant few of the places pike inhabited during winter's first three to six weeks maintain fish populations. About the time northern pike migrate to deeper water, their compulsion to feed diminishes to some degree. Foraging occurs less frequently, and their willingness to pursue prey subsides. Anglers must react by focusing on peak periods, investigating deeper haunts, and adjusting presentations.

Another notion regarding midwinter pike is that deeper generally translates into larger. It's possible to persist hooking one-, two-, and three-pound pike amid the shallows. Small pike are far less troubled by winter's progression than big pike; snakes are highly adaptable. Giant pike refuse to nibble on what's left in shallow environs, there-

Deep-water pike are frequent bonuses while jigging for walleyes, perch, and trout. This well-fed gator struck a maggot-tipped drop line, which was intended for jumbo perch.

fore, they vamoose. The moral of this narrative is that shallow locations are sufficient for fishermen who choose quantity versus quality. Trophy hunters venturing into deeper water won't hook as many fish, but their odds of setting into tape measure pike are greatly improved.

Remaining Weeds

Pike are reluctant to abandon shallow weed zones. In fact, during mild winters with minimal snow cover, some weeds remain intact throughout, and in such an event, a number of northerns elect not to leave. Weeds perish progressively from inside out. Shortened daylight hours, thickening ice, and a deepening blanket of snow cause weeds to brown, wither, and eventually die. Inside weeds lay down first, next come the middle weed flats, and last, deep weeds and the outside edge turn lifeless. On many clear lakes, deep weeds endure the entire hardwater period. Conversely, all or most weeds in murky and stained-water lakes have perished by midwinter; forsake such lakes after winter's first four to six weeks.

It's the deep outside edge you'll want to focus on, especially on clear lakes. Waters supporting an outside weededge in the 15- to 25-foot range are desirous. Pike use the weed wall as a travel route while sniffing out forage. Panfish, perch, and baitfish mistake deep weeds as a sanctuary from predators—they'll pay for it! As stated earlier, fingers and cuts along a deep outside edge are favorable. Be sure to punch a few holes beyond the outside edge; big pike frequently lurk just off the weedline.

Big Points and Bars

Simply stated, northern pike go wherever the food goes, and previous chapters ascertained that walleyes, baitfish, and various immature game fish species gravitate toward large shoreline points and offshore bars. Choose the largest and most structure-intense point on a lake. Identify its outside weededge, rock structure, deep breaks, and any section of the point facing secondary structure (i.e., a nearby rock pile or hump).

Lakeside of Bays

Bays and backwaters hosted pike earlier in the winter. However, once conditions compel them to drive deeper, pike exit the bays and search for the nearest favorable habitat just outside the mouth.

Northern pike move to deep outside weededges beyond the mouth, nearby offshore structure, as well as deep breaks beyond the weedline. Outside weededges funneling into the main lake are the first places to explore. Offshore formations take a close second, and your third option is to probe for big fish holding over deep breaks outside the bay's mouth.

Weedy Humps and Deep Rock Piles

About the time you recognize a decrease in pike activity among shore-line vegetation, it's time to look at offshore humps. They are my first choice once shoreline areas dry up. What makes one hump more attractive than another? Many hump characteristics divulged in the walleye and panfish chapters also ring true for northern pike. Massiveness is always good. Because pike seldom school and big pike tend to be territorial, more space equals increased fish numbers.

Weeds and rocks are two other components that make a hump engaging. A deep outside weedline skirting the perimeter of an off-shore hump is likely pike territory. Vegetation creeping up a hump's crown adds to the allure. Toss in a rocky break or random pile of stones and you're sure to find northerns on the prowl.

Here are a couple final notes on offshore humps: Opt for humps covered with bulrushes or lush, submerged vegetation, and ones that are 100-percent useable, meaning humps cresting at depths that al-low pike to crisscross the tops. Humps near other structure, such as points or bars, proffer even better results. This is another example of compiling structural elements to build better habitat.

Offshore rock piles, known for tempting walleyes, perch, and even lake trout, also have a knack for hosting big pike. It's rare to chance upon strong numbers of fish, but what the structure might lack in volume, it surely compensates for in hugeness. Deep rock piles may be the best spot to track a lake's biggest northerns.

Deep Flats and Basin Areas

I won't pretend that tracking pike in wide-open spaces is easy; it's not. However, there are a handful of clues to guide you, and sacrific-ing numbers for a chance at the fish of a lifetime is reward enough. Consider drifting back to simpler shoreline locations if you're after northerns for meat-eating purposes only; this is trophy country. By midwinter many of a lake's largest northerns meander out to the main basin and deep flats. Here, solitary fish roam about searching for perch, tullibee, and occasionally suspending panfish. These giant fish seldom cruise more than a foot or two from the bottom, unless in hot pursuit of suspended prey.

Typically, its proximity to structure determines what portion of a flat or basin presents the greatest opportunity to find northern pike. For example, picture a deep flat that bounces from 28 to 31 feet for acre, after acre, after acre. In the middle of the flat, sits an enormous rock reef that climbs to 15 feet. On the flat's shoreline-facing edge, the 28-foot mark jumps quickly to 15 feet (deep break). This illustration offers a couple clues. First, the rock reef is an obvious target. The reef itself is a natural reference point for nomadic pike. The 15- to 28-foot break is the reef's greatest feature. Deep-ranging pike often follow such contours as they scour for food. The 15-foot crown warrants exploration during morning and evening hours.

Late Winter

A little while back meat eaters were encouraged to pick on smaller fish and leave the deep-water pigs alone. This suggestion was in part to protect titanic pike, and at the same time give anglers a better chance of scoring a meal. I want to make something clear, I'm not a vegetarian. I like beer-battered fillets as much as the next person, but I am a staunch conservationist—not an environmentalist, a conservationist.

Pardon me while I jump down from my soapbox. Late winter is an angler's principal period to catch and release gigantic northerns, and potentially numbers of them. Hefty, egg-filled females begin swimming toward breeding areas, which often duplicate their early ice haunts. Northern pike spawn over shallow, soft bottoms occurring in bays, sloughs, and backwaters adjoining tributaries. Shallow in this discussion means shallow. Pike, even large specimens, will procreate in as little as a foot or two of water.

In bays and sloughs, ones that likely produced at first ice, keen winter anglers can track pike entering from the main lake. Work from the outside in. Look for encroaching pike within or just outside a bay or slough mouth. From there, move right into the murkiest, shallowest, and weediest surroundings; somewhere along the line you'll engage fish.

Building a Better Rod

Gather all ice-fishing poles that consist of wood dowels, thick black line, and metal spikes. Stuff them in a box, mark it "Free for Kids," and set it on the front lawn during your next garage sale. These simple poles remain one of the best starter outfits for young anglers, but for the masses, the sport of ice fishing is evolving and so are its tools.

Along with the appeal for overall quality is a need for species-specific rods. In the early 1980s Gregg and Paul Thorne, founders of Thorne Bros. in Fridley, Minnesota, with anglers such as Dave Genz, Pat Smith, and the In-Fisherman boys, began designing and building high-end ice-fishing rods to meet burgeoning demands. The tradition continues today as Thorne Bros.' lineup of winter poles currently contains more than 30 customized models, each geared for specific situations. Experienced rod builders, Paul Gausman, Bill Fiebranz, and Lonnie Murphy maintain the legacy.

What makes a rod better? "Better action through better design and better materials," says the staff at Thorne Bros. Thorne Bros. Rod Builders starts by using only the finest graphite and fiberglass blanks. Several of their winter rods originate from solid graphite blanks. Solid graphite provides superior action, durability, and sensitivity in a lightweight package. Solid graphite blanks are excellent for jigging panfish and walleyes. Hollow graphite is often preferred in rods exceeding 42 inches in length. Custom-tapered, solid-glass blanks have undergone a recent explosion in popularity. Solid glass, like solid graphite, offers sensitivity and durability, but the soft tip and smooth hook sets separate glass from graphite. Longer glass poles are phenomenal for working walleyes, northern pike, bass, and lake trout.

Thorne Bros. matches their premium blanks with quality guides and handles. Only the best Fuji guides and preformed cork handles find their way onto Thorne Bros. ice-fishing rods. A generous number of guides raised high off the blank keeps line

102

running smoothly while lowering a jig or battling a trophy, and the short, customized cork handle sets the reel back and puts the power in your hands.

Many sporting goods outfitters and small rod-building businesses now manufacture high-quality ice-fishing rods. Likewise, major rod manufactures such as Berkley and Shimano have introduced select products, and you can expect the trend to continue.

The art of custom rod building has spread into the realm of ice fishing. Fishermen now demand the same quality from their winter gear as they do from their summer stuff.

Northern pike are forever attracted to current. Figure 5.1 shows creek inlets, coulees, and forced water areas where two sections of a lake merge, setting the stage for outstanding winter action. In this diagram, a coulee dumps into a large bay. Pike will position themselves along the current break anticipating passing forage. The stump fields, sharp breaks, and shoreline riprap provide prime structure near or adjacent to the vaunted current line. Areas similar to this are known to host the biggest pike a lake or reservoir has to offer, especially early and late in the ice-fishing season.

Creek and river mouths are other venues pike set their sites on. Backwater areas conducive to pike spawning are usually upstream. An effective strategy is to position yourself outside the mouth and cut off pike attempting to enter the flowage. Catch a fish, take a picture, and quickly release her; keeping disturbances to a minimum promotes successful breeding. Again, be cautious of shaky ice quality.

Rivers, Backwaters, and Reservoirs

Nurturing Tremendous Pike.   I want to address the subject of reservoirs. You may have noticed that I referenced lakes nearly exclusively throughout this chapter. Although lakes dominate the range of northern pike, many of North America's greatest pike waters are reservoirs. Well, relax, because the collective information regarding weedlines, rocks, humps, points, and so on is transferable. Reservoirs feature many of the same structures.

Rivers sometimes sport enough ice to permit ice fishing. Backwaters and hardened slack water areas are recognized pike haunts. Major river systems such as the Mississippi maintain extensive backwater areas, where some sectors are so large they bear distinct identities (i.e., Lake Pepin and Lake Onalaska), and they fish similar to lakes.

Vast backwater labyrinths complete with channels, pockets, bends, and holes can be challenging to fish without first analyzing the situation. Explore any backwaters directly contacting the main channel (mouth) again, when ice conditions allow. Pike are known to hunker just off the current, awaiting incoming and outgoing victims. Deeper into a backwater, you'll want to focus on bottleneck areas and junctions. Bottlenecks, as described earlier, are narrows where traveling fish are forced to pass through a confined area. Junctions are where two, three, or more backwater arteries converge, creating a situation where fish traffic likely concentrates.

104

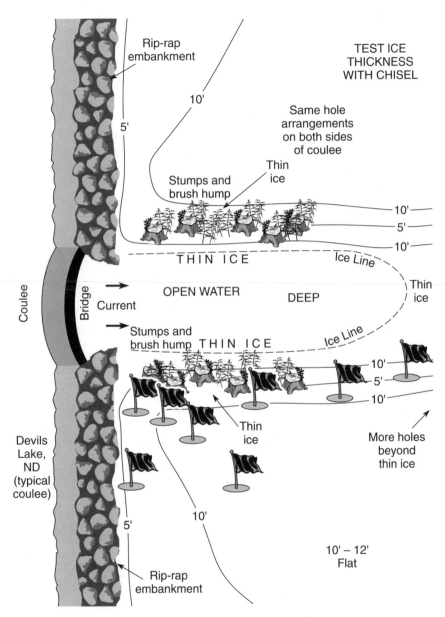

Rip-rap embankment

TEST ICE
THICKNESS
WITH CHISEL

10'

5'

Same hole
arrangements
on both sides
of coulee

Thin
ice

Stumps and
brush hump

10'
5'
10'

THIN ICE   Ice Line

Coulee

Bridge

Current

OPEN WATER   DEEP

Thin
ice

Stumps and
brush hump   THIN ICE   Ice Line

10'
5'
10'

Thin
ice

More holes
beyond
thin ice

Devils
Lake,
ND
(typical
coulee)

5'

10'

Rip-rap
embankment

10' – 12'
Flat

Figure 5.1   Places where northern pike might be found.

Submerged timber is a hallmark of river backwaters, and in a back-water maintaining acres and acres of flooded hardwoods, selecting a starting point is arduous. You can distinguish probable haunts from the maybes by incorporating the aforementioned bottlenecks, mouths,

105

and junctions with submerged timber. Also, deeper wood, standing or downed, tends to attract river pike, chiefly because backwaters as a whole are predominately shallow.

Slack-water zones usually take the form of a river eddy. Often, what's labeled an inlet on a lake translates to an eddy on a river. By definition, an eddy is any currentless section adjacent to the main channel. Downed timber or shoreline debris creates eddies, river bends create eddies, and dams also create eddies. River eddies offer fantastic pike fishing, but time is limited because the ice won't be around for long.

How to Ice Winter Pike

The Tools and Techniques. Unlike species such as perch, panfish, walleyes, and trout that feast on a wealth of aquatic edibles, everything in a pike's diet has fins. They don't eat zooplankton, bloodworms, or mayfly larvae, except teeny northerns. Instead, northern pike consume a potpourri of fish species. This knowledge allows ice fishermen to concentrate their efforts. See the fish, be the fish. I present dead bait, live bait, and spoons to dupe pike into believing it's natural forage.

Setlines

Jigging, jigging, and more jigging—have you had enough? Want panfish, go jig. Chasing walleyes, tie on a jig. Perch jerking, you guessed it—jig 'em. Northern pike also succumb to tantalizing jigging spoons and minnows, but setline tactics that have taken a backseat thus far now ride shotgun.

First, setlines, chiefly tip-ups, don't have to be the fully stationary devices they're perceived to be. A previous analogy spoke about a couple fellows tossing out flags and sipping beverages. True, this is what tip-up fishing means to many ice fishermen. However, if you treat tip-up placement and rigging with the same consideration you give to jigging tactics, the results will be surprising.

Tip-Up Varieties

I've been remiss to not offer any definition of a tip-up. Here we go. In its most basic form, a tip-up is a stationary contraption used to catch fish remotely, meaning placement a distance from anglers jigging or

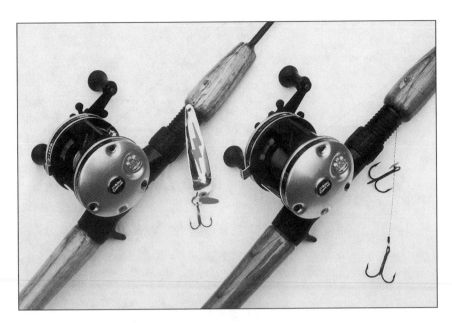

Jigging has risen in popularity with serious winter pike anglers, and rightly so. In head-to-head competition, jigging usually outproduces setline fishing. Pictured are a pair of Red Barn Rods matched with Abu Garcia 5500 bait-cast reels; one is rigged with a Bay de Noc Coho-Laker Taker spoon and the other with a Thorne Bros. quick-strike rig. Both packages are ideal for jigging northern pike and lake trout.

waiting for flags to fly. Bait or a lure is suspended beneath the device and strikes are indicated via an unfurling flag—truly a Reader's Digest condensed version.

You can address every conceivable tip-up circumstance with three specific models. I carry hundreds of jigs, nearly a dozen rod and reel combinations, but at most three tip-up types, and usually only two.

The first tip-up to pencil onto your must-have list is the Arctic Fisherman made in Beaver Dam, Wisconsin. The reason Beaver Dam is germane to this discussion is that some circles of ice anglers refer to them as Beaver Dams.

The phrase "time honored" comes to mind when I think about Arctic Fisherman tip-ups. These super-duty boards have been taking fish for decades, and little has changed since the original models first hit the ice. The baseboard is constructed of a wide pine plank that spans even the broadest hole. Freezing, a common tip-up foible, is remedied with a one-two punch. First, the line spool stays underwater where

The HT Enterprises' Windlass is the ultimate tool for presenting dead bait to northern pike, muskies, and lake trout. Adjusted properly, the slightest breeze causes dead minnows or cut bait to temptingly pulse up and down.

laws of nature deny icing. Second, that spool is suspended by a seamless steel tube that's filled with a special freeze-proof lubricant. Sitting on top of the tube is a double-sided spinner-trigger that, when teamed with the flag arm, offers four tension settings. Beaver Dams are incredibly reliable and durable, and you can implement them in any winter pike program.

The Polar Tip-Up by HT Enterprises is similar in design, but a little lighter in weight as well as on the pocketbook. Their lightness results from the fact that a Polar Tip-Up's baseboard is a synthetic frame, not a solid hunk of wood. A Polar Tip-Up, like an Arctic Fisherman, features a spring-driven arm or flag and a submerged line spool. A five-gallon bucket of Beaver Dams and Polars is like heading out deer hunting with a machine gun.

The final entry into tip-up stardom is HT Enterprises Windlass Tip-Up. The Windlass isn't as versatile as Polar or Arctic Fisherman, but it satisfies a specific need. It looks and behaves like an active Texas oil well. The upper cross member features a metal foil that pumps up and down in response to winds. The effect is hands-free jigging, and a Windlass is best suited for situations when dead bait is on the menu.

Live Bait Applications

More often than not, pike-oriented tip-ups are dressed with live minnows. I made the point earlier that northerns feed primarily on fish, and a high percentage of these fish are true baitfish (i.e., chubs, shiners, etc.). Consequently, bait shop variety minnows suffice.

Hooking a minnow beneath a tip-up introduces the vaunted injured minnow element. Pike thrive on injury and misery, albeit not their own perils. The unorthodox twisting and flipping of a hooked minnow spurs curiosity. The combination of flashing scales, fleshy wounds, and a throbbing motion are appealing sights, smells, and sounds to passing pike.

Minnow selection is contingent on what's available and how active the pike are. Always procure two or three different types of pike bait through a local establishment. Most winter anglers choose sucker minnows. Suckers are hardy, readily available, and come in a wide range of sizes. Bait shops regularly sort sucker minnows and separate them into small, medium, and decoy sizes. Small suckers, usually four to six inches long, work well on small northerns, inactive northerns, and bass. Medium suckers, those in that six- to nine-inch range, are a good all-around size for tip-up pike fishing; few pike, regardless of size, will disregard a medium sucker. Last, the decoy sucker tag is reserved for anything over eight inches in length; employ such big baits for pursuing huge pike and muskies.

Shiner minnows have rapidly gained favor as northern pike bait. Pike love the tender and brilliant flesh of shiners. Certain bait shops handle oversized shiner minnows specifically geared for taking northern pike and winter bass. Four-, five-, and six-inch golden or spot-tail shiners are fantastic offerings. I'll take a giant shiner over a sucker minnow any day!

Soft chubs, of the red-tail or creek variety, also come in many sizes. Without question, I'll take a dozen chubs over suckers, but big chubs can be difficult to locate. In some regions, creeks and rivers have been overharvested, and chub populations are in jeopardy.

Here is some advice on minnow size: Seldom is a minnow too small, but too large an offering can dissuade strikes. Many 10-pound and larger pike have smacked panfish jigs and crappie minnows. Unless you're sure that gigantic minnows are the way to go, carry some midsize bait. Bait is inexpensive, so I always carry a mix.

You can present a live minnow either on a solitary hook, or what's known as a quick-strike rig, or multihook set. The designation of solitary hook encompasses true singular hooks and individual treble hooks. With a single hook, use something that matches the size of the minnow, offers a wide gap (distance between the hook point and line tie), and is exceedingly sharp. I turn to VMC, Owner, Mustad, and Gamakatsu. A couple favorites are Gamakatsu Shiner Hooks and VMC cone-cut, high-carbon, wide-gap hooks; sizes 1/0, 2/0, and 3/0 generally make the grade.

The most common way to thread a minnow on is to run the hook point through the minnow's back, just behind the dorsal (back) fin. Hooking it this way permits the minnow to swim freely, doesn't mortally wound it by puncturing entrails, and grabs enough meat so light biters can't easily steal bait. As morbid as this sounds, hobbling is in order when it's apparent that pike aren't interested in chasing energetic minnows. Do this by cutting or damaging the minnow's tail so it no longer swims uncontrollably, but still offers some movement.

Single treble hooks provide a great hook-setting percentage, but they don't conceal well when fish are picky. Hook sizes ranging from a #8 up to a 1/0 do the job. Again, go with the same brands cited earlier and match hook size to bait size. Use a #8 or #6 with small minnows, upgrade to a #4 or #2 treble with giant shiners or medium suckers, and tie on a #1 or 1/0 when lowering a big sucker. Bury one of the treble's barbs into the minnow's back, similar to positioning a single hook. The remaining exposed hook points provide firm and immediate hook setting.

Quick strike is a broad term describing a multihooked rig designed to offer sure and fast hook sets. The drawbacks of using single hooks are twofold. Number one, hooking percentage using a single hook doesn't approach what a quick-strike rig achieves. Second, pike readily inhale single hooks, potentially resulting in injured or dead game.

A characteristic quick-strike rig consists of a pair of treble, or specialty two-barb hooks, fastened or tied in-line on a single leader, which can be either steel wire or braided wire. The primary hook is crimped or wrapped to one end of the leader, and the other treble sits above it. Some rigs feature a fixed secondary hook, and others have an adjustable crimp, thus allowing you to match bait size. With a treble-hook quick-strike rig, bury the first hook (bottom hook) just behind the minnow's snout, and the secondary, or upper treble, somewhere into the minnow's back. Pike prefer to take forage head first, and this quick-strike arrangement puts the primary hook's points in place for instantaneous contact with a pike's mouth (more on quick-strike rigs and leaders later).

Dead Bait Applications

Most living organisms are mourned or disposed of once dead. Minnows are not one of them when northern pike are part of the equation. Pike forage on expired baitfish and smaller game fish. Dead eats are especially desirable to larger pike that'd prefer not to expend energy hunting spry forage.

Dead bait usually means big bait. Why? One reason is that pike can take their time clamping down and repositioning something that doesn't struggle to escape. Second, as I just mentioned, big pike favor dead bait.

The leading dead bait contenders are smelt, herring, ciscoes, and sucker minnows. Smelt and ciscoes are my top choices. Both species naturally occur in many of North America's finest pike fisheries; also, dead smelt and ciscoes produce a rancid odor that, although offensive to humans, invites pike to feed.

Without debate, quick-strike rigs are the best way to present dead bait. Hook dead smelt, herring, ciscoes, or suckers just as you would a live sucker minnow, bottom hook in minnow's head and top hook across its back. HT Enterprises, Thorne Bros., and Bait Rigs Tackle Company manufacture exceptional prefab quick-strike rigs.

A word of warning—the legal use of quick-strike rigs is not universal. In Minnesota, for instance, double treble hooks in a setline presentation are only legal if the rig is considered a lure. You achieve this by adding a small in-line spinner blade above the secondary hook. In neighboring Wisconsin, quick-strike rigs are perfectly legal. Make sure to check the current rules and regulations in your state or province.

Tip-Up Rigging

Pike are voracious creatures with great bodily strength and barbed teeth. It's possible to counteract a pike's strength by using equally as strong line. Spool your tip-ups with 20- to 40-pound test strength braided nylon or Dacron line. These heavy-duty lines are impervious to nicking, unlike mono, and a single spooling can last several seasons. Coated Dacron is excellent. The slick black coating prevents freezing, and it doesn't hang up on the ice like an exposed braid.

Quick-strike rigs pro-
vide instantaneous and
high-percentage hook
sets. A typical quick
strike consists of a wire
leader and pair of treble
hooks. In places where
quick-strike rigs are illegal, adding a spinner
blade usually converts
the rig into a legal pre-
sentation.

Coated lines play a special role on Windlass Tip-Ups because the spool is exposed to the elements.

The downside of heavy tip-up lines is that they're visually displeasing to approaching fish. Overcome this obstacle by tying in a segment of thin wire between the hook and braid. Thin wire doubles as a leader, preventing sharp-teethed pike from cutting away. Wire strengths of 20 and 30 pounds are remarkably transparent in the water. With a single or treble hook, cut off an 18- to 24-inch section of wire. Next, tie a barrel swivel to the free end of the tip-up line. Take the wire segment and thread one end through the barrel swivel's open eye, loop the end back around the wire, and twist it six or eight times with a pair of hemostats or pliers; some anglers prefer using crimps versus twisting the wire. Attach the hook to the open wire end in the same manner. Again, you can substitute a crimp for wrapping.

The marketplace is brimming with preassembled and neatly packaged leaders. They're strong and simple to use, but most are too thick and visible beneath the ice. Fishing wire, which is available at most sporting goods stores, is a far better choice.

Keeping a minnow down is another topic. Wire's inherent weight will slow a minnow some but not hold it down and maintain control. You'll need to add split-shot or other sinker types to restrain a big minnow; experiment with weight. Dead bait usually works best without sinkers, because the body mass of a deceased minnow is weight enough.

Tip-Up Placement

Previously, I introduced mobility into the realm of winter pike fishing. How does a stationary method such as tip-up fishing blend with a mobile approach? Cut plenty of holes and be prepared to shuffle flags around!

Effective tip-up fishing is an exercise in covering ice. Most states and provinces afford ice fishermen two lines, if not more. Another thing to consider is legal distance an angler can be away from a setline. In Minnesota, for example, you can stray as far away as 200 feet from an active line, which is a long way. Exercise your rights when pursuing pike, as long as the fish don't suffer because you're not paying attention.

Drilling more than one hole per line is a good start. For instance, two anglers with four lines should drill eight or more holes. Their holes should blanket a variety of depths and structures, if available. Imagine you're fishing a lush weed flat with a distinct outside edge and plenty of pockets within the bed. Pop several holes across the flat, sticking to clearings if possible. Blast the next set of holes along the outside edge, and finish with a few holes well off the weedline. Spread the field out! An exploratory tip-up field needs to address all surrounding circumstances.

In our example, let's say the weed flat ranges from 6 to 8 feet in depth. Set the bait on these shallow tip-ups about halfway down. Shallow weed–orienting pike tend to cruise midway down the water column. Position your next couple flags along the outside weededge, but at least 20 yards apart. In this example, the outside weededge lies in 12 feet of water. Fix one tip-up so the bait is only a foot from the bottom and the other three to four feet up. Generally, the deeper the water, the closer pike hug to the bottom. Drop the last couple tip-ups over holes drilled beyond the weedline. Here, run one along the bottom and the other four feet off. The outside depth in this illustration ranges between 12 and 16 feet.

I designed this scenario to demonstrate the importance of using a wide tip-up field. Now, if only the weed-flat holes produce fish, the obvious response is to move all or most tip-ups inside. Thankfully you already popped extra holes, right? Inversely, if an hour or so passes without any action, the situation calls for moving flags around, but in an even, looser assembly. Attacking a hump, bar, or rock pile is comparable. Set tip-ups over the top, along the break, and just off the structure.

One last thought on tip-ups and northern pike. As I reported earlier in the book, most jigging situations call for using one line, possibly two, but never three. Instead, I prefer to turn my secondary line, regardless of what species I'm after, into a remote pike line. Most productive panfish, perch, trout, and walleye spots also attract hungry northern pike. Rig a pike tip-up and place it 20, 30, or more yards away from the jigging holes. The auxiliary line often yields bonus pike. Nothing tops off a successful day of jigging perch or panfish like the catch and release of a mammoth northern!

Jigging Pike

At the onset, I touted setline fishing as the leading method for procuring winter pike. That fact hasn't changed, but with the passing of each hardwater season, I hook an increasing number of the northerns while jigging.

I have already established that northern pike are meat eaters. This means that pike are constantly looking for the flashy and fleshy. Jigging imitates the action of wounded forage, and at the same time throws beacons of color and flash well beyond the means of real baitfish.

Pike jigging presentations fall into three categories: big spoons, big swimming jigs, and dead bait rigs. Opening with big spoons, we're dealing with blown up versions of walleye jigging spoons. In fact, several pike spoons are large renditions of the models used on walleyes. The largest size Deadly Dart (System Tackle by Lindy Little Joe) and 1/2-ounce Do-Jigger from Bay de Noc Lure Co. are good examples of oversized walleye spoons.

A couple other jigging spoons to look for are the Coho-Laker Taker from Bay de Noc Lure Co. and Ivan's Glo Tackle Smasher. The incredibly showy Bay de Noc Spoon is geared for lake trout and salmon, but performs wonders on pike. These elongated spoons are available in a wealth of patterns and weights. The smaller Ivan's Glo Tackle Smasher is an intricately painted lure that also comes in several patterns. A Smasher's finest features are its aggressive wobble and havoc-wreaking Mustad Triple-Grip hook. A host of other jigging spoons perform admirably, but these models comprise the bulk of my big-spoon arsenal.

You can pump big jigging spoons in virtually any depth and circumstance. Your task is to match lure size and weight to the condi-

Tip-ups are the accepted means for bagging hardwater pike, but in head-to-head competition, jigging usually reigns supreme.

tions at hand. Heavy and large match well with deep and aggressive; inversely, small and light go with shallow and lethargic. Deep and inactive requires that you jig a smaller spoon with enough weight to get it down. You can challenge aggressive fish in shallow water with a big-bodied but light lure, such as a Bay de Noc Lure Co. Flutter-Laker Taker. It pays to carry a wealth of sizes and weights. Smaller spoons might also be necessary during cold-front periods and in the dead of winter; both circumstances can slow pike down.

Tipping a pike jigging spoon is similar to dressing a walleye spoon, except the size of bait used. Instead of a fathead or small shiner head, you'll be gunning for a severed sucker or oversized shiner cranium. You want just enough meat to effectively cover the hook, but not so much that pike have an opportunity to undershoot hook points. A decent size shiner, sucker, or chub clipped off just behind the gill plates still leaves one to three inches of tastiness. A little trick is to leave some entrails connected to the head; the jellyfish-like action of pulsating innards is extremely tempting.

115

The next group of pike lures are the big swimming jigs. These jigs horizontally hung treat dart, dive, and swim like real baitfish, assuming the user operates them with authority. The large vertical jigging Rapalas and Nils Master Jiggers aren't often thought of by winter pike anglers, but they should be. Their intense action, authentic baitfish profile, and vivid colors and patterns make them difficult for northerns to ignore.

As an attraction lure, it's not necessary to tip swimming jigs with bait, because hostile pike will smack them as is. However, a smidgen of bait bolsters angler confidence. One baiting method is to slide a hunk of minnow meat or a head onto the jig's dangling treble hook. Smaller sucker and shiner heads give it enough flare to induce strikes, while not interfering with the lure's performance. A second formula is to take the jig's fixed rear barb and lip hook a small sucker, shiner, or even a fathead so the presentation mimics a fish chasing a fish. Make sure to run the hook into the minnow's mouth, and punch it out through the back of the head. This technique secures the bait so it does not break free while jigging or when a pike short strikes.

Lead-head swimming jigs are simpler and less expensive alternatives. Large winged jigs like the Flyer (System Tackle by Lindy Little Joe) and the Mini Air-Plane Jig Head by Northland Tackle don't dance as magically as a Rapala or Nils Master, but when fitted with a minnow and jigged intently, they do catch a lot of pike. The best method for tipping a lead-head swimming jig is to stick the single hook into a minnow's mouth, thread it, and pop the hook point back out somewhere behind the head. Bait is a necessary component while working lead swimming jigs.

A subgroup of swimming jigs includes the upsized Air-Plane Jig by Northland Tackle. The gigantic version of their smaller Mini Air-Plane Jig Head is riddled with hooks and gaudy in appearance. Originally intended for lake trout in deep water, air-plane-type jigs are fantastic lures for jigging pike in deep water. They work best with dead bait. Take a deceased minnow, bury the forged single hook through the minnow's jaw and out the back of the head, and stick the trailing treble hook stinger somewhere into the minnow's back. A steady lift and fall approach through a deep column of water creates a tantalizing circling pattern, which also covers a great deal of horizontal space.

You also can jig the same quick-strike rig and dead minnow package that commonly hangs beneath a tip-up. Take your dead minnow, double treble quick-strike rig, wire leader, and tie it to a heavy-duty jigging outfit. Gently raise and lower the dead bait rig at any depth or circumstance, or install it as a deadstick and lay the minnow on or near the bottom. Big pike regularly comb the bottom for expired forage.

Jigging in a Sea of Flags

No two snowflakes are alike, and no two anglers within a fishing party are entirely alike. Use this to your advantage. Let the guys who prefer lying back and waiting for flags to unfurl relax and twiddle their thumbs. In the meantime, you, or the group's most energetic member, should quietly walk from hole to hole with a jigging outfit. We know of course that you drilled plenty of extra holes, right?

Jigging inside or outside a field of tip-ups is incredibly effective! Jigging in holes just outside a tip-up field pulls pike into the strike zone or cuts them off before entering. Jigging amid active tip-ups draws fish right into the gauntlet or offers them an alternative to idle baits. Jigging sometimes triggers a response when pike are in the vicinity, but not interested in stationary offerings.

Specialized Gear

Other chapters promote the fact that you can use panfish gear for perch fishing, and some walleye equipment is also permissible while jigging perch. Unfortunately, the only outfit mentioned so far that suffices for jigging pike is a rugged walleye setup. You'll need to procure one or two specialized combos for jigging pike.

Because tip-ups play such an important role in winter pike fishing, I won't spend much time on rods, reels, and line. However, don't interpret this to mean that rod, reel, and line selection isn't important, because it is; you just don't need as much of it.

Rod Selection

Picture your favorite walleye pole with another 6 to 18 inches of length and added strength. Maintaining sensitivity is fine, but not in lieu of strength. I still favor high-quality graphite and fiberglass blanks. Rod length is a factor during both the hook set and the battle. Setting jigs into the iron jaws of a pike is challenging with a short pole. Long rods provide a smoother delivery in which the lure impacts jaw tissue with allied strength rather than a quick snap. The rod's role in the battle

117

relates to a pike's brute force. When big pike run, your equipment must absorb the energy. A long rod, particularly glass, disseminates a pike's power, hence not placing too much demand on the line and reel.

Another consideration for purchasing a pike pole is whether to lean toward spinning or baitcast. To this point, every reel we've recommended or referenced was of the spinning variety. Big spinning combos do a fine job, but in the case of winter pike fishing, I vote for baitcast setups. Most manufacturers produce spinning and baitcast rods that, other than reel seat type and guides, are essentially the same.

Reel Selection

Not to bore anyone with rehashing the entire reel selection process, I'll simply say this: Larger models of the spinning reels discussed in the walleye and perch chapters will meet the demands of winter pike fishing. Larger is necessary for holding heavier line (spool size), counteracting the power of a surging northern (longer handle and greater line pickup), and to balance a longer pole. Qualities such as a smooth front drag and multipoint antireverse also deserve recognition.

Concerning the baitcast versus spinning argument, I could fish an entire winter without touching a baitcast outfit and get along fine. In fact, I own only two baitcast rod and reel combos, but they're awfully good ones. There are a couple upsides to baitcast reels, or level winders, as they're sometimes called. First, there's no comparison; line spools off much easier from a baitcast reel than it does from a spinning reel. Second, there's a great deal more line stress with a spinning reel. The oscillating bail on a spinning reel twists the line, and this can be especially damaging while fighting a big fish or numbers of small ones. Tried and true Abu Garcia 5500s and larger 6500s are fantastic wintertime baitcast reels.

Line Selection

Many of the same lines that ice other species will do the trick on pike, although an increase in test strength is in order. Beginning with monofilament or nylon line, you'll want to increase test strength to the 10- to 20-pound range. I spool my spinning and jigging outfits with stiff 12- or 14-pound test strength Berkley Trilene or Stren nylon lines; upgrade to a stiffer 17- or 20-pound test on baitcast reels. Whenever targeting trophy-caliber pike, I want heavy line and a baitcast reel in my hands.

The advent of superlines also wages some influence on pike jigging. The innate strength, sensitivity, and abrasion resistance of lines such as Berkley Fireline and SpiderWire Fusion meet the demands of winter pike fishing. Any line stiffness problems can be relieved by using a long fiberglass rod, however, you still have to deal with line icing and freezing in wintry weather.

Muskies

The Other Pike.   Muskies fall into a category of freshwater species that are occasionally hooked by winter anglers, but infrequently sought. Most hardwater muskies materialize while angling for other species. Oh sure, there are a handful of winter fishermen who intently pursue muskies on selected waters, but they are a rare breed. Nonetheless, muskies pose enough of a wintertime threat to warrant some discussion.

The first thing anyone serious about hooking hard-water muskies needs to do is return to the beginning of this chapter and reread it with muskies in mind. For the most part, muskies look like pike, feed like pike, and inhabit similar environments. However, at some juncture, muskies slump into a lethargic state while northern pike continue stalking and foraging.

Serious muskie fishermen recognize autumn as the principal season for nailing trophy-class fish. Giant muskies prepare for the off-season by gorging themselves before ice over. Fortunately for early ice enthusiasts, the fall muskie bite doesn't end abruptly when the surface seals. Instead, feeding gradually diminishes throughout the hardwater season, and by midwinter muskies seemingly disappear. The obvious advice is to focus your energy on winter's front side.

I just drew a parallel between the looks, behaviors, and preferred habitats of northern pike and muskies. A little clarification is in order. In waters where muskies and northern pike coexist, it's possible to hook both species while standing over a single hole. Understand first and foremost that muskies are genetically predisposed for life in warm water; the odds are not stacked in your favor. Counteract this natural barrier by choosing an optimum piece of water—not all muskie lakes are created equal. Opt for lakes, rivers, and reservoirs known for bearing large muskies and numbers of them. Consult with bait shops and regional fisheries offices to determine where the strongest muskie populations thrive. Some of North America's finest muskie waters are beneficiaries of routine stocking programs.

As in the case of northern pike, big structure and big water equals big muskies. Not to say that smaller lakes and rivers can't support muskies, because they do, but larger waters have a greater capacity to yield both volume and size. Within a given environment, it's in your best interest to explore the grandest structural elements available (i.e., huge bays, massive weed flats, and giant offshore humps and bars).

Wintertime muskie fishing affords an opportunity to catch one of the world's largest and most ravenous freshwater species. Few outdoor experiences compare with the battle, landing, and subsequent release of a gigantic muskie or northern pike through a hole in the ice. Releasing top-of-the-food-chain, predatory fish is critical to maintaining balance in a fragile underwater environment.

A Final Thought

Northern pike and muskies are the largest and fiercest predators beneath the hard glassy layer. And to the benefit of winter fishermen, they remain frisky throughout the hardwater season. By employing the recommended tools and techniques, and locating previously defined pike habitat, it's possible become a northern pike expert over the course of a single ice-fishing season. You will often find hardwater pike in the following locations:

- Bays
- Points and bars
- Channels
- Narrows
- Inlets
- Outlets
- Weededges and pockets
- River backwaters
- Humps and rock piles

Chapter 6

Panfish

EVERYBODY LOVES PANFISH. Both crappies and sunfish, predominant members of the class known as panfish, are universally admired. These abundant freshwater species are generously distributed throughout North America, and aside from Canada's upper reaches, panfish inhabit just about every viable body of water across ice-fishing country.

Crappies, both black and white, are an especially popular target for wintertime anglers. The cold-weather months encourage crappies into predictable habits and environments. Elusive slab-size crappies, which seem to disappear during the summer, materialize beneath the ice. They school and suspend over holes and off structure while feeding on baitfish or zooplankton. Hardwater season presents a window into the world of paper mouths.

Even more plenteous and sought after are sunfish. Bluegills, the reigning member of the sunfish family, behave like cold-water crappies, and throughout this chapter, I'll interchange the names sunfish and bluegill. Like crappies, bluegills swarm, school, suspend, and larger members emerge at wintertime. Their propensity to scour weed beds for aquatic delicacies, sift the bottom for invertebrates, and hover beneath schooling crappies are distinguishing behaviors. A common thread among panfish factions is the tastiness of their fillets when lightly battered and panfried.

Choosing a Premium Body of Water

Good Lakes, Bad Lakes, and Great Lakes. There is no other category of freshwater fish for which choosing the right lake, pond, or river is as critical to success. Picking a poor panfish lake results in either no fish or potato chip size pans. Most conventional walleye-managed lakes harbor a mix of year classes, whether they're stocked or naturally occurring. Likewise, lakes that maintain a respectable northern pike population seem to churn out a variety of sizes, including trophies. Obviously there are specific bodies of water known for producing bigger than average pike or walleyes, but generally, there's distribution of size. Flourishing populations of big panfish, on the other hand, occur only in certain lakes and during certain years.

Panfish populations rely on natural propagation, whereas walleye, northern pike, and trout populations can be, and commonly are, bolstered through stocking programs. Artificial panfish replenishment on public waters is nonexistent. In order for a lake to produce quality panfish, it must display exceptional physical merits and receive a helping hand from Mother Nature. Assistance arrives in the form of warm spring breeding conditions, high water, and ample forage.

Focus on Habitat

First understand that lakes in northern Wisconsin are far different than farm ponds in central Iowa. It's impossible to generate the perfect template and universally apply it. Instead, we're offering a batch of proven lake characteristics, which have a history of proliferating and maintaining strong panfish populations.

Fertility is the first element required of a potential panfish water. Fertility manifests as in the form of abundant underwater vegetation; rich shoreline vegetation; stained water; tons of baitfish; oodles of aquatic insects; critter-laden bottoms, springs, and flowages. The perfect panfish water is built from the above list, but legitimate crappie and sunfish waters can get by with some of these features.

A lake's lifeblood is pumped through the leaves and stems of underwater vegetation. Weeds breathe oxygen into a body of water, as well as provide habitat for panfish, and what panfish consume. It's rare to encounter a prolific panfish lake having scarce vegetation. Thick shoreline vegetation is also symbolic of fertility. Heavy cattails,

Outdoor writer and guide, Brian "Bro" Brosdahl spends countless hours research-ing and fishing over 100 local lakes; the results are evident.

reeds, and rushes mark places that are littered with aquatic organ-isms; many of these organisms panfish eat.

Stained- to murky-water conditions also characterize fertility. Wa-ters imbedded with organic particles commonly host impressive panfish populations. Zooplankton and phytoplankton, staple compo-nents in a panfish diet, prosper in dingy water. Sometimes stained water is a product of an inlet or water seeping through a bog, both of which encourage the presence of aquatic edibles.

Crappies in particular benefit from the existence of a stable baitfish population. No doubt crappies eat zooplankton, bottom-dwelling in-vertebrates, and aquatic insects, but most lakes with a history for producing large crappies also contain an ample residency of fatheads, chubs, shiner minnows, or even small perch.

Abundant numbers of strange-looking underwater critters go hand in hand with fertile waters. Mature aquatic insects and even freshwa-ter shrimp in some cases inhabit the greenery. Hellgrammites, blood-worms, and insect larvae require rich fields of silt, clay, and marl to prosper, and zooplankton colonies enjoy deep columns of water near breaks and the littoral zone (a littoral zone is the measured area in a lake residing in depths of 15 feet and under).

These characteristics find their way into North America's finest panfish waters, but the list isn't done yet. The topography of a lake is as important as anything mentioned to this point. Features such as bays, bars, flats, and holes work in union with weeds, water clarity, bottom content, oxygenation, and forage. We'll dig deeper into lake types later.

Maps and Tips

Hot panfish lakes come and go. Studies reveal that panfish populations are cyclical in nature, meaning they go through ups and down in numbers as well as average sizes. Factors such as pressure from predators (i.e., bass, northern pike, etc.) low water levels, cool breeding conditions, winterkills, and overharvest can adversely affect panfish numbers. It's important to consider these factors when choosing a prospective panfish water.

Winterkill occurs when dissolved oxygen levels shrink to the point that fish begin dying off. Exceptionally long winters with heavy snow and thicker than normal ice take their toll on shallow lakes. Total winterkills are rare, but partial winterkills are common. Partial winterkills leave a body of water with fewer fish, but the surviving fish grow rapidly due to a decrease in food competition. Boom lakes are venues that winterkill with regularity, but because of their incredible fertility, solid panfish populations can build following a succession of mild winters. Keep an eye on boom lakes in your area.

How is it possible for the average angler to keep comprehensive records of environmental and climatic conditions relating to his or her favorite lakes? It's not, but in many states the department of natural resources (DNR) keeps a close watch on lakes within its jurisdiction. In Minnesota, the DNR keeps extensive records on most lakes with public accesses. Other than maintaining fisheries through stocking, the Minnesota DNR conducts gill net surveys, trap net surveys, and conducts angler censuses. The results of such testing reveal average numbers and sizes for all fish species present. The information is public record and you can obtain it through regional offices, the central office, and on their outstanding Internet site **http://www.dnr.state.mn.us**. The Minnesota DNR Web site also in-

124

cludes lake maps, which you can download at no charge. Most, if not all, state DNRs now offer Web sites.

Gill net and trap net results give ice-fishing enthusiasts a glimpse of a lake's overall panfish populations. A specific lake's results are compared with a median divined from results on similar lakes. A creel census, or sampling of fish caught, offers further evidence of a lake's potential. Creel censuses also reveal fish sizes through length measurements. For instance, if anglers catch more 9- to 11-inch crappies on Lake A than Lake B, even though volume is similar, the choice is obvious.

Typically, a lake summary accompanies DNR test results. Summaries disclose which years had the strongest breeding classes, what species and sizes are most prevalent, the area fishery manager's opinions and forecasts, and so on. Often more useful than DNR data is information you collect at local bait and tackle establishments. It's important to leave your driveway with some idea of what lake and what part of the lake you're heading to, but never, and I mean never, bypass the local bait establishment. They provide a wealth of information, and current at that. You can improve your odds of getting the best advice by making the cash register ring, if you know what I mean.

I like to purchase a map of the lake in addition to recommended live bait and tackle. Lay the map out on the counter and have the proprietor mark a few spots for you. Ask questions such as where can I access the lake? How deep of water should I look for? Is it a day bite or night bite? Can I move away from the crowds and still catch fish? Are the fish suspended? Is there a mix of crappies and bluegills? Have the fish been aggressive? Ask questions that might cut down on search time.

Winter Panfish Location

The Right Lake at the Right Time. Before you get too caught up in dissecting your beloved local lake, make sure it's the right lake for the moment. Bodies of water that churn out fabulous panfish during winter's first few weeks shrivel to a shadow of themselves after the holidays. Likewise, lakes where clusters of fish houses appear during the heart of hardwater season seldom explode at first ice. Your job is to match a lake to current conditions—we'll help you sort things out.

Walking on water? No, but from a distance the transparent surfaces of early ice appear nearly fluid. Early winter welcomes fast crappie action, but take caution when treading on the season's first glaze.

Early Winter

Earlier, we expounded on the inherent connection between late fall and early winter (see sidebar on page 56). In general, panfish location at first ice mirrors the week or two preceding hardwater season. So the first step in tracking sunfish and crappies at first ice is to understand their fall patterns.

Just because you've got a handle on their whereabouts doesn't mean catching panfish is automatic. Some plenteous panfish waters simply don't burst with activity at first ice. Typically, it's the larger, clearer, and deeper lakes, which require several weeks of wintertime conditions before firing up. Even if you identify an early winter panfish bite on a big, deep lake, there's a good chance it pales in comparison with what's happening on smaller lakes.

Small bodies of water are the first to freeze, and subsequently the first to produce hardwater action. Small in panfish terms means anything oxygenated and deep enough to support sunfish or crappie populations. Deep farm ponds, deep sloughs or ones with current, river backwaters, and small lakes are excellent examples of first ice panfish targets. Getting access to a private farm pond is something special. Minimal fishing pressure combined with ultrafertile conditions foster incredible panfish growth rates. A slough featuring a deep trough or continuous current from a feeder creek is another diamond in the rough when it comes to cultivating panfish in a secretive environment. We'll elaborate on ice-fishing river systems later, but for now, it's time to focus on small lakes, the kind everyone has access to.

Figure 6.1 outlines the following structures:

a. Creek inlets usually forge a subtle sand or gravel bar that in its best possible form also features weed growth. The current sweeps in forage as well as oxygen. Panfish, especially sunfish, will use the weeds, bottom-content transitions, and any breaks associated with an inlet.

b. The deepest hole in a small lake or farm pond is unquestionably the first place to look for fish—employ an "inside-out" search method. Earlier in the winter, panfish will use various depths heading down the break, but by midwinter you can nearly bet both sunfish and crappies will be suspending over the hole—look for sunfish closer to the bottom and relating to the hole's steepest drop.

c. Secondary holes provide desirable temporary surroundings for fish migrating to deeper water—many secondary holes maintain panfish populations throughout the winter. And alternate, less obvious spots receive diminished angler pressure.

d. Narrows or "bottlenecks" host migrating panfish all winter long. The most widely used narrows are deeper cuts featuring steep breaks.

e. Any rock pile found inside a small lake or farm pond is lethal. Crappies in particular love hanging around rocks—the deeper the better.

f. The deepest point in a secondary section of a lake or pond is worthy of at least a brief look. Such places are especially attractive if they graze a weedline, hump, or any other viable structure.

127

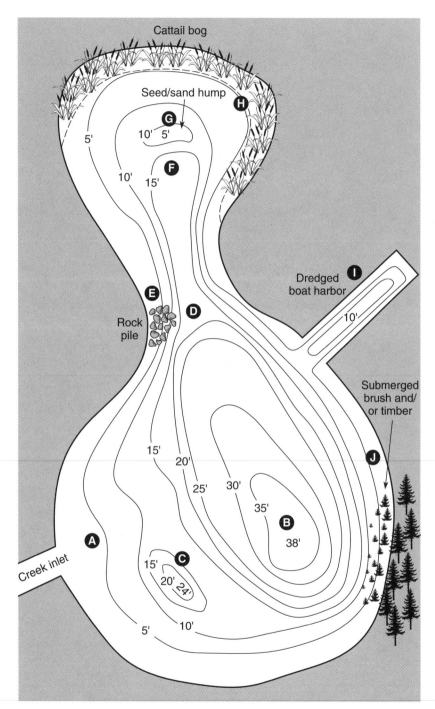

Figure 6.1 Check these structures for panfish.

g. Shallow sand and weed humps are favored feeding zones during low-light periods. Both crappies and sunfish will move to the edges and on top of said structure at dawn and dusk.

h. The perimeter of a cattail bog oftentimes suspends, forming a "lip," which hangs a couple of feet or more from the bottom. Panfish, sunfish in particular, will tuck beneath the flange for protection and to procure a meal. Seepage from bogs is known to stain surrounding waters, thus permitting panfish to range quite shallow.

i. Gorged out boat harbors and channels offer panfish supplemental early winter habitat—the deeper and steeper the better.

j. Hardwater panfish frequent submerged timber and brush piles—again, deep is good. Fish will vacate shoreline timber once oxygen levels fade, opting for deeper wood, breaks, or holes.

Kick off the ice-fishing season on the smallest legitimate lake at your disposal. If possible, track down one of those 50- to 100-acre beauties, but the right 200-, 300-, or 400-acre lake will suffice. Lesser surface acreage furnishes a manageable destination, which means it's possible for an angler to explore various locations during a single outing.

Hitting the Hole

Once you select a lake, the next step is identifying the deepest water. Small, fertile bodies of water usually contain one or two deep holes. In an ultrashallow lake, the deepest point might only be 10 or 15 feet, but the type of lake we're searching for bottoms out at 20 to 35 feet of water. From a scientific standpoint, lakes having eutrophic (shallow, fertile, soft-bottomed) characteristics to late mesotrophic (fairly shallow, fertile, primarily soft bottomed) are most desirable.

Work a true bowl-shaped eutrophic lake from the inside out. Let's say a 75-acre gem maintains a maximum depth of 22 feet. The shoreline filters uniformly to a midlake hole, except a steep break on its northern edge. An effective approach would be to cut holes at 22 feet and move north, across the break, until engaging fish. Panfish, particularly sunfish, gravitate to the sheerest slope of a cavity.

Presence or Absence of Weeds Tells a Story

It's no secret, without weeds a lake is merely a lifeless puddle. They oxygenate, provide protective cover, and harbor innumerable varieties of aquatic foodstuffs. At first ice, an angler needs to establish if there's a presence of lively green weeds. In a stained- to murky-water lake, most underwater weeds brown and lay down before ice forms. Although clear lakes sustain weed growth well into winter or until thickening ice, dense snow cover and shortening daylight hours team up to eradicate vegetation. The kind of lake best suited for early winter action is one in which weeds have perished, or at least are on their way out. In this situation, it's a safe bet that panfish are hovering somewhere beyond the former outside weededge. As weeds die, panfish cluster and move deeper.

Speaking of weededges, the outside edge itself provides applicable clues about a lake. An outside weededge is the point where weeds cease to exist because of a lack of sunlight. As a rule, the darker the water, the shallower its weededge. Conversely, clear lakes sustain weeds in much deeper water. The outside weededge on cloudy lakes might reside in only three or four feet of water. In such an event, weeds play little or no role during the winter because they've long since died.

Weeds demand attention on lakes sporting thick vegetation and a distinct outside weedline. Beneath the ice, patches and groves of lush vegetation commonly host sunfish, and the outside edge is the place to start probing. From there, move across the weed bed searching for any pockets or lanes within the greenery. Clearings within an otherwise thick plot give anglers prime access. The transparent quality of winter's first glazing of ice enables you to see chasms within a weed mass. Tread quietly, because shallow-water panfish spook easily!

Although crappies occasionally burrow inside a weed bed, they're more inclined to forage along the outside edge or suspend just beyond it. Crappies can track a mixed bag of zooplankton and baitfish outside the weeds. Sunfish, having minimal interest in minnows, prefer weed-oriented critters, including mayfly larvae and invertebrates that may be imbedded in the sediment floor below towering weeds.

Bays, Coves, and Harbors

Regardless of whether a lake's classification is small and fertile or deep and clear, certain bays, coves, and harbors will have what it takes to produce panfish at first ice. Offshoots of a main lake maintain their own ecosystem, and these ecosystems peak with activity at first ice, and last ice.

Bays off a main lake can vary in magnitude from supershallow sloughlike appendages to deep structure-filled bodies, which behave like autonomous lakes. What you're looking for is something in between. The perfect bay on a midsize to large lake looks a lot like the small fertile lake described earlier. For example, imagine a sprawling 1,500-acre lake that offers a 50-acre weedy bay. The teardrop-shaped bay plummets to 18 feet, and the main lake reaches a maximum depth of 65 feet. The bay is a winner for first ice panfish!

Inside our hypothetical bay, you'll want to focus on the 18-foot hole, the outside weededge, and mouth area leading into the main lake. The 18-foot hole is unquestionably the first place to explore. Here, panfish likely suspend while feeding on zooplankton and baitfish. The deep cavity may also hold larval-stage insects and invertebrates, so look for panfish close to the bottom as well.

The outside weededge within our bay may not be consistent with that of the main lake. Shallow bays frequently contain darker water than adjacent lakes because of bog staining, runoff, or incoming feeder creeks. As stated earlier, water clarity is directly proportionate to depth of the weedline. In our illustration, the main lake's outer weeds fade at about 14 feet, and weeds inside the bay cease growing in only 8 feet of water. Our bay is rimmed by a rich tamarack bog. Expect to find crappies lingering between 8 and 18 feet. Sunfish might be mingling with the crappies, but don't ignore green vegetation inside 8 feet of water.

The mouth leading into the main lake is another venue worth examining. Back to our model bay, let's say the 18-foot chasm is situated close to the mouth. Also, the steepest slope leading down to 18 feet faces the mouth. In this scenario, the greatest concentration of fish should be between 18 feet and the break closest to the mouth. The mouth itself maintains a midchannel depth of 10 feet before it opens into the main lake. You should also consider this narrows section, particularly at dawn and dusk. Fish will pass back and forth during peak feeding periods.

Coves by definition are essentially small bays. Some might even call a long, slender cove a channel. Regardless of the vernacular, it's prudent to keep these structures in mind. Their shallow, mud-bottomed, and fertile composition makes them attractive for a brief stint at first ice, but all it takes is a little foot traffic and weed decomposition (lowered oxygenation) to drive panfish deeper.

You have to love the smile on a kid's face when he or she pulls a fish through the ice. Panfish, due to their abundance and willingness to hit, are the perfect target for introducing youth to ice fishing.

Constructed harbors are another potential and frequently ignored first ice hot spot. A dredged channel within a harbor might be 8 to 12 feet deep, while the surrounding murk lies in only a couple feet of water. Panfish stack up along the break while picking through the mud. Harbors catering to large vessels often feature aerators, a serious panfish magnet. However, be cautious of unsafe ice around oxygenating devices. Again, as in the case of coves and channels, the bite inside a harbor is short lived.

Points and Bars

The preceding chapter on walleyes asserted the importance of points and bars to early winter walleye location; the same holds true for panfish. Whether you cut holes on a stained-water pond or a large, deep lake, identifying primary shoreline points and underwater bars is crucial. As a rule, more is better when it comes to available structure. A simple shoreline point might be all that's required to corral panfish on an otherwise featureless piece of water.

As expected, when investigating a potential shoreline point, look for thriving underwater vegetation and breaks. Check for crappies suspending along or just outside the weedline and sunfish either stacked up along the edge or ferreting amid the shallower weed flat. The difference between combining a shoreline point with a weedline versus a stand-alone weedline is, once again, the benefit of compiling structural elements.

Most shoreline points, even on relatively featureless waters, offer a segment or two with steeper breaks than the balance. Always begin your panfish quest over the point's sharpest break. On a tiny farm lake, steep and deep might mean a quick snap from 5 to 12 feet of water. In this instance, look for panfish along the 5- to 12-foot break. If not there, shift outside the break and toward the deepest available water.

Finding a shoreline point that directs toward a deep hole is of special interest. Take the previous illustration, and imagine that 12 feet marks the beginning of a 50-yard flat, where at 13 feet it plunges to the lake's deepest spot at 25 feet. Explore the original 5- to 12-foot break, the deeper break from 13 to 25 feet, and even the 12- to 13-foot flat between breaks. It's possible to scour this entire range during a single outing. Address shoreline points on larger, deeper lakes later in the winter.

Standard shoreline points work fine, but lengthy underwater bars do an even better job. In the chapter on walleyes, I drew a distinction between bars and points. In summary, think of a point as a physical shoreline jettison, attached break, and structure descending beneath the surface. A bar, on the other hand, can be an extension of a shoreline point, an underwater annex that juts nondescriptly from shore and is surrounded by deeper water, or a randomly occurring offshore elevation. Why do bars outperform points? For one, underwater bars generally cover more area than the submerged portion of a point, and because panfish like to roam, larger structures attract more fish. Second, underwater bars usually host heavier vegetation, and third, bars probe farther into the basin—increased deep-water access.

A typical bar on a desirable first ice lake bulges from shore, then twists and curls 50 to 100 yards out into the lake. Preferred bars crest at depths that offer useable terrain on top. An ideal bar might peak at 5 to 10 feet of water. Sunfish and crappies are known to assault a bar's summit at dawn and dusk. A bar that breaks the surface or comes up to only a foot or two of water doesn't provide nearly the feeding opportunities.

Weeds and mixed bottom content are other features that make a bar appealing. If weeds are present, there'll also be a weededge and a shallower weed flat. Probe the outside weededge and weed flat for sunfish, and anticipate finding crappies beyond the foliage—sound familiar? In the case of an ultrashallow lake where weeds have already checked out, you need to identify deep breaks off the bar or a nearby hole.

Midwinter

At the onset, I recommended handpicking a lake rather than forcing your favorite water into an unfamiliar role. Also, I encouraged you to solicit a tiny, nearly swampy destination. Well, if you followed protocol, dividends were probably paid in the form of tasty fillets, but don't rest on your laurels. If you want the fun to continue, it's time to scrap those dinky lakes.

Winter takes its toll on eutrophic and late mesotrophic lakes. Ice and snow cover thicken, weeds die off, oxygen levels drop, and panfish push toward midlake. Eventually, oxygenation wanes to a point where panfish activity nearly ceases; they almost enter suspended animation. It's possible to mark fish all day and never induce a strike. Quit beating yourself up—it's time for a change.

You know that lake I discouraged you from trying earlier in the winter? Put it back on the menu for the duration. Selecting bodies of water is a progression, and it's time to start thinking bigger, deeper, and maybe clearer. Not every slice of water falls neatly into our earlier definition of the perfect lake. In fact, most lakes lie somewhere between a farm pond and a glacial lake.

The panfish bite on most northern lakes doesn't entirely vanish at midwinter. Instead, the fish simply migrate to deeper, warmer, and more oxygenated sectors.

Deep-Water Abundance

There's never been a better interval to explore deep water. Panfish are attracted to depths of 30, 40, 50 feet, and sometimes more. If earlier in the season, sunfish or crappies were engaged near or along the edges of a 40-foot hole, chances are by midwinter (January and February), they're hovering right over the pit. The bigger the pit the better—more fish.

In a 40-foot deep column of water, it's unlikely that all the fish wallow near bottom. In fact, odds are they'll be elevated off the lake floor, depending on what's for dinner. In a mixed panfish situation, sunfish generally range beneath suspending crappies. Deep holes, such as our 40-foot model, offer food, oxygen, and a preferred water temperature. Zooplankton is the primary component in the diet of suspending panfish. Crappies might cruise at 35, 30, and 25 feet, or whatever depth connects them with the greatest concentration of zooplankton. Expect to mark fish much closer to the bottom if invertebrates or insect larva litter the sediment.

The oxygen factor is as important as the forage issue. Shallower areas of a lake that were favored earlier in the winter are no longer habitable. Panfish are compelled to push deeper. Warmth is the final determinant. Under the ice, a lake's warmest temperatures rest in the deepest water; 39-degrees Fahrenheit is as warm as it gets. In our illustration, the 40-foot cavity harbors the warmest water.

Deep Weeds

By midwinter, submerged weeds on small, shallow, and stained-water lakes have expired. However, the larger, deeper class of lakes, which take precedence at this time of year, often maintain weed growth. Tall stalks of cabbage commonly form the deep outside weededge on clear lakes. Their lush foliage can reach depths of 15 to 20 feet or more, depending on overall water clarity. Panfish, particularly sunfish, reside along or just inside this deep wall of greenery.

Tracking panfish amid deep weeds is challenging during daytime hours. Fish bury themselves inside the weed bed while on full predator alert. You stand the greatest chance of confronting panfish at dawn and dusk when panfish activate and predators such as northern pike mellow out.

Deep Bars

Depth is the distinction between bars that hold midwinter panfish and those that played a role earlier in the winter. Both the crown and surrounding water range deeper. Choose deep bars, whether they're offshore or not, that top out at depths of 10 to 20 feet or so and are encircled by wide-ranging depths. The key element is that a bar's top and breaks are deep enough to interest midwinter panfish.

135

On a clear-water lake, it's common to encounter weed growth across a bar's top, and a weedline down the break. Deep, weed-covered bars provide prime habitat for sunfish and crappies. To no surprise, you'll likely find sunfish inside or just outside the weeds and their crappie counterparts either piled up along the weedline or suspended nearby.

Humps

Humps are to bluegills what rock reefs are to walleyes. Digressing for a moment, a hump is a pushup is a sunken island, depending on whom you talk to. All three titles can refer to the same structural object. What we're speaking about is an offshore elevation that may or may not exist with another piece of structure. Humps are big and humps are small. Some are bald and others boom with foliage. Humps can be composed of gravel, marl, muck, sand, rock, or a combination of these.

The author had success working a System Tackle Fat Boy by Lindy Little Joe and wax worm over a sandy offshore hump. The tops of humps attract bluegills during morning and evening.

It's evident that humps come in all shapes and sizes, so let's narrow things down. Large humps hold more panfish than small humps, just like expansive, deep holes and long bars outperform smaller versions. Bigger is better for attracting volumes of fish.

The next thing to look for in a hump is its proximity to other structures or deeper safe havens. For example, a hump close to shore or off a shoreline bar, but still surrounded by deep water, is preferred. The mix of structural elements grants panfish the opportunity to range either shallow or deep.

Let's expound on a scenario where a hump lies somewhere off the tip of an underwater bar. Imagine that a weedy, fingerlike bar extends 50 yards from shore. The bulk of the bar tops off at 10 feet, but at its tip the bar nose-dives to 18 feet. From there, an 18-foot saddle runs for about 40 yards before creeping up the break of an offshore hump, where 18 feet rises to 12 feet, the top of the hump. The entire saddle area between the bar and hump is a panfish hunter's dream! Look for crappies and sunfish along the bar's break leading down to the saddle, across the saddle itself, and up the slope of the offshore hump.

Another characteristic common to offshore bars is their propensity to draw panfish at sunup and sundown. The crown acts as a buffet line for about an hour at the beginning and end of a day. Even if you locate a hump at midday but do not mark fish, return at dusk because an invasion may be planned. During the day, explore beyond the hump looking for suspended panfish.

A final consideration for judging a hump is whether it lies within a deep flat. A hump that plateaus at 10 or 12 feet, breaks, and merges with a midlake flat in 15 to 30 feet is prime. The deep flat offers panfish plenty of schooling, roaming, and suspending space, and the hump gives them both structure to cling to and a part-time feeding station.

Deep Flats

Deep, main basin flats can vary in size from an acre or two on smaller lakes to several miles on gigantic bodies of water. Once panfish enter their midwinter mode, they may spend several weeks traversing deep flats while inhaling zooplankton, vacuuming the bottom for invertebrates, or ambushing baitfish. A typical flat occurs in 15 to 35 feet of water and rambles along with little alteration in depth. Also, flats usually don't mark a lake's deepest point; instead they often form the main basin and bridge spaces between deeper holes.

Regarding holes, anytime you discover a depression within a flat, it deserves exploration. For instance, if a 25-foot flat gives way to a 30-foot depression, it's probable that panfish will either hover over the five-foot dimple or refer to it while cruising the flat.

Deep Bays

On several of the North Country's larger lakes, the only palpable places to track panfish are bays. The main lake is overrun with predator species, thus limiting panfish to secluded areas. Most big, deep lakes aren't known for producing volumes of panfish, but their rich forage bases have the power to nurture giant sunfish and crappies. Treat bays of large lakes like small, but self-sufficient lakes, and look for deep weeds, bars, humps, deep flats, and holes within.

Late Winter

By late winter, walleyes, bass, and northern pike seasons have closed, except certain states and regions with continuous or extended seasons. Certain winter trout seasons remain open, but not everybody lives near stocked or natural trout waters. What's a person to do? You could abandon ice fishing altogether and start tinkering with summer gear, but I think not. A better alternative is to retool your ice-fishing gear and hunt late ice panfish.

Reverse migration is underway. This is a period when panfish return to areas inhabited at first ice. Sunfish and crappies revisit shallower haunts for many reasons. Shallower reaches once again become livable. Longer and warmer days eat away at snow cover. At the same time, old frozen holes reopen. The result is a continuous stream of oxygenated water flowing back into shallow regions that were pronounced dead several weeks ago. Increased sunlight and warming water also stimulate new plant growth, bettering oxygen levels even more. Panfish respond to the reoxygenation by coming home.

Delectable aquatic morsels start to awaken. Larval-stage insects become restless, and ravenous panfish answer by picking off as many as possible. As old, rotting ice slowly rises, it uproots dead weeds that froze into it earlier in the winter. Revealed in this phenomenon are even more insects and invertebrates.

These circumstances alone are lure enough to draw panfish shallow, but there's one more item that's as influential: breeding. Both sunfish and crappies gravitate toward respective spawning grounds.

Depending on the lake, panfish will either move right into spawning areas or stage just outside them. Crappies generally spawn over soft bottoms in supershallow water; the darker the water, the shallower they'll breed. Sunfish prefer excavating spawning beds in sand or light gravel.

An illustrative crappie spawning area would be a shallow soft-bottomed bay on a lake's north side. During the late ice period, crappies will either stage in middepth ranges just outside the bay, suspend over a deep hole in the bay, hang along deep weedlines inside the bay, or roam shallower weed flats if new growth is present. Sunfish follow the same patterns because they also recognize that shallow bays teem with food. The only distinction being that sunfish may look elsewhere for suitable spawning grounds when their time comes.

A final option to consider while chasing late ice panfish is revisiting any spot where you found fish at first ice. Late winter's reverse migration deposits panfish right back where they came from.

Rivers and Backwaters

A Logical Alternative to Lakes.   Panfish aren't the foremost residents in most rivers. However, in some parts of the country, ice-fishing regions or not, river systems hold the finest crappie and sunfish action around. In hardwater river fishing, your choices are backwater tracts or a deep main channel.

Twisting, turning river backwaters are a hotbed at first ice. Both crappies and sunfish invade these fertile, current-free sectors to feed with reckless abandon. Viable backwaters vary in size from a small cut off the main channel to sprawling networks that wander on for miles.

Key ingredients within a backwater are weeds, timber, depressions, and the mouth area leading into the main channel. Weeds are far scarcer in rivers than in lakes, so if you find the green stuff in a backwater, give it a thorough work over. Submerged timber, on the other hand, is abundant in most river systems, and things look good anytime you locate deep timber or the outer edge of a timber field. Depressions or holes within a backwater are significant because most backwater areas are flat and shallow; depressions offer an attractive change of scenery. The mouth of a backwater yields panfish access to a constant flow of forage. Both crappies and sunfish often suspend in slack water off the current break waiting for a passing meal.

Deep stretches along the main channel are a better bet in the middle of winter. You will find the warmest water and the least current in 20-, 30-, and 40-foot holes. Panfish, particularly crappies, linger in these deep, lazy current expanses while plucking insects and aquatic worms from the sediment and chasing suspended schools of baitfish. Generally speaking, anglers are drilling holes on lakes long before nearby rivers ice up, and frozen rivers usually reopen long before surrounding lakes. Ice-fishing season can be short lived for river rats, but for what it lacks in length it more than makes up for in intensity. A word of warning, river ice conditions can be volatile, so please familiarize yourself with the system before embarking.

How to Ice Winter Panfish

The Tools and Techniques.   If you've applied the location suggestions forwarded to this point, there should be fish swimming beneath your feet. Without question, finding panfish is job one. Owning the finest equipment on the ice is meaningless if there aren't any fish to use it on. So first and foremost, locate some fish. The next step is pulling a few of those fish through the hole.

Ice fishing has come a long way over the past couple decades, and anglers now have access to equipment and tested techniques that nearly guarantee success—as ironclad a guarantee as fishing will allow. There's a reason it's called fishing and not catching.

The Foundation for Catching Panfish

Jigging is a synonym for movement, and motion is what induces panfish to strike. Everything in the diet of a sunfish or crappie advances through the water in some fashion. Baitfish dart and dodge with silvery flashes at every turn. Zooplankton chug, pulse, and swirl in long, open-water columns. Insect larvae crawl and invertebrates slither—motion, motion, motion.

Jigging is the answer. There's a jig design and matching technique to duplicate the look and feel of just about everything in a panfish's diet. Your assignment is to present panfish something that either emulates forage or renders itself so tantalizing they can't resist.

Before you get caught up in personalizing a jigging method, it's important to be sure that you have the right lure for the assignment. The realm of jig makes and models is enormous. During the 1980s

Dave Genz, ice fishing's foremost ambassador, advocates an active approach to finding and catching wintertime panfish; jigging tactics ice nearly all Dave's hardwater fish.

ice fishermen had only a sparse selection of jigs to choose from. As the 1990s progressed the ice fishing marketplace soared, and there appears to be no slowdown in the future.

Size, shape, and color are all important. Too big might discourage takers. Too small might encourage less than sizable suitors. The wrong color can deter bites, and even if your lure meets the size demand, if its shape doesn't stimulate interest, the going will be tough. Certain classes of panfish jigs fit specific situations. Carry an assortment of jigs, match the lure to the situation, and be prepared to experiment.

Horizontal Jigs

Jigs that sit up and down are known as vertical jigs, and those that ride left to right, anglers dub horizontal jigs. Horizontal jigs perform

141

Imagine having to differentiate between vertical and horizontal panfish jigs in this assortment. Renowned ice-fishing guide, Dick "the Griz" Gryzwinski, possesses a knack for reaching in his pocket-sized box and plucking out lucky lures.

best in shallow reaches where their innate left-to-right swimming action flourishes. Sunfish in particular have a knack for slamming horizontal jigs, but that's not to say crappies ignore them.

Anglers can dictate how a horizontal jig hangs by sliding the knot back, straight up and down, or forward on the line tie (eye). Sliding the knot back, meaning toward the hook, causes the jig head to point down while elevating the hook. Centering the knot permits the lure to ride flush, and pushing the knot forward, toward the head, makes the hook drop below the head. A simple modification of how a jig rests can trigger a reponse. Also, the lure's action changes each time you move the knot around, which is another means for finding the ideal motion.

Several manufacturers produce horizontal ice-fishing jigs and good ones at that, but don't get caught out on the ice without the following. Wisconsin's HT Enterprises manufactures the heralded Marmooska. It's the modern reproduction of an ice-fishing jig made famous in Europe decades ago, and the Marmooska is a panfish slayer. Its unique obtuse shape and interesting coloration drive sunfish nuts. The oblong shape also creates a luring wobble when jigged.

An upturned light-wire Aberdeen hook effectively penetrates fish mouths and pierces through live bait effortlessly. Hook setting is further improved because of the spacious gap between the line tie and hook point, as well as the fact that the line tie is set far forward on the jig head, causing the jig to pivot and provide solid hook sets. Wisconsin ice-fishing legend Tom Gruenwald starts every ice-fishing expedition with a twitch or two of a Marmooska.

Another tried and true horizontal jig is the Rat Finkee by Custom Jigs & Spins of Illinois. This monumental panfish lure comes in vivid florescent colors that seem to infuriate panfish. A Rat Finkee's soft midsection and unusual head shape add to the overall luster. A Rat Finkee stuffed with maggots is tough to beat.

Ice-fishing icon Dave Genz offers anglers the Fat Boy and Genz Worm, both heralding from System Tackle by Lindy Little Joe. These fascinating lead jigs are amazingly heavy for their size. Genz's reasoning behind the extra heft is to make his jigs effective in deep water. Plus, the added weight takes kinks out of monofilament line when the jig is stationary; detecting strikes is easier with taunt line. Both designs also present a wide profile, which is easily detected on a flasher. The Fat Boy is a fantastic all-around panfish producer, and

An HT Enterprises Marmooska sticks firmly into the jaw of this hefty bluegill; the legendary Marmooska is a standard piece of tackle for serious bluegill anglers.

the Genz Worm draws attention because of its segmented body. Aside from minnows, nearly every aquatic morsel has identifiable body segments.

Plain, horizontal lead-head jigs should also find their way into your tackle arsenal. Sometimes the only lures finicky panfish will take are small, plain lead-head jigs tipped with a single wax worm or maggot. Shearwater Fishing Tackle Powerball Jigs are specifically made for wintertime panfish, and they come in diminutive 1/32-, 1/64-, and even 1/80-ounce weights.

You'll need to experiment with hook size and lure weight independently. Use just enough weight to keep the line tight, with consideration for reaching a specified depth in a reasonable time. You can place tiny split-shot sinkers six inches to a foot above a jig to increase descent time. Hook size for panfish varies from minuscule #12 and #14 sunfish applications to gaudy #8s and #6s for aggressive crappies.

Most of Dave Genz's hard-water sunfish inhale System Tackle Fat Boys. The heavy for its size horizontal jig is a panfish killer. Note Dave's closed-face, underhand reel; it's his favorite for jigging panfish with light line.

144

Vertical Jigs Are Favored by Crappies
and Rarely Denied by Bluegills

Vertical jigs run up and down with a line tie at the top and hook below; they're perfect for covering a towering column of water. Vertical jigs move effortlessly through deep water due to a lack of water resistance. Compared with a horizontal jig, the pillar-like design of a vertical jig glides up and down easily.

Vertical jig options are as diverse as those of horizontal jigs, and it's impossible to list every make and model that has put fish on the ice. However, you'll be in good shape if your tackle box contains the following:

Custom Jigs & Spins offers another essential ice-fishing lure—the reliable Demon. These vertically hung two-tone jigs feature gold hooks and boast a storied history of catching panfish, especially crappies. Their body design begins with a line tie, which connects to a small colored head. The head widens into rounded shoulders that eventually taper inward at the hook. The head displays one color and the main body gets painted another. The hottest crappie patterns feature a hot pink or bright green head with a glow (phosphorescent) body.

A couple notable vertical jigs originate from the mind of Dave Genz. The Pounder and Coped, again from System Tackle by Lindy Little Joe, are highly effective vertical jigs. Pounders are cylindrical two-tone jigs that feature a flat top. Genz has found that the flat surface enables electronic flashers to pick them up. To a degree, a Coped looks like a horizontal Genz Worm standing on its tail. The segmented body is visually attractive to panfish, and when jigged, the irregular shape transmits appealing vibrations. Both models use fine wire hooks that cleanly penetrate wax worms and maggots. Genz recommends using Copeds in shallow situations and Pounders in deep water.

JB Lures Lunar Grub, like a Coped, has distinct body segments. What makes this lure unique is that the segmented lead body is forged onto a traditional round live bait hook. Colored Gamakatsu hooks form the base of a Lunar Grub. The lure's other notable features are its resemblance to a freshwater shrimp and its remarkable multitoned paint job. They come in a wealth of sizes and colors, and I've caught everything from bluegills to a 26-inch Mille Lacs Lake walleye on a tiny Lunar Grub.

Ants and spiders are another group of vertical lures. Realistically, panfish don't feed on spiders and ants during the winter months, but the flowing motion of their tentacles, either rubber or feather, mesmerizes approaching panfish. Additionally, the skirts act like a parachute when the jig drops; at times, slow-dropping lures are the ticket. Bad Dog Lures and Shearwater Fishing Tackle manufacture awesome looking rubber-legged spiders. Northland Tackle makes as impressive feathered ants.

The lexicon of panfish jigs is extensive. I couldn't begin to name every model that's iced panfish for this angler, but when my reputation is on the line, the aforementioned jigs get the nod.

Drop Lines

For the most part, jigs are attractants and live bait is a triggering device. A jig has the power to draw panfish in but not always enough charm to generate hits. Plain live bait can trigger action, but alone, live bait struggles to lure fish in from a distance. What if there was a presentation that fused the merits of live bait and jigs? There is. The dropline combines a flamboyant jigging spoon with a plain hook (or small jig) and live bait.

Begin by removing the hook from a jigging spoon and attaching a six-inch to one-foot segment of four-pound test nylon line to the O-ring that holds the hook. Next, tie on a plain hook or tiny ice jig to the open end of the nylon drop segment. Finish by dressing the hook or jig with some live bait, and you've got a drop line.

Several variations are at hand. Spoon size needn't be large, but choose the same colors you would for a jig. The length of the line is a matter of personal preference, but the six-inch to one-foot range suffices. Anything longer encourages tangles when you pump the presentation up and down. For line weight, use the same two- or four-pound test as on your jigging outfits. Hook selection mirrors that of your bobber setups—Aberdeen for sunfish and Octopus for crappies, and it doesn't hurt to try a wee ice jig as an alternative to a plain hook.

Drop lines are notorious for inducing action in previously dead zones. Panfish are drawn to the commotion an aggressively jigged dropline creates. Pump it a few times, then let it stand still, allowing panfish a few seconds to strike. Try wax worms, maggots, or a small minnow. Once I engage fish, I usually revert to jigging equipment and see if they'll accept traditional fare.

Another means for attracting and holding panfish is loading a single-hook jigging spoon (1/16th ounce) with wax worms and thrashing it violently. Six or eight wax worms on a single hook won't last long when pumped feverishly, but it plays a role. Bits and pieces break free and create a natural chum cloud. Curiosity forces panfish into the area, and they'll either strike the spoon or a smaller jig lowered down a nearby second hole. Panfishing maestro Brian "Bro" Brosdahl tipped me to this technique a couple seasons ago.

Color Selection

The importance of color seems to be directly proportionate to fish activity, meaning when panfish feed with reckless abandon, they'll take a swing at everything. Conversely, desperate times call for desperate measures, and that translates to experimenting with colors and patterns. There are a few broad brush strokes that you can apply to panfish, though. Two-tone patterns, regardless of how you mix and match, give panfish variety, as well as contrast, and contrast fosters enhanced visibility.

Bright florescent colors give anglers an edge in both stained and deep water. Sunfish seem to prefer yellows and oranges, and crappies lean toward greens and pinks. Again, these aren't hard rules, but tendencies. A number of experienced panfish enthusiasts have reverted to earthier colors. Subtle blues, greens, browns, and mellow reds can do the trick on finicky sunfish, and basic black has seen a boom in recent years. I've found that subtle patterns work best on pressured fish, situations in which they've seen every flashy lure known. Bad Dog Lures is a specialist in applying detailed, but subtle paint jobs.

Hail to the jig that glows! The arrival of phosphorescent paint revolutionized ice fishing. It's now possible for panfish to see your presentation in the deepest, cloudiest water and in the middle of the night. Phosphorescent paint absorbs natural and artificial light, then emits a greenish glow into the blackness. The amount of time a lure maintains its glow depends on the intensity in which it was charged. Flashlights and lanterns adequately pump up a glow jig, but nothing illuminates like the short burst of a camera flash.

Live Bait Tipping

Live bait selection is as critical as choosing the right lure, and contrary to what you might think, there are several options. Bait stores carry wax worms, maggots, spikes, mousies, grass shrimp, mayfly larvae, minnows, and a smattering of other local oddities.

Look ↑

The mother of all panfish baits, Eurolarvae or maggots, when accessible, are the leading presentation for both sunfish and crappies. Availability makes wax worms more popular, but maggots usually outproduce waxies.

Wax worms are the universal favorite because they're effective and readily available. These puffy little half-inch critters are the larval stage of a bee moth. Both crappies and sunfish seldom turn down the opportunity to inhale waxies. Hook a wax worm by pushing the hook point through their tail end; this holds true for vertical and horizontal jigs. The tail puncture releases just enough inner ooze (flavor) to stimulate panfish, while leaving the main body to move freely. Start jigging with two or three wax worms, and go up or down from there. If you're taking hits without hooking fish, try threading a single wax worm up the hook. Puncture the tail and insert the hook until the hook point reaches the wax worm's head. Sometimes covering the hook point prevails with picky fish or in ultraclear water.

Maggots, or Eurolarvae, are another essential panfish bait. Maggots are the larval stage of blue and green bottle flies. Compared with wax worms that prosper at room temperature, maggots keep better when refrigerated. Maggots are smaller and tougher than wax worms. Toughness refers to their sausagelike skin that pops when stabbed. Carefully pierce their flat end between what looks like but aren't eyes. An extra-sharp, thin, wire hook slices cleanly through a maggot. Put on two to four maggots and modify numbers from there. It's nearly impossible to thread a maggot, because they tend to explode, so in the case of shy fish, you're better off with a single wax worm. Maggots come in a variety of colors, which are determined by what they're fed before packaging. Experiment with colors. Spikes look like short, fat maggots with fleshy wax worm coloration. Their application is interchangeable with maggots.

Exotics such as mayfly larvae (wigglers) and grass shrimp deserve a chance if local anglers or bait shop owners recommend them. However, don't go out of your way to track down oddities if traditional wax worms and maggots will take fish. In my estimation, minnows are overused as panfish bait. Sure enough, crappies eat them and in some cases prefer them, but I've never experienced a crappie that would take a minnow but wouldn't accept a jig covered with maggots. Rarely will a sunfish engulf even a small minnow; they only like to pick at them. So in situations where crappies and sunfish mix, which is often, wax worms or maggots prove the better bait.

Small minnows, shiners, or crappie minnows are most effective on a plain hook and bobber used as a secondary line. A minnow's undulating action will attract and hold fish even if they refuse to strike it. Minnows also gain prominence during low-light periods. Crappies forage for minnows at dawn, dusk, and overnight, because at these times they have a distinct vision advantage. Also, larger foods, such as minnows, are easier to target in a dark environment, and crappies can detect, via their lateral line, what they cannot fully see. I prefer horizontal jigs when using a minnow and jig combination. Take a jig such as a Rat Finkee and reverse hook a minnow so it swims away from the jig head. Do this by pushing the hook point through the minnow's underside, behind the vitals, and continue working it through until the point pops back out behind the dorsal (back) fin. If you leave the entrails undisturbed, your minnow will agitate for a long time. The theory behind reverse hooking a minnow is that foraging fish take their game head first, so by presenting your bait this way, incoming fish have an unabated path to the hook point.

A closing note regarding live bait—bait is cheap, especially when you consider the cost of a gas auger, fish house, and possibly the $30,000 pickup truck that got you to the lake. Buy a variety of bait and lots of it. Carrying ample bait allows you to refresh regularly. Replace dead or sickly minnows, chewed up wax worms, and maggots when all that's left are fluidless skins. Fresh, live bait catches more fish!

Look!

In general, you can divide panfish tackle into two categories, vertical and horizontal. Starting at the far left and traveling clockwise, you see a Shearwater Tackle Helgamite, which is in its own class; sometimes you need small jigging spoons to trigger inactive panfish and challenge larger ones. Next comes the first entry into the horizontal classification, Gopher Tackle's Tiny Mite. Along with it are the Shearwater Tackle Powerball Jig, Bad Dog Lures Gremlin, Shearwater Tackle Starlite, System Tackle by Lindy Little Joe Genz Worm and Fat Boy, and Custom Jigs & Spins Rat Finkee. The Sumner Bros. Flirty Girty and Gapen's Mr. Waxy hang at angle somewhere between horizontal and vertical. Moving along, the vertical entries are as follows: Gapen's Egg-N-Eye, Shearwater Tackle Punkin, Bad Dog Lures Banshee, Custom Jigs & Spins Demon, Northland Tackle Hackled Ant, Shearwater Tackle Ant, Gapen's Bead Bluegill Bug, JB Lures Lunar Grub, System Tackle by Lindy Little Joe Coped and Pounder, and a Custom Jigs & Spins Peeper.

Jigging Methodology

There is no definitive jigging motion that fools all the fish, all the time. You'd be hard pressed to walk from angler to angler on any day and find uniformity. This isn't to say that every angler's jigging pattern is revolutionary, but that successful anglers take a few basic motions and incorporate a little personalization. That little something usually changes from trip to trip, and even hour to hour.

The first principle in panfish jigging is motion. Think about walleye jigging patterns for a moment; pauses and rests are common. Pauses and rests are rare when jigging panfish. A jigging motion might take the form of aggressive snaps, or at the opposite end of the continuum, subtle pulses.

Another significant variance between walleye jigging and panfish jigging is reference to the bottom. Walleye jigging sequences usually begin and end on or near the bottom. While jigging suspended panfish, your lure may never contact the bottom. Also, an angler usually jigs walleyes inside a two- to four-foot column of water, which is not true with panfish. It's often necessary to cover 10, 15, 20 feet of water, or more to jig through a massive or scattered school of suspended panfish.

A basic jigging pattern begins with a couple short snaps (attraction), followed by a series of small pulses (triggering). The snaps can be six-inch to one-foot rapid lifts, followed by limp-line free falls. Panfish, crappies in particular, sometimes snatch up a lure during an unrestrained drop. If not, gentle pulsing usually triggers a response. From this basic process, all jigging methods are born.

Suspending panfish like to fill up on zooplankton, and most open-water species of zooplankton progress through the water with short bursts and twitching motions. Their daily travels take them up and down a column of water while feeding on smaller phytoplankton. You can reproduce this aquatic dance with a jig and grub. Starting from the bottom, crack your rod tip upward in six-inch increments. Follow each lift with a two- to four-inch free fall. Prolong this series until you reach the surface, take a strike, or your jig encounters fish on the flasher.

Another way to trigger strikes is to swim a jig back and forth by simply moving the rod tip from side to side of the hole. This is particularly effective when a flasher reveals that prospective panfish are sitting right in front of your presentation. Swimming is a potent alternative to still periods between jigging motions.

One of the most effective jigging methods you'll ever employ is what Dave Genz calls pounding. Pounding requires using a sensitive rod and heavy enough jig to eliminate line kinks. The motion is a continuous pumping of the rod tip in short but smooth pulses. The jig hops up and down in an appetizing fashion. Experiment by pounding faster or slower and with longer or shorter strokes.

Sight fishing isn't as much a jigging technique as it is an ice-fishing method. Sight fishing, as the name implies, means watching and fishing simultaneously. In shallow or clear water, many panfish anglers, particularly bluegill zealots, will sit over a hole while peering down and jigging. Critical components to sight fishing are a short, sensitive rod and a large 10- to 12-inch hole; you can see more through a big hole. It's an exciting way to fish, and kids really love viewing the underwater world. Not to mention all you can learn by watching how fish react to lures, what they naturally forage on, and identifying weeds and structure.

Setlines

No matter how many articles are written about jigging, there will always be a contingency of anglers who rely on bobbers and plain hooks. Why not? They have been catching panfish that way for eons. Bobber fishing is underrated, and some ice anglers in the wake of technology have abandoned the technique. It's time to revisit your childhood.

Realism is the driving force behind a setline and live bait. You're taking a lively minnow or wad of wax worms and offering it in as natural a fashion as possible. However, the presentation needs to not only look ingenuous, but also feel real. A basic setline consists of a bobber (float), sinker (weight), hook, and some type of live bait. Let's work in reverse by first addressing bait selection. Most panfish setline situations call for minnows. Crappies eat minnows, giant bluegills will sometimes take baitfish, and panfish of all sorts and sizes at least show interest. In addition, an energetic minnow generates enough commotion so that jigging isn't required. Other free-swimming critters such as mayfly larvae are worthy alternatives. A batch of wax worms or maggots on a small hook sometimes stimulates lethargic panfish.

The realism of live bait is forfeited if improperly paired with the wrong hook. Tiny hooks and big minnows or big hooks and tiny minnows simply don't cut it; matching hook size to bait size is critical. In general, plain #12, #10, and #8 hooks work well for crappies, and #14, #12, and #10 hooks do the trick on sunfish. Size up when confronted with big, aggressive fish, and drop down when confronted with the opposite.

Opting for the right style and make of hook is also important. Small hooks need to be super sharp and thin wired. Hooks by Gamakatsu, Owner, and VMC are incredibly sharp right out of the package. High-carbon steel and state-of-the-art sharpening techniques merge to make Gamakatsu, Owner, and VMC hooks industry standards. Their panfish-size models are thin, and thinness is important for carefully hooking live bait. Thin also translates into reduced visibility.

I prefer octopus and Aberdeen hook styles. Rounded octopus hooks are perfect for crappie fishing with live minnows. The wide gap offers high hook-setting percentages, and the short shank nearly disappears when buried in a minnow. Aberdeen hooks are favorites of bluegill enthusiasts. The long-shank, thin-wire design sets firmly, unhooks with ease, camouflages beneath the ice, and effortlessly penetrates even the stubborn skin of maggots. A trick giving an Aberdeen hook a little boost is wrapping part of the shank with narrow diameter copper wire. Painting the wire wrap gives the hook even more piz-zazz. Speaking of color, the new wave of colored hooks has been well received by anglers and their quarry. Energizing a plain hook is as simple as slipping on a colored bead before tying up. Tiny colored beads give live bait presentations a dash of excitement that might make the difference.

Hooking live bait on a plain hook is akin to how you thread bait on a jig. Tail hook or singly thread wax worms. You should lance mag-gots between their eyes, and hook small minnows from belly to back so the minnow swims away from the shank. Experiment with min-now positioning by hooking it crosswise just behind the head (min-now swims up), crosswise near the tail (minnow swims down), or through the lips from bottom to top (minnow swims erratically).

Next in line is the sinker or weight. How much weight you add to the line depends on the bobber's buoyancy. Other than volume of weight, the other sinker-related consideration is how high to pinch them above the hook. With a minnow, the greater the distance be-tween the hook and sinker, the more freedom a minnow is afforded. Aggressive panfish don't mind chasing wily minnows, but cautious fish prefer a shorter leash. Obviously, swim control isn't important when using maggots or wax worms. Authenticity is a good reason to keep sinkers as far from the hook as possible; it just looks funny when a jig and sinker are too close together. Thill (Lindy Little Joe) and Water Gremlin market pocket-size containers of mixed split-shot sinkers.

The last element in a setline is the bobber. I grew up calling them bobbers so it's difficult for me to utter the word float. Start by choos-ing an in-line or slip bobber. You can rig in-line bobbers as a slip bobber or one that's pegged. Pegging means inserting a small wooden peg or similar object (toothpick tip) into the top of a slip bobber to hold it in a fixed position. Pegging works fine in shallow water, but it's a headache if your bait is set more than four or five feet down. A true slip-bobber setup holds its depth with a thread knot or other in-line bobber stop. Sliding the bobber stop farther up the line, pulling line down through it, lowers your presentation. Some ultrasensitive slip bobbers, such as those by Thill, thread through their bases.

The key to choosing a specific bobber style and size is buoyancy. The goal is to have just enough buoyancy to keep the rig from sinking. Start by matching bobber size to the situation at hand. Small bait with minimal weight demands a small bobber. Conversely, upsizing the bobber is necessary when fishing with a bigger minnow and several sinkers. Too often ice anglers employ giant bobbers that even the most hostile crappie couldn't drag down. Cautious panfish will immediately drop the bait if resistance is too great. You can counteract this circumstance by adding weight to an oversized bobber. Pinch on enough split shot so the bobber's crest rides just above the surface. I call this neutral buoyancy. However, a better solution to modifying an incompatible bobber is starting with the right size. Thill floats and Slip-N-Lock floats from Gapen's are the industry's finest. Both companies offer several models specifically geared for panfish. Their exquisitely finished balsa wood floats feature bright, strike-detecting colors, and like most things in life, you get what you pay for.

Specialized Gear

So often it's the subtle differences that determine whether you leave the ice with a meal of panfish or a bucket still full of minnows. We've already looked at the particulars of panfish location, lure and bait preferences, and technique. It's time to complete the equation by selecting the right rods, reels, and line.

Rod Selection

The quality of ice-fishing rods has improved dramatically over the past couple decades. Panfish rods are probably the chief beneficiaries of industry advancements, and that's good because ice fishermen demand more from panfish poles than they do from anything else in their arsenal.

Jigging is the predominant panfish technique; therefore jigging rods should dominate your inventory. Short ones, medium ones, and long ones each have their place in time, and quality is as important as correct length. Most panfish rods are between 24 and 36 inches in length. Certain circumstances demand using models outside this range, but a good 24- to 36-inch pole meets most challenges.

Top-notch panfish rods usually start with a solid or tubular graphite blank. Graphite offers stiffness, which translates into sensitivity, and sensitivity is crucial to detecting strikes. Graphite blanks are also strong; strength and stiffness team up to provide solid hook sets. Most mid- to low-priced graphite jigging rods are constructed from tubular graphite. However, if finances permit, opt for something in solid graphite, because overall strength and sensitivity are superior.

Even a graphite blank is useless if matched with a junky handle and misplaced or too few guides (eyes). Cork is unquestionably the best handle material. Cork repels water, warms quickly upon contact, and doesn't reduce feel like foam. A good jigging pole also features four to six guides including the tip. The right number of guides keeps line traveling smoothly and parallel to the blank, even under pressure. Thorne Bros. in Fridley, Minnesota, comes to the table with a few outstanding panfish rods. Their 28-inch Sweet Heart (tubular) and Sweet Heart Plus (solid) graphite rods detect nibbles better and set firmer than anything else I've used. The 19-inch Finesse Plus is a shorter solid graphite rod that's perfect for both jigging and sight fishing. HT Enterprises, Shimano, South Bend, and Red Barn Rods of Dodge Center, Minnesota, are a few other rod makers worthy of time on the ice.

An instant ago I named the Thorne Bros. Finesse Plus jigging rod. Well, the one sitting in my rod bag is modified a tad; the top guide (tip) now sports a customized spring bobber. I could have included the topic of spring bobbers in the technique section, but the topic pertains as much to equipment as it does to technique. A week or so before writing this chapter, I picked up a customized Finesse Plus rod, and with my brother Andy, headed to a southern Minnesota water looking for slab crappies. Upon arrival, we found crappies stacked up like Havana cigars over a 50-foot hole, but there was a problem with the 15-foot wall of crappies. The area was filthy with zooplankton. The few crappies we managed to land with traditional jigging

Tools of the trade, clockwise from left to right, beginning with the hemostat, you're eyeing a cluster of simple, yet essential ice-fishing supplies: hemostat (hook removal), eye buster (opening the eyes on paint-covered lures), hook sharpener (hook maintenance), clippers (cutting line), and line weights (setting depth for slip bobbers and tip-ups). Gemini Sports Products of Grand Rapids, Minnesota vends the eye-buster, hook sharpener, and clippers combo.

poles spewed out globs of partially digested zooplankton. So I rigged up the Finesse Plus spring bobber rod with two-pound fluorocarbon line and a tiny glow jig. For the next few hours, I iced crappie after crappie while my brother watched in dismay. He couldn't feel any bites. I couldn't either, but I was able to see them. Every time the spring tip deviated from its smooth pulsing motion, I lifted and hooked another crappie.

You can add after-market spring bobbers to just about any jigging rod. There are several designs available, but they all achieve the same result, to show strikes. It's possible to convert a cheap pole into a panfish killer by simply adding a spring bobber. Spring bobbers also enable you to jig with a smoothness and control that's unachievable with a naked rod. Spring bobbers put an interesting twist on Genz's pounding method.

A second category of panfish poles is referred to as noodle rods. As the name indicates, the rod blank is noodle-like in its dexterity. The tip of a noodle rod acts much like a spring bobber. Even light bites are telegraphed via slight movements of a colored tip. A noodle rod makes an ideal deadstick for panfishing. Winter anglers often jig over one hole while watching a noodle rod positioned over a secondary hole. Position the noodle rod horizontally with the tip directly over the hole. Fix it in place by stuffing the butt in a snow or slush pile, draping it over a five-gallon bucket, or use one of numerous customized rod holders now on the market.

Reel Selection

Earlier I encouraged anglers to abandon their jiggle sticks. Well, the subsequent move is to dump everything but spinning reels. The optimum reels for wintertime panfish are small, open-face models featuring a front drag and multipoint antireverse. Small reels operate better with light fishing line, and they also balance well when paired with a jigging rod. A large reel feels awkward on a small pole.

Other than a few closed-face spinning reels by Zebco, Quantum, and Shakespeare, open-face models dominate the market. Dave Genz favors closed-face reels because of their smooth line delivery and effectiveness with one- and two-pound test line. Line loops and tangling are more common on open-face reels, but the fact remains that there's a far greater selection of open-face models.

Often it's the drag system that separates the good from the bad. For starters, stick to models featuring a front drag; they're more reliable in cold and icy conditions. Second, reels with multipoint antireverse offer superior control while battling fish; plus they engage faster. Multipoint antireverse means that the drag engages and handle locks immediately once the bail is closed. Traditional reels lock in only a few places, and this margin of error is often responsible for lost fish.

I tote several rigs onto the ice, and it seems that reels by Silstar/Pinnacle, Shimano, Abu Garcia, Quantum, and South Bend usually make the cut. This brings me to something I should have included earlier. In lieu of having to frequently tie and retie jig after jig, I prefer to carry several prerigged outfits. Nothing's more frustrating than attempting to tie on minuscule lures with numb hands. Fix several outfits with various lures before heading out.

157

Tapping into a school of wintertime panfish is exciting and rewarding. The sport is further enjoyed outside a shelter on mild winter days.

Line Selection

The topic of fishing line selection can get complicated, but I won't let it. Start with the notion that nylon or monofilament lines have been working fine for years, and with the passing of each ice-fishing season, manufacturers make marked improvements on their existing products.

Winter panfishing demands that fishing line be strong, but not too stiff, and low diameter for minimal visibility. Limp casting line seizes up a bit in cold water, leaving it with just about the right amount of stretch. Low-stretch lines, particularly in shallow water, tend to be too rigid for use on soft-mouthed crappies. Overall stretch increases in deep water so you can get away with inelastic line in some situations. Low-diameter lines are more transparent than thicker lines of equal test strength. Colored lines can improve the camouflage illusion if used with the right backdrop. Greens and browns do the job in stained water, and smoke or gray lines seem to disappear with cloud cover or beneath deep snow. And plain old clear line remains a good choice for general use.

Choosing the correct line weight is as important as finding the perfect color and line type; 90 percent of my panfish poles are equipped with either two-pound or four-pound test strength nylon line. Oh sure, line weights drop to one-pound test strength and less, but demand for such fine line is minimal. Instead, a high-quality, two-pound test line will do what a lighter line does but without spiderweb messes or the risk of snapping when a big bluegill or crappie takes. A formidable two-pound test line is effective for jigging sunfish and crappies, bobber fishing at any depth, and catching a hog bluegill with a noodle rod. Consider using four-pound test line in stained water, thick weeds, and when confronted with passing walleyes or hostile panfish that show no regard for line transparency. Berkley SensiThin, Berkley XL, Berkley Tournament Strength, Cabela's Tectan, Stren Magnathin, and HT Enterprises Polar Line have performed well for this ice angler, but don't hesitate to experiment with new and improved models as they appear.

Aside from nylon line, your other possibilities are fused spectra (superlines) and fluorocarbon. The incredible strength, sensitivity, and low diameter found in SpiderWire Fusion by JWA is remarkable, but it's sometimes too stiff and ices up and kinks when fishing in temperatures below the freezing mark. Braided superlines are out of the question because they absorb water into the line. Fluorocarbon lines by manufacturers such as Seaguar are slowly taking hold. I experimented with two-pound fluorocarbon while writing this book and found it to be strong, sensitive, and more transparent than nylon lines. It is more expensive, but you can simply tie 50 yards or so onto an existing line backer of cheaper monofilament.

Even the best nylon or fluorocarbon lines need refreshing every now and then. Old line gets brittle and becomes impregnated with memory (coils). Brittleness equals breakage, and line memory results in decreased sensitivity. At the least, replace line on your reels before each winter. An avid winter angler should change line a couple times during the winter, and that's not an expensive endeavor if you only replace the outside 50 to 75 yards.

A Final Thought

Flourishing panfish populations can be traced to particular lakes and even to certain years. Plentiful vegetation, structure, and deep-water escapes are hallmarks of the consummate panfish water. Specialized rods, reels, tackle, and bait help to make the pursuit of hardwater sunfish and crappies enjoyable and successful.

Chapter 7

Jumbo Perch

LET'S GET SOMETHING STRAIGHT FROM THE START: PERCH ARE NOT PANFISH. Sunfish and crappies, as described in the previous chapter, comprise the group affectionately known as panfish. Too often authors and anglers lump perch into the same classification. When you shake things down, perch behave more like walleyes than crappies or sunfish. Genetically, walleyes and perch coexist on the same family tree.

Perch are predominately meat eaters, whereas panfish depend more on zooplankton, insect larvae, and aquatic invertebrates (worms). Perch reside on or just off the bottom, while panfish typically suspend. Perch roam great expanses, and panfish habitually stick to more finite zones. Crappies and sunfish often commingle, but rarely will a legitimate panfish hole produce perch. In fact, the presence of pesky perch is a signal encouraging panfish purists to relocate.

The reference to pesky perch is another item that I need to address. The perch notorious for pecking and tearing at bait aren't what we're looking for. We use the adjective jumbo to describe perch worthy of tracking beneath the ice. Jumbo is a relative term though. Some anglers call 6-, 7-, and 8-inch perch jumbos. Other anglers need a perch to hit the 9-, 10-, and 11-inch mark before they achieve jumbodom, and a few elite winter anglers aren't impressed by perch until they measure at least a foot. Regardless of what jumbo looks like through

Ice fishermen travel far hoping to harvest a two-pound perch. A jumbo such as this two-pound (plus) fish from Devils Lake, North Dakota, is the catch of a lifetime.

your eyes, the techniques in this chapter will help you hunt down the biggest perch available.

What else makes winter perch fishing so popular? Perch are a fish of volumes. They occur in massive schools that once engaged offer hours of nonstop action. Also, North America's finest perch waters are the most accessible. Big waters such as Mille Lacs Lake, Lake Erie, and Devils Lake maintain enormous perch populations and provide ample access to the ice.

Tastiness is another factor that invites anglers to pursue perch. The aroma and succulent flavor of cracker-crumb battered perch fillets are icons in the outdoor world. Anglers travel hundreds of miles to hook a meal or two of freshwater perch.

The frequency that perch feed is also at issue. Many experts believe it's not a matter of when perch feed, but rather how much and to what intensity. Plainly stated, perch eat continually, but the size of preferred forage and vigor to which they feed fluctuates. "Perch are to eating what ants are to working." A result of their eating habits is that perch aren't as subject to peak and off-peak feeding periods as other freshwater species. Certainly, activity rises and falls during a day, but not to the extent of walleyes, which forage mainly in short bursts at dawn and dusk. Generally speaking, perch feeding intensifies for a two- to three-hour period beginning about an hour after sunup. Midday hours offer ebbs and flows in activity, but rarely will they completely shut down. The evening bite seldom rivals morning performances, yet activity escalates just before the sun goes down. In dark water or extremely deep conditions, feeding can fade an hour or more before dusk.

What's in a Name?

Choosing a Premium Body of Water.   The preceding walleye, northern pike, and panfish chapters delved into handpicking a body of water that has what it takes to produce quality fish and numbers of them. For perch, some lakes are perch free, others turn up jumbos infrequently, most hold only diminutive specimens, but a few elite destinations harbor strong numbers and sizes.

Big Water and Open Spaces

Room to Grow, Room to Roam.   It takes a special body of water to nurture jumbo perch, and lake size is the fundamental component in building a perch fishery. Perch are nomadic by nature. In scavenging packs, perch scour great expanses to score meals. They gravitate toward wide-open flats and basin areas, which are synonymous with large lakes. Big places also host richer food supplies while giving perch populations opportunity to expand.

Large flats or a useable basin are more important than overall surface acreage. For instance, imagine a 10,000- to 20,000-acre lake with a maximum depth of 100 feet and a basic funnel or upside-down cone shape. The basin steps downward without presenting any extensive flats or shelves between 15 and 60 feet of water. It's dominated by rocky shoreline breaks, and it has water clarity comparable to rubbing alcohol. This is not the lake you're searching for! Such lakes can maintain isolated groups of jumbo perch, but usually

The author discovered several jumbo perch while fishing seemingly featureless deep-water stretches on Lake of the Woods. Subtle depth changes and bottom-content transitions often magnetize perch over wide-open basins.

you're either dealing with a preponderance of tiny perch and trout domination.

Make believe you're confronted with a second lake of identical surface acreage and maximum depth, but this venue maintains a couple huge flats, at different depths, in less than 60 feet of water. In addition, the shoreline is a mix of rocks, sand, and prairie pasture or bog, and there's a hint of color to the water—a far superior choice!

A lake's basin doubles as a flat if it's inside a useable range. Useable is relative to the body of water in question. On some shallow prairie-type lakes, the basin and deepest point are the same. Clear, well-oxygenated waters can hold perch in 40, 50, 60 feet, and more, providing there's space to roam and oxygen and food at such depths.

There are exceptions to the size issue. For example, several small lakes in north-central Minnesota harbor outstanding perch populations, chiefly due to having the perfect blend of lake characteristics. Similar lakes occur in the northern reaches of states such as Wisconsin, Michigan, and New York. Prairie lakes to the west likewise nurture big fish in small places. Highly fertile bodies of water in Iowa, North Dakota, and South Dakota have the power to cultivate perch in unsuspecting environments.

Working hand in hand with favorable lake features is bountiful forage. Whether the staple food source is crayfish, baitfish, freshwater shrimp, or bottom-dwelling creatures, abundance is the key. Most prolific perch lakes contain plentiful numbers of shiner minnows, ciscoes, or other large baitfish. Large lakes like Mille Lacs Lake, Leech Lake, Lake Erie, and Lake of the Woods are loaded with forage fish, and bigger foods foster accelerated perch growth. Out west, the alkalinity and fertility of prairie lakes are conducive to freshwater shrimp. Perch in Devils Lake, for instance, rely on a seemingly infinite supply of freshwater shrimp, even though baitfish are present. Freshwater shrimp make up a high-protein diet that's easy to capture.

Knowledge is another corridor that leads anglers to the promised land. Bait store and resort owners, as well as DNR agents, can point you in the right direction. Their input is important because merely locating a perchy lake isn't enough if two- to four-inch perch are the norm. These local experts usually know which lakes contain the most and biggest perch.

Winter Perch Location

Isolating Hot Spots on Big Water. We've established that size is important in creating a viable perch fishery. The obvious by-product of dealing with massive bodies of water is the challenge of pinpointing fish. When miles of water potentially harbor perch, how and where do anglers approach it? I cover the where component in detail over the next several pages and reveal a large portion of the how when I discuss perch methods. I want to elaborate on a specific aspect of perch fishing before going further.

It's evident that mobility is a desirable trait while fishing any hardwater species. Probable locations are numerous, and fish tend to move. Therefore, an efficient ice angler must counteract by following their lead, but with no other species, aside from possibly lake trout, is mobility as critical to success. Perch fishermen must be able to turn on a dime. No fish—move. Fish turn off—move. Only small fish—move. It's that simple. Perch fishing is a proactive and reactive sport!

First, mobility applies to targeting perch across a large, but continuous slice of water. For example, say your lake has a huge midlake bar that crests at 24 feet of water and remains at that depth for several hundred yards. You've marked perch across the top and along a break leading down to 30 feet. Start cutting holes, and I'm talking about lots of them. Plug holes in long strings across the flat, down the break, and onto the basin. Drill no less than a dozen holes per person! Mobility in this instance means hopping from hole to hole searching for active perch.

A second form of mobility is completely relocating when a spot doesn't produce or dries up. Be willing, and prepared, to pack up the truck, ATV, or sled; move; and reestablish camp elsewhere. On giant lakes, it's possible to strike out at your first location (that's why it's important to have a backup plan). Maybe it'll be the second or third destination that finally puts smiles on faces. Don't be lazy, because history substantiates the fact that a few hours of productive fishing in a supplementary location beats a full day of fishlessness back at the starting gate.

Early Winter

I have woven the roaming and spaciousness themes into the entire discussion thus far, and the proposition continues. The early ice period finds positive-minded perch perusing classic shoreline locations. A customary feeding frenzy makes first ice perch fishing highly desirable. Adding to the bounty, large female perch mix with lesser males, affording the opportunity to catch big fish and quantities.

I spelled out the attraction of shallow water at first ice in the walleye and panfish chapters. A sidebar on page 56 details the relationship between late fall and early winter as it pertains to lake metamorphosis. So to be brief, perch prefer shallow haunts for the same reasons as other fish: favorable water temperature, abundant food, and plenty of oxygen.

The next step is to identify premium places within the shallow zone, and depending on the overall lake picture, you've got several options.

Early winter affords the opportunity to engage numbers of perch in shallow water. Big fish invade the shallows to feast on baitfish and various aquatic edibles.

Shoreline Flats and Breaks Mean Abundant Perch in Accessible Areas

Shallow is relative to the lake in question. For instance, shallow means only 5 to 8 feet of water when looking at shoreline areas on Leech Lake, whereas shallow translates to 10 or 15 feet on nearby Mille Lacs Lake. You'll need to establish how shallow is shallow on your chosen lake.

Most preferred shoreline flats are gravel or sand. Slowly tapering sand or gravel bottoms are common on open-basin, perch-type waters. Typically, shorelines fade into gradually tapering bottoms that eventually hit a break, or steeper slope. Imagine a lake where the shoreline slides ever so slowly from 0 to 10 feet of water, then abruptly falls to 15 feet; the 10- to 15-foot gap forms the first break. This break becomes a structural element that corrals nomadic perch and offers a tangible point to begin fishing. Look for fish concentrating just above, over, or at the base of the break. This scenario calls for aggressive augering with the result being numerous holes forged across the entire depth range. Again, perch fishing is an activity, not a pastime.

Breaks sometimes appear as subtle one- or two-foot changes along a shoreline flat. Often a broad shoreline flat bounces up and down in six-inch to one-foot intervals, then at some point drops two or three feet. A subtle change such as this won't usually attract all the fish, but when they scatter across a shallow flat, you can bet even a minor break lures perch.

Another interesting occurrence within a flat is a trough. You can find cuts or depressions, as they're also known, over sand or gravel flats and gently tapering shorelines. An example is where a sandy shoreline flat hovers around 8 or 9 feet of water, but at some juncture a rectangular trough dips to about 12 feet, then rises back to 8 or 9 feet. When perch favor expansive flats, all it takes is a little dip here and there to gather fish.

Any irregularity, besides a break, within a shallow zone also appeals to vagrant perch. A couple rocks here and there, a minor underwater bar, weed patch, or bottom-content change are all capable of holding perch (more on rocks and weeds in a moment).

Shoreline Points

As stated in the walleye chapter, nothing improves the promise of a shoreline break like a merger with a point. Shoreline points are the most reliable and recognizable early ice locations, and bigger is better. Giant points render abundant forage and usually more contours, depth variations, and structure than smaller versions. Refer to the walleye chapter for an extensive discussion of shoreline points, and because early winter perch and walleye behavior is similar, the bulk of the data is transferable.

Bays and Coves

About the same time perch invade shoreline areas, usually late fall, some fish also migrate into certain bays, coves, and harbors. Such shallow offshoots of a main lake benefit from the same favorable conditions that make shoreline sections attractive. Bays, coves, and harbors hold forage, are oxygenated for the time being, and have yet to reach uncomfortably low temperatures.

A shallow sand- or gravel-bottomed bay featuring some weed growth is prime. Inside the bay, look for classic holding structures such as breaks adjacent to flats, scattered rocks, bars, and any place weed growth forms a distinct edge. The mouth area leading in and out of a bay also deserves attention. A bay's mouth offers the best of both worlds, meaning the outer mouth likely greets favorable shallow shorelines on the big lakeside, and the inner mouth offers perch a staging zone between big water and small water habitats.

Coves and harbors, especially spacious ones on big lakes, often experience a short burst of activity at first ice. Baitfish flock to fertile coves and dredged harbors during autumn, and they'll usually hang around for a week or two following ice up. Perch are able to find bountiful forage within the finite environment of a cove or harbor; stuffing their bellies requires less effort here than on the main lake.

Shallow Weeds

More often than not, lakes recognized as perch factories aren't weed choked. Weeds seldom receive consideration during perch fishing discussions, but like diamonds, scarcity is what drives up the value. Early winter often allows a few lush beds of cabbage, coontail, or milfoil to persist for at least a few weeks. Thick mats of such greenery form an outside edge, and wandering perch will fall in line and cruise along the perimeter. Perch also use clear lanes and pockets within an otherwise dense mat. Here, fish have a venue to trap and ambush prey, and anglers are able to jig without constant snagging.

In situations where weed formations are patchy and scraggly, look for perch using them as temporary holding and feeding stations. Towering weeds such as cabbage do sprout in scattered arrangements, but it's usually shorter grass-type weeds that litter sand and gravel flats. Carpet grass, as these weeds are sometimes known, tends to grow in erratic patterns across massive flats. Roaming perch stop at these plots looking for aquatic insects and crayfish, two regular residents of grassy weed zones.

Shallow Rocks

Shallow rocks provide structure and a feeding area. As structure, rocks create a natural margin for perch to follow. As a lunch wagon, rocks harbor crayfish, baitfish, and sometimes insect larvae.

Watch for rock bars and shoreline reefs that either greet a large flat or are contained within it. Picture a 50-yard long rocky jettison emerging from an otherwise contour-free shoreline. The rock bar dips beneath the surface and slopes to 8 feet, where the tip quickly drops to 15 feet. The surrounding shoreline taper is sandy and slopes from 0 to 15 feet. Expect to find early ice perch clinging to the base of the bar, where rock gives way to sand. Early and late in the day, fish might probe across the top of the bar searching for baitfish or crayfish.

An isolated rocky reef situated over shallow sand or gravel is also attractive. Again, you're dealing with something that keeps perch from endlessly roving. Like our rock bar example, anticipate engaging perch around the base (transition), up the break, and over the top during low-light periods.

Imperfections within a rock structure are always a bonus. Probe for supplementary fingers (extensions), varieties of rock sizes, barren or hardpan sections within a bar or reef, and of course weeds.

Midwinter

Most freshwater fish species reluctantly migrate to deeper climes. Midwinter's wrath, as described previously, makes shallow reaches either uninhabitable or at least unpleasant. Walleyes and northern pike lose access to a great deal of structure when they're pushed deep. Shoreline rocks, weeds, and bars go from being lush terrain to a nearly desolate ghost town, but perch, being far less structure oriented, willingly accept the change. Instead of roaming shallow flats and breaks, perch simply drop down and continue on their merry way. Their tolerance for adversity is what makes perch catchable throughout the hardwater season.

Angling for migrant fish in deep water is challenging, but not impossible. Knowledge is a powerful tool. Regardless of a lake's size, diversity of structure, and what winter period is at hand, a properly equipped and educated winter angler can always hook a meal of perch.

Deep Flats and Breaks

The previous section listed early winter perch haunts, and it opened with shoreline breaks and flats. Flats and breaks are also important during the midwinter period, but sought-after locations range deeper. Deep in this case means anything deeper than areas perch inhabited through the first three to six weeks of winter. In a shallow bowl-shaped

170

Ward Julien of Shearwater Fishing Tackle probed deep flats just off a major rock structure and hit the jackpot. Midwinter often finds perch roving junctures where deep flats greet rock piles and bars.

prairie lake, where perch foraged previously in 8 to 12 feet of water, deep might mean sliding down to 15, 20, or 25 feet. In clear lakes, deep lakes, and rugged northern lakes, deep can run all the way down to 40, 50, 60 feet, or more.

Beginning with breaks, deep refers to a second or third shoreline break, or a solitary break found quite a ways offshore. Our earlier mental diagram offered a shoreline break (first break) that ramped from 10 down to 15 feet of water. Imagine that from 15 to 25 feet, the bottom tapers slowly and uniformly. Then at the 25-foot mark, it breaks dramatically to 32 feet of water, which consequently scores the edge of an enormous flat covering several hundred acres. This 25- to 32-foot slide is our deep break.

The environmental products of bone-chilling winter weather (lowered water temperature, oxygen deficiency, etc.) drive perch to deep water. They'll roam and feed in no particular pattern other than to trace forage movements and find comfortable temperatures. However, as stated previously, any object or structure gives them a reference point, and a deep break is just that.

In our example, the base of the 25- to 32-foot break is an obvious juncture to explore. The base of the break is exactly what an angler needs to pen perch. Perch will cruise back and forth along the aquatic fence line. Actively feeding perch might climb up and down the break, especially around sunup and sundown.

You've punched holes across the break and at the base, but what about the adjoining flat? Remember, perch are nomadic creatures that treasure wide-open places, and our hypothetical 32-foot flat is large, deep, and livable. Go ahead and scatter holes across the flat. An able-bodied person, snow conditions permitting, should be able to tote an auger 50 to 100 yards away from the break. Sometimes schools of perch loiter at midflat during midday hours and range closer to the break for morning and evening runs.

A gradually tapering shoreline behaves like a flat when depth change is subtle. For instance, if overall depth changes by only 1 foot for every 50 yards moving away from shore, you might as well call it a flat. This phenomenon is common on extremely large bodies of water.

When deep-water perch aren't referencing any particular structure, it's important to distinguish a preferred depth or depth range. Bait shops, resorts, and local anglers are a tremendous resource to gather such information; without a little assistance you could blow an entire day trying to determine what depth to fish.

Bottom-Content Transitions

On a contour map, the basin of a lake and huge flats appear featureless and downright intimidating. Combing acres of uniform depth is laborious. Well, if depth is consistent and there's an apparent lack of structure, you need another clue. What about bottom content?

Deep flats and basins vary in composition. Gravel, hardpan (dense clay), sand, and muck (mud or silt) compose the basins of lakes in perch country. Five miles of hardpan is interesting but not intriguing. Five miles of hardpan with a 10-acre patch of gravel is absolutely fascinating! First, a bottom-content transition gives perch a physical reference point in an otherwise unvarying environment. Plus, a secondary bottom type, such as gravel, hosts different life forms (forage).

The perimeter of a bottom-content transition is what you're looking for. The edge gives perch access to two unique environments, in addition to a pathway. Sometimes the transitional edge also forms a break line. Many large-basin lakes feature elevated gravel and mudflats, which rise above the main basin. On Mille Lacs Lake, for instance, the basin ranges from 30 to 35 feet deep, and scattered about its northern half are mudflats. These irregularly shaped plateaus rise sharply, cresting at 20 to 24 feet. Mille Lacs Lake's mudflats are famous for producing wintertime perch and walleyes.

Mud zones are particularly interesting because of what lies within. Various invertebrates and larval insects make their home in mud, silt, and soft clay. Aquatic worms and mayfly larvae are a couple inhabitants of deep soft bottoms. Minnows and young perch also forage on critters in the mud, making such areas more attractive to jumbo perch.

Deep Rocks and Bars

In the walleye chapter, I described deep rock piles and bars in detail. As offshore perch structure, they provide both a feeding post and formation to hang around, and once again, the larger the structure the better. Big, deep rock piles, or reefs as they're also known, offer a plethora of forage, including baitfish, crayfish, and insect larvae. The deep edge or break of a rock pile is the first place to rummage for perch. The base usually marks a transition point where rock converts to gravel, sand, or hardpan. Finally, explore beyond the reef, looking for perch roaming the adjacent flat or basin.

View huge offshore bars similarly to deep rocks. First identify the top, which is commonly sand or gravel based, check depths leading down the break, and finish at the base. Deep bars can hold fish on top, along the break, at the base, and just off into the basin. The deeper the water over the crown, the greater the chance perch will use the entire depth range.

Late Winter

This is as good as it gets! The weather can be springlike during the climax of hardwater season. Air temperatures are escalating, the sun's path arcs higher in the sky, snow reverts to its liquid form and runs down old fishing holes—sure beats a January windchill. Late ice perch enthusiasts will creep onto lakes until the ice turns black and rots away; the author of course encourages readers to exercise caution.

By late winter game fish seasons, those pertaining to walleyes, bass, trout, northern pike, and muskies, have closed, aside from a couple states with liberal continuous seasons. Perch, like panfish, provide year-round fishing possibilities. The late ice period yields the biggest and most fish of the hardwater season.

Earlier I used the term reverse migration to describe how walleyes and panfish venture back to shallow areas before ice out; perch follow the same pattern. Their impetus to migrate is food related and, of course, nature's calling. The food part connects to the entire chain of events that now make shallow locales habitable. Reoxygenation and rising water temperatures are the two chief reasons that baitfish and subsequently perch storm the shallows.

A genetic urge to breed is the other factor drawing perch tighter to shore. Perch are one of the first species to spawn. In the northern states, perch commence spawning when water temperatures hit the lower 50s, and temperatures usually touch that range soon after ice out. What this tells fishermen is that long before breeding occurs, perch make their way toward spawning areas.

Perch, like walleyes, spawn over shallow gravel, but they'll also use shallow sand, a little deeper sand, gravel that's not quite shallow, and occasionally sand or gravel that's deep. The point is that perch aren't as selective about spawning terrain as walleyes. Your objective is to learn what area perch use to spawn and start drilling holes, or reuse old ones. Local fishing businesses can help narrow things down.

Another upside of late ice is the increased presence of big fish. Larger female perch prepare for the rigors of spawning by eating like crazy. Not to say you can't catch big fish all winter, but the ratio of ho-hum perch to jumbo perch swings your way at winter's end.

Still not convinced? Late winter also sees smaller perch schools (pods) bonding to form massive throngs of perch. As schools migrate inward from deeper locales, they join other groups heading in the same direction. It's a volume thing. The odds of catching great numbers of perch improve as spring approaches.

What's Old Is New

I'll make this easy on you and on me for that matter. Every location I offered as an early ice prospect comes back into play during the late ice period. The same breaks, flats, points, and rocks that held perch earlier in the winter regain their status, and there will be plenty of old holes to go around if you or others fished those areas previously.

Keep in mind that the transition from early winter, to midwinter, to late winter isn't neatly divided into trimesters. Perch don't suddenly leave one spot and materialize in another. There's usually a gray area between periods when fish are scattered. Late ice isn't immune to this grayness either. If you start jigging proven shallows but cannot locate fish, work your way back to midwinter haunts. Somewhere along the line you'll engage perch—another call for mobility.

How to Ice Winter Perch

The Tools and Techniques.   You wouldn't think that any forethought or savvy is necessary to catch jumbo perch, being how they are. After all, everyone knows that perch numbers are nearly infinite, combined with the notion that perch feed with reckless abandon. Such is not always the case. Dinky perch are capable of hitting anything and everything, but true jumbos can be far more selective and stubborn. You have to give them what they want. Certain colors, sizes, and patterns perform better in certain situations. The following methods and related gear have a storied history of consistently taking big perch.

Jigging

Surprise, surprise! Jigging once again takes precedence as the leading method for catching hardwater perch. Flash and movement easily dupe perch. Their innate curiosity and incessant desire to feed make dancing spoons irresistible. Baitfish, a dietary staple, juke and jive in a tireless effort to keep from being digested by predators. Each twist and turn emits attracting sights and sounds. Perch, being largely meat eaters, respond to the commotion by closing in for a kill.

Jigging spoons aim to re-create the action of baitfish. A spoon's size, shape, coloration, and how it behaves when jigged capture the realism. For the most part, spoons used on perch are smaller versions of walleye spoons. Take a color and pattern that's proved effective on walleyes, downsize, and the smaller rendition should perform as well on perch.

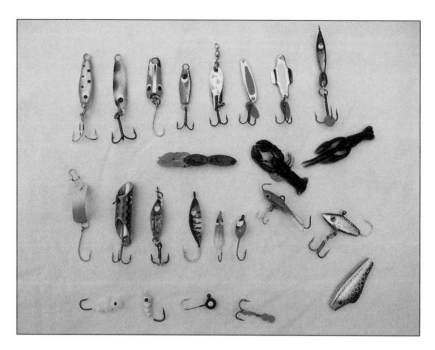

The complete perch arsenal can fit in a single pocket-sized tackle box. Row 1: A selection containing a heavy-pounding Ivan's Glo Tackle Slammer, Ivan's Glo Tackle Jigging Spoon, Jig-A-Whopper Hawger Spoon, Jig-A-Whopper Rocker Minnow, Luhr-Jensen Champ, Bay de Noc Swedish Pimple, and Bay de Noc Vingla. Bad Dog Lures Pin Minnow is the perfect low-profile spoon. Row 2: The Shearwater Tackle Helgamite, Outdoor Creations Torpedo Lure, Bad Dog Lures Willow Spoon, and Bad Dog Lures Crippled Minnow are exemplary wide-flashing spoons for shallow water. Ivan's Glo Tackle Swimming Jig and Northland Tackle's Jig-let are effective downsized vertical jigs. The Nils Master Jigger and Ivan's Glo Tackle Minnow are perfectly sized swimming jigs. Row 3: System Tackle by Lindy Little Joe Genz Worm, JB Lures Lunar Grub, and Gopher Tackle Tiny Mite work wonders on light-biting perch. Shearwater Tackle Double Trouble is an excellent pre-packaged drop-line system. Also pictured between rows 1 and 2 are soft plastic crayfish, which you can substitute for live bait.

During those moments when perch refuse to inhale spoons, panfish tactics are in order. You can trick light-biting or nonresponsive perch into feeding by charming them with ultralight tackle. Another reason panfish strategies sometimes produce is that perch aren't exclusively minnow eaters. They'll take advantage of bug hatches, bottom-dwelling worms, freshwater shrimp, and even zooplankton in a bind.

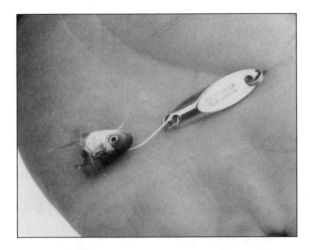

An elementary jigging spoon and minnow head still take more wintertime perch than all other presentations combined. Pictured is a Kastmaster spoon and the head of a small fathead.

Jigging Spoons and Walleye Tackle

We just spoke to the fact that perch spoons are essentially shrunken walleye spoons. Inside the walleye chapter, I dispensed great detail distinguishing categories of jigging spoons. I attempted to match design to the conditions at hand, and subsequently offer several exceptional makes and models that fall into each category. You can apply the same spoon categories to perch fishing. So we'll revisit the subject as it pertains to perch, but if you crave greater details, please hearken back to the walleye chapter.

Wide-flashing spoons are broad-bodied but light lures that work magic in shallow water. Without adding sinkers, they're effective down to about 12 feet. Their wide profile resembles larger baitfish, and the added size is a bonus when aggressive perch invade. Using thin, lightweight metal permits wide-flashing spoons to glint and flutter during the descent. The intense action draws fish in from great distances. No doubt, such spoons are meant for hostile perch. Northland Flash'n Fire-Eye Minnow and willow spoon series by Bad Dog Lures and Ivan's Glo Tackle are fantastic examples.

The second classification of jigging spoons is dubbed heavy pounding. These oblong, leaden lures comprise most of what's found in bait shops. The pounding designation relates to how they're used; go to the bottom and pound (jig) until something strikes. Anglers can choose from a wealth of sizes, colors, and patterns from dozens of manufacturers. A few favorites are System Tackle by Lindy Little Joe

Small but weighty, miniature heavy-pounding spoons are attractive in size and coloration and can contact deep bottoms in a hurry.

Deadly Dart, Shearwater Fishing Tackle Thumper, and Swedish Pimple by Bay de Noc Lure Co.

Low-profile spoons are mellow variations of heavy-pounding spoons. Their slender design renders enough weight to reach deep perch, while throwing out just a taste of flash—perfect lures for lethargic fish. Pin Minnows by Bad Dog Lures are worth looking for.

Nothing more accurately portrays baitfish than swimming jigs. These minnow-looking lures are basically wintertime crank baits. Fishing them properly is an art form. Swimming jigs bob, weave, swirl, and jerk, and with a seasoned angler at the helm, few perch can resist. Rapala, Nils Master, and Bad Dog Lures manufacture perch-sized swimming jigs.

Consider Color and Hooks

Color selection is personal. At any time, on any lake, you'll find anglers experiencing similar success while working lures of completely different colors. Having said that, at times, selecting the right color most certainly increases your catch. Perch tend to like fancy, brightly colored lures; florescent orange, lime green, and chartreuse are favorites. Florescent combinations reduce the possibility of picking the wrong color. Interestingly, another productive pattern is perch. You heard it. Perch are cannibals, and big ones love to prey on smaller ones.

The metallic aspect of jigging spoons caters to a perch's hunger for minnows. When jigged, silver, gold, and bronze spoons emulate injured baitfish. Try silver in clear water and on sunny days; switch to bronze and gold in stained water and when it's overcast. Spoons sporting a metallic base with fluorescent accents are especially effective. Glow-in-the-dark paint (phosphorescent) has its time and place. A little illumination can go a long way. Perch residing in deep or murky water react favorably to glowing spoons. Glow also comes into play early in the morning and just before dark. Several manufacturers combine glow paint with florescent colors and metallic finishes.

Pay attention to hook type and size. The problem with walleye-size jigging spoons is that their hooks are too large for perch; juicy #4 and #6 treble hooks are difficult to chomp. Downsize to #8, #10, and #12 models; Mustad, VMC, Owner, and Gamakatsu forge fantastic replacement treble hooks. There's nothing wrong with large jigging spoons if you have downsized the hooks. The voluptuous lure draws fish in, and the smaller hook won't discriminate against the size of a fish's mouth.

Factoring in a single Aberdeen or long-shank hook is an alternative to using small treble hooks. Single hooks do a better job of presenting whole live minnows, wax worms, and maggots, and the long shank keeps bait away from the spoon to ensure that fish strike the hook, not the spoon. Few jigging spoons come equipped with single hooks, but swapping a treble for an Aberdeen is a simple modification. Shearwater Fishing Tackle Helgamite is factory rigged with a single hook, and Bay de Noc Lure Co. Swedish Pimples are packaged with both a treble and single hook.

Drop Lines and Panfish Tactics

I revealed the drop line in the panfish chapter. A drop line's merit is that it combines the luring capabilities of a jigging spoon with the

Drop lines combine the attracting attributes of a jigging spoon with the triggering component of live bait.

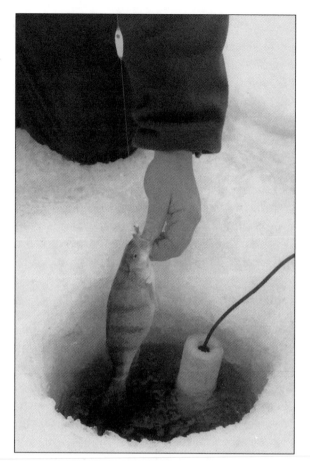

natural appeal of live bait. Perch, because of their inquisitive nature and propensity to feed, are as well suited for drop line fishing as anything under the ice.

Drop lines are highly effective in deep-water situations when perch seem hesitant to smack a jigging spoon. Take your favorite perch spoon (vertical), and remove the hook. From the vacant O-ring, tie on a 6- to 12-inch segment of two- to four-pound test monofilament or fluorocarbon line. On the other end, tie on a single hook, bait it up, and you've got yourself a drop line.

From this basic setup, there are a few modifications that you can implement. Beginning at the top, spoon options are wide ranging. Large spoons give it plenty of flash, but they're heavy. Small spoons attract with a subtle flair, but they may be too light for angling in deep water. Just be sure to use a spoon heavy enough to hastily reach the bottom. After size, color is another area in which experimentation can be rewarding.

The length of the line dropper is discretionary, but as a rule, use a longer line with light biters and a shorter segment when perch are snapping. One positive effect of using a long line is that the bait and hook portion have a longer leash for free falling. The hook section of drop line takes several forms. A basic perch drop line employs an Aberdeen (wax worm or maggot) or Octopus (minnow) hook. From there, experiment with colored hooks or slide the line through a single colored bead before tying on a hook. Tiny #10 and #12 treble hooks afford a nearly zero-miss hook-setting percentage, but they're visibly displeasing when fishing is tough.

A unique alternative to rigging a plain hook is instituting a small panfish lure. A Custom Jigs & Spins Demon System Tackle by Lindy Little Joe Genz Worm, and Shearwater Fishing Tackle's Powerball Jig make perfect lures for a drop line. Two things happen by using a jig rather than a plain hook. Number one, you benefit from the visual attractiveness and movement of the jig. Two, the lure makes a pendulum-like swing when it's jigged, resulting in fewer tangles because it sways away from the overhanging spoon.

Spending a lot of time covering panfish methods for perch would duplicate the Tools and Techniques section in the panfish chapter. What you do need to understand though is that when perch are present, as established by a depth finder, but not responsive, it's time to downsize.

Just about any panfish jig discussed earlier will generate interest; your task is figuring out how to get a small lure in front of deep fish. Drop lines, as stated, are one means of taking a tiny presentation to great depths. A second option is to pinch just enough split shot above the jig (6 to 12 inches) to efficiently reach the lake floor.

Live Bait Tipping

Minnows and maggots—it's as elementary as that. Offer aggressive perch minnows, and drop down to wax worms and maggots when perch seem sluggish. There's no need to fill up on expensive minnows, because bulk-run fatheads or a comparable local strain do well. Size down to crappie minnows when you're confident they want finned forage, but are ignoring or only picking at whole fatheads. Jump up to whole shiners if you find gigantic perch or set a remote tip-up.

Heads, tails, or should you hook a whole minnow? Usually, minnow heads prove more effective than whole live bodies. After all, perch strive to inhale baitfish head first, and a lone head hooked beneath a jigging spoon looks like an upside-down, vertically hung minnow. A head, chiefly the eyes, gives perch an appetizing target, and one that's small enough to engulf in one slurp. Minnow heads work best on jigging spoons, regardless of whether they feature a treble hook or single point. In the case of a treble hook, simply bury one or two barbs deep into the head; threading a head on from cut to mouth does a better job with a single hook.

Pinch or cut off a minnow's head just behind the gills; leave a little extra body and dangling entrails intact if you want more meat. A trick is to precut several dozen minnow heads before hitting the ice. Slip the heads into a pocket-sized Ziploc bag, and you're ready for fast and efficient angling.

Switch to whole minnows while fishing with a setline, drop line, or jigging spoon with a single hook. A setline, or bobber rig and hook, is functional as a backup package, and a free-swimming minnow matches up well. A live minnow also makes the grade while jigging a drop-line rig featuring a single hook. The same is true for spoons with attached single hooks; it's difficult for perch to grab a whole minnow stuck on a treble hook.

When the going gets tough, the tough opt for waxies and maggots. You can remedy even the worst case of lockjaw by floating a couple grubs in a perch's face. Maggots or wax worms? Perch don't seem to demonstrate favoritism like sunfish and crappies, but understand that you should never hit the ice without toting at least one tin of waxies or maggots.

Jigging Methodology

The science of jigging perch is a mixture of what I presented in the walleye and panfish chapters. At best, perch behave like dwarf walleyes, and at least, they simply live and eat as do panfish. Previously published ice-fishing books isolated the topic of jigging and built a freestanding chapter around it. I chose to inject jigging into individual species-related chapters. Why? Because, although jigging techniques used on walleyes are similar to those for panfish, there are many differences. However, when perch enter the fold, similarities outnumber differences.

To refrain from reinventing the wheel, I recommend that you re-visit the Jigging Methodology section within the walleye chapter. Techniques such as quivering and desert storming accomplish the same results on perch as they do on walleyes. The only exceptions being that you may use smaller spoons and subtler motions.

The same goes for applying panfish jigging tactics to perch. You can easily transfer jigging methods unveiled in the panfish chapter to perch fishing. Such motions take precedence, as stated previously, when perch dismiss traditional meat-and-potatoes jigging spoons and minnows.

Expounding on Jigging

By now you should be strapping an arsenal of jigging techniques—walleyes, panfish, and perch beware! However, class hasn't let out yet. How you incorporate specific jigging methods into fishing situations also warrants attention.

We've established that perch are drawn to movement and flash. Imagine if you could multiply the effect of a single jigging spoon. You can! Sometimes a group of perch anglers have better results by sticking together. Throughout this book, I preach mobility, but perching affords one of those rare opportunities that merit staying put.

I call it tight flashing. It's when a group of anglers hunker over a cluster of holes. Their cumulative jigging has the power to lure and hold nomadic perch. Four, five, six, or more spoons pumping up and down within a small area have tremendous capabilities. Regardless of how many fish you hook, someone always has a line down. A common problem for solitary anglers is that schooling perch will vacate an area while he or she is busy unhooking fish and rebaiting.

Another instance when tight flashing or staying put takes precedence is when fishing featureless expanses. It's possible to run and gun to excess. I've seen anglers try to outguess perch movements by dashing from hole to hole while others, sitting patiently on buckets, iced more fish. Sometimes you just need to wait for another wave of fish to pass through.

The opposite of this system is leapfrogging. This is a rapid search-and-destroy method for initially locating perch. Start by drilling a long line or circle of holes spaced approximately 10 to 15 yards apart; form one line or circle for every two anglers. Place angler one over the first hole and angler two at the second. Angler one jigs for no longer than a minute or two without catching a fish, then hops to the third hole. Angler two leaps past angler one to hole four, and so on. This is an efficient means for eliminating water. Once you engage perch, blast additional holes nearby and commence tight flashing. The two schemes work well together.

Sight fishing is one last component I'll throw into the mix. Being able to watch perch while jigging over shallow water is instructive. In clear water, it's possible to plainly see fish down to 10 feet or more. You can observe structure, natural forage, fish sizes, and most important, how perch react to lures. In situations where mixed-size perch travel together, sight fishing permits you to pull bait away from small fish and dutifully entice jumbos.

Setlines

The demand for setlines is less when chasing perch than walleyes or panfish. A perch's dynamic predisposition calls for jigging roughly 90 percent of the time. You can easily fulfill the other 10 percent with a drop line, which is essentially a stationary approach. My fishing buddies and I live by a little credo that goes, "If you need two lines to catch perch, it's probably time to move." Trying to monkey with two lines in heavy fish traffic creates nothing but havoc.

However, if you elect to go the bobber route, follow a few basic suggestions. Upsize bait and treat your bobber rig as both an experiment and a decoy. The experimental component aims to attract big perch. From a decoy standpoint, a thrashing minnow does a tremendous job of drawing and holding curious perch, even if they don't strike.

Tie on a #6 or #8 Octopus (minnow) hook while using shiners or chubs. Thread a colored bead or two onto the line before tying up for attraction purposes; colored hooks provide similar results.

Far superior to soaking a bobber is implementing a remote tip-up strategy. Rarely are tip-ups associated with perch, but they should be. There's no better way to research an area. Place tip-ups in shallower or deeper water than your primary jigging holes, affording the ability to identify fish passing at various depths. A distant tip-up lets an angler get a line down away from traffic and commotion; older, wiser, and bigger fish can be wary of fishermen walking around.

Speaking of big fish, rig your tip-ups so that they encourage jumbo perch and discourage annoying smaller ones. You don't want to be chasing flags that are tripped by diminutive perch. Dress it with a #8

Never underestimate the feeding abilities of hungry perch. This specimen engulfed a whole shiner minnow suspended beneath a tip-up.

or #6 kahle or Octopus hook teamed with a shiner minnow or chub. The larger setup aims to please big perch and potentially a bonus walleye or northern pike.

Specialized Walleye and Panfish Gear

The beauty of assembling perch fishing equipment is that you shouldn't have to look any farther than your existing inventory, assuming it contains both panfish and walleye stuff. Panfish instruments prevail on days when perch prefer small jigs and grubs. Inversely, when they're smacking jigging spoons with ballistic intensity, you'd better grab a heavier rod and reel package.

The perfect all-around perch pole exhibits the characteristics of a walleye rod in a lighter, but not necessarily shorter, blank. Added length initiates sweeping hook sets. Opt for poles with a 32- to 42-inch graphite blank, and you should be able to see and feel the difference between midweight perch poles and heavier walleye or lighter panfish rods.

Choosing a reel for perch fishing isn't complicated either. Key components to look for are front drag, multipoint antireverse, and balance with a rod. Front drags tend to be more reliable in wintry weather. A multipoint antireverse allows you to engage the bail and drag instantaneously; it also improves hook setting and control while fighting a fish. The balance issue is seldom discussed but incredibly important when matching a rod and reel. Overly large reels interfere with comfort and feel of the rod. Also, a mismatched reel, leaning toward the big side, won't feed line smoothly through the guides (eyes). If anything, tend toward smaller reels. Stick to name brands such as Shimano, Abu Garcia, South Bend, Silstar/Pinnacle, Diawa, and Shakespeare, and you'll be fine.

The question of line selection shouldn't be responsible for sleepless nights either. The two- to six-pound window covers any circumstance a perch angler greets. In stained water or when perch attack without caution, six-pound test nylon or fluorocarbon lines are permissible. You can ferret out superlight biting perch with two-pound test line, but it's scary to use if walleyes or pike lurk about. The foremost line from end to end is four-pound test monofilament or fluorocarbon. Four-pound line is strong enough to tangle with walleyes and perch, while presenting a narrow diameter that seldom offends even finicky perch.

A Final Thought

Perch, freshwater's striped meat eaters, have a special place in the hearts of ice fishermen. They feed with regularity and winter finds them in predictable locations such as:

- shallow and deep flats
- breaks
- points
- bars
- reefs
- bays
- weedlines

A mixed bag of basic walleye and panfish gear will bring them up.

Chapter 8

Trout

A FEW YEARS BACK, A MOVIE TITLED *A RIVER RUNS THROUGH IT* PROLIFERATED A TROUT-FISHING RENAISSANCE. The Robert Redford film secularized what was formerly considered an elite pastime. Funny though, I don't remember having seen Brad Pitt, the movie's lead character, hunkered over an eight-inch hole dressed in worn Carharts. Oh no, Mr. Pitt, cloaked in L.L. Bean fashions, waded through a sparkling stream all the while Victoria's Secret-like classical music provided peace and tranquillity. Where was the *Grumpy Old Men* ice-fishing scene?

Fortunately for real-life anglers, the popularity of trout fishing has spread to the hardwater. More winter anglers add trout to their list of targeted species each season. In response to the ever-increasing interest in winter trout fishing, area fisheries divisions and departments of natural resources strive to protect and expand the resource. Programs involving fisheries, habitat improvement, special designations, and restrictions ensure the survival of the sport and the species.

To effectively pursue wintertime trout, you first need to understand the nature of the beast. Essentially, the large group referred to as trout is divided into two categories, stream trout and lake trout. Stream trout are just that, current-oriented trout, but a contingency of them, predominately rainbow trout, brook trout, and brown trout, have successfully adapted to

Stream trout have adapted well to life in certain lakes and ponds, and under the right conditions, they're able to develop into trophy class fish.

lakes and ponds. Lake trout are actual lake trout, the species—pretty cut and dried.

Before examining any defining criteria regarding individual trout species, I want to mention some universal truths. First, trout as a whole favor colder water temperatures than most freshwater fish. Their ideal temperature range lies somewhere between 45- and 60-degrees Fahrenheit, but nonetheless, even cooler conditions beneath the ice are still more comfortable to trout than most fish.

Another common feature among trout is their nomadic lifestyle. Seldom does a school of lake trout or rainbows suspend motionless. Trout, like sharks, prefer to cruise terrain while hunting forage; even while in a neutral to inactive state, trout remain in motion.

Sheer speed is one of a trout's greatest attributes, and they use this proficiency to track baitfish. Working in harmony with swiftness is a trout's exceptional vision. It's amazing that a stream-dwelling trout is able to spy helpless midge drifting across a turbulent surface. These visual skills further permit trout to distinguish between favorable and unfavorable artificial offerings. Have you heard about matching the hatch? A trout's visual powers also demand consideration from ice anglers, because most trout waters are exceptionally clear, particularly in the winter.

Another common thread among trout species is their tendency to range shallower in the winter than during the warm-water months. As cited earlier, frozen waters display minimal temperature stratification; therefore trout are able to reside in shallows, which are too warm during the summer months. For example, a brook trout that spends much of the open-water season confined to deep environments opts for forage-rich shallows in the winter.

Trout feeding patterns also seem to transgress species. In general, trout feeding peaks around sunrise and remains positive for most of the morning. Evening provides a second, but clearly secondary rise in activity, and throughout the daytime hours, trout activity ebbs and flows. Coupled with a trout's 24-hour feeding cycle is a typical migratory pattern, which places them in shallow haunts during the morning and evening feeding binges and deeper during their afternoon respite.

Stream Trout

A Successful Transplant.   Wily river- and stream-populating rainbows, browns, and brooks are notoriously fickle. Factors such as siltation; rapid changes in acidity; and influxes of agricultural fertilizer, livestock waste, and various chemicals can, and often do, have immediate and long-term effects on the environment of a trout. This notion of fragility applies to lakes and ponds; trout require the same near-pristine conditions in a lake or pond as they do in a stream or river.

A brief look at stream trout species, which inhabit lakes, starts with rainbow trout. Rainbows are the most widely distributed stream trout, and many believe them to be the tastiest table fare. These highly aggressive feeders are also known to put up quite a scrap. Sizes vary greatly, but common wintertime catches range from one to three pounds. When identifying a rainbow trout, look for well-distributed black dots over silvery to greenish sides, and possibly a reddish to pink vertical bar that runs along the midriff.

Next in line comes brook trout. Brookies, as they're affectionately known, run larger in lakes than they do in streams (a bonus for ice anglers). What stream-going trout, such as brookies, lack in physical stature, they more than compensate for in voraciousness. Colorful brook trout usually exhibit orangeish lower fins, which are edged with black and white, and a dark body patched with white and red spots that are encased with blue.

Brown trout have the honor of being the fastest growing, longest lived, and hardiest of all stream trout species. Browns prefer low light for feeding, which they accomplish almost exclusively near the bottom. Football-shaped brown trout maintain a mixture of red and black spots over a brownish background, and browns carry a squared rather than curved tail.

A more recent entry into the glossary of trout living in lakes are splake, a crossbreed between lake trout and brook trout. Deep-ranging splake have made quite a splash as a stocked fish in several northern waters because of their size and tenacity.

Reclaim Lakes

Rarely will random selection deposit trout in a lake where they'll prosper. You need to address factors such as water quality, predation, and available forage before trout can be stocked into a prospective lake or pond. With this in mind, state or provincial fisheries biologists sometimes elect to create favorable trout environments from existing bodies of water. The resulting waters are known as reclaim lakes.

Proposed lakes and ponds are first chemically treated to eliminate undesirable species such as carp, suckers, and bowfin. After a settling period, officials then stock the reclaim lake with rainbows, browns, or brook trout, and desirable baitfish species. To maintain the newly created trout lake, they implement fish barriers (traps), aeration systems, and pollution-control policies. Reclaim lakes often receive designation status, and they're subjected to special seasons and regulations. Most states and provinces publish lists of designated trout waters and corresponding regulations.

Reclaim lakes come in all shapes and sizes. Neighborhood ponds are sometimes reclaimed and maintained as trout fisheries, small to midsize lakes have been reclaimed and managed for trout, and, in areas where mining is a way of life, former strip or mine pits are filled and converted into fantastic trout fisheries. Mining pits make choice trout waters because they're usually deep, steep, and receive minimal erosive runoff.

A commonality among reclaim waters is their lack of structure. From pits to ponds, most reclaim waters are funnel-like in shape. This fact places premium value on any existing structure.

First, expect most action to occur inside the littoral zone (water shallower than 15 feet). Within this range, dissect things further by locating any available submerged weeds. Weed flats, weedlines, and randomly occurring pockets are obvious holding features; look for rainbows and brookies amid the weeds and browns lying deeper beyond the greenery. Other hotbeds for locating fish in reclaim lakes are inlets and outlets. Usually capped by fish barriers, these current areas provide a déjà vu venue for stocked trout that are genetically predisposed to thrive in current. Also, current areas are natural feeding stations because of their ability to attract and hold baitfish.

Other traits to look for on reclaim lakes are shoreline points, even subtle ones, sunken timber, dock or pier pilings, and any rocks or offshore irregularities. In the case of mining pits where nearly everything is steep and rocky, gravel flats, sand flats, and weeds make attractive alternatives.

Two-Story Lakes

Every now and then along comes a body of water that's suitable for both warm- and cold-water species; we dub such habitats two-story lakes. Cold-loving trout, sometimes both stream and lakers, share waters with walleyes, smallmouth bass, northern pike, and even panfish.

Two-story lakes offer structures discussed in previous chapters (i.e., points, bars). As a rule, stream trout in two-story lakes relate to the same areas walleyes do. Key locations are shoreline points and breaks, the mouths of bays, inlets and outlets, outside weedlines, and various rock formations. Of these potential locations, points and weedy bays are most notable. Shoreline points have a natural corralling effect on meandering trout.

The mouths of weedy bays also deserve recognition. Shallow weeds are prime foraging grounds during low-light periods. Rainbows, brookies, and even brown trout invade weed beds searching for minnows and various invertebrates. Following a shallow morning flurry, expect to find these light-sensitive fish retreating to deeper water outside the mouth of the bay; count on them to slide back in at dusk.

Annually, a two-story lake's cold-water and warm-water species twice flip-flop primary depth ranges. In late fall or early winter, as water temperatures reach maximum chill, trout migrate up from deep summer haunts, while species such as bass and panfish dip down. The reverse occurs following ice out as water temperatures ascend.

Many bays on the Great Lakes also behave like two-story lakes. Deep bays and inlets attract several freshwater species, including both stream trout and lake trout. Brook trout are the only stream-dwelling trout native to the Great Lakes, but successful stocking programs have introduced brown trout, rainbow trout, splake, and others. Lake trout populations on the Great Lakes have made a serious recovery since sea lampreys, a lethal exotic parasite, were held in check. Hardwater season on the Great Lakes can be short lived because ice conditions fluctuate greatly, and in some years, a walkable thickness refuses to form.

How to Ice Winter Trout

The Tools and Techniques.   If you were looking for a drawn out section featuring unique trout tactics and specialized gear, I'm sorry to disappoint. Because, as any honest winter trout fisherman recognizes, effective panfish strategies ice trout most of the time (see chapter 6), although there are a few subtle modifications designed to increase your booty.

Jigging is the overwhelming favorite method for yanking hardwater trout. Stream trout species are aggressive sight feeders that respond well to movement. Additionally, browns, rainbows, brookies, and splake maintain a diverse diet that consists of baitfish, insect larvae, and various invertebrates. Your task is to present them with something that's intriguing and realistic enough to spank. The combination of a trout's excellent vision with typically clear water demands a careful presentation.

In clear, shallow water, less than 10 feet, lean toward the small side when choosing a lure. Don't be misled into believing trout will pass on tiny lures or that a diminutive bait will go unnoticed. Again, trout are keen eyed, and a great deal of their natural forage are also tiny; anatomically, the mouths of trout are small compared with their bodies, unlike bass or northern pike.

Start with a small horizontal jig, such as a Custom Jigs & Spins Rat Finkee, System Tackle by Lindy Little Joe Fat Boy, HT Enterprises

Marmooska, or Shearwater Fishing Tackle Powerball Jig; each of these lures are proven trout catchers. A vertically hung Custom Jigs & Spins Demon or System Tackle by Lindy Little Joe Coped are prime up-and-down lures. As a rule, open with horizontal jigs, and carry vertical offerings as backup.

Trout tend to be color sensitive, so it's in your best interest to tote an assortment of pigments, even of the same lure model. Experience reveals that reddish jigs or jigs with red accents are trout slayers. Also, the flash of metallic silver and gold seems to spur trout on; painted jigs with exposed metallic patches are particularly interesting. A final lure suggestion is the dwarf W2 Normark Jigging Rapala. This 1-1/4-inch stick of dynamite, preferably in firetiger, can be a trout's nemesis.

Sight fishing is often a component of pursuing trout in shallow water. Gin-clear water permits anglers to see leaping lures and prospective trout entering the strike zone. Based on how trout react, an angler can upsize, downsize, speed up, slow down, or ultimately relocate if needed.

Jigging in deeper water, over 10 feet, requires heavier lures. Tie on larger versions of the jigs already named. Extra weight is necessary in deeper water to keep a taut line and to reach a desired depth in a reasonable time. Larger profiled lures also have added alluring capabilities in deeper, darker locations. If conditions call for using small or light jigs in deep water, it's necessary to pinch a split-shot sinker six inches to one foot above.

Bait choice is also similar to what's used for panfish. Small minnows where legal, wax worms, maggots, mayfly larvae, and other local favorites cause trout to salivate. Always ask area bait shop merchants for a recommendation. There are a few commercial jig dressings deserving recognition. Berkley's crack research team has developed a wealth of effective, commercial live bait substitutes. Their Power Bait lineup includes several items that hardwater trout find appealing. Power Eggs, a glittered salmon egg reproduction, emit a tantalizing lifelike scent that maintains potency longer than the real thing. Berkley Trout Bait is soft and moldable to a hook, and it's available in tasty natural corn, salmon egg, nymph, and night crawler flavors. Last, Berkley Power Wigglers make you wonder if live wax worms and maggots are dispensable. Power Baits come in resealing plastic packets, making them perfect for transporting on remote trout-fishing expeditions or simply crunching up in your pocket while hole hopping.

Setlines, as stated in previous chapters, provide the ideal support component in a comprehensive jigging program. Trout will fall prey to a properly equipped tip-up or bobber rig, and there's no better way to explore nearby, but different, depths and structure while jigging.

The keys to rigging a tip-up or bobber line are using a small hook and making the presentation as delectable as possible. Tie on a fine-wire Aberdeen hook (#8, #10, or #12), and match it with a small, live minnow (where legal), salmon egg, wad of maggots, or various Berkley Power Baits. Realism is essential because a trout has ample opportunity to examine an offering fixed on a remote line.

The tackle, rod, reel, and line ingredients duplicate your panfish gear. Stick with smooth-spinning reels and sensitive graphite or fiberglass poles. The only elements regarding line selection I want to stress are to go light and low diameter; trout can ferret out thick line in clear water. Four-pound test is universally accepted, but it may be necessary to move up to six-pound test when engaging bigger fish and drop to skinny two-pound test with scrupulous trout.

Lake Trout

Icy Barracudas. Serious lake trout fishermen are passionate like none other; they'll do whatever it takes to find fish. No distance is too great, no snow too deep, and no weather too foul. Winter camping, 100-mile snowmobile tours, snowshoe treks, cross-country ski portages, and an occasional dog sled expedition—all for the love of lake trout. Luckily, pain and endurance aren't required to locate and catch lake trout, but some of the finest waters are the hardest to reach.

What makes lake trout fishing so addicting? Maybe it's that lakers are the biggest and nastiest members of the freshwater trout family. You won't find 25-pound brook trout swimming around a courthouse pond. Could it be their hostile foraging tactics and proclivity to consume everything? Maybe it hearkens to the intrinsic drive within all men and women to commune with 60-foot Norway pines, lichen-covered shoreline cliffs, and the twilight howl of a timber wolf.

Correctly speaking, lake trout are grayish in appearance with smatterings of white spots. Unlike stream trout, lakers sport distinct forked tails, which enable them to reach impressive attack speeds. These

The chance of icing giant lakers lures folks to Canadian waters every winter.

long-living trout frequently travel in small schools or pods, and depth is rarely a concern; lake trout use a lake's entire water column. Lakers are highly tolerant of depth change, and inside a 100-foot hole, it's possible to mark fish at 80, 60, 40, and 20 feet.

Ice-fishing legend Dave Genz says that lake trout fishing is a group effort. As opposed to panfishing, in which catching fish tends to be individual, the whole gang gets involved when someone hooks a laker. You've got the catcher, gaffer, and, of course, moral support by cheerleaders. Dave also notes that part of an effective lake trout strategy is drilling plenty of holes that cover wide-ranging depths.

Winter Lake Trout Location

Tracking Their Royal Nastiness. Shakespeare asked, "What's in a name?" For purposes of lake trout discovery, I'll ask, "What's in a lake?" First, quintessential lake trout waters are cool and deep, which normally go hand in hand. Lakers retreat to deep and cool zones during the summer when shallower reaches become intolerable. Size and structure are two other components built into a complete lake

195

The Tools of All Tools—Chisels and Augers

When the chisel and when the auger? It's a study of inches. A hole can be readily chiseled in anything between walkable ice (typically four inches) and roughly eight inches. The Jiffy Mille Lacs and Straasburg Kathadin are heavy-duty classics; Lacko makes a dandy lightweight version.

Chisels also act as probing devices for testing overall ice thickness. Tread lightly while striking the chisel before you. After breaking through, it's possible to reach down and take a finger measurement of the ice. Always begin ice evaluations close to shore in only a foot or two of water.

Chisels can also reopen holes, but old holes tend to refreeze with harder, denser ice, so if a refrozen hole is especially thick, popping a fresh hole is sometimes faster.

After chisels, hand augers enter the scene. Hand augers are lighter than gas-powered augers and therefore preferable for traveling light on early ice. Hand augers will drill holes efficiently in ice ranging from walkable levels to a foot of thickness, but once you get past a foot, you're better off with a gas-powered unit.

Narrow cutting diameters make hand drilling easy. Small four-inch drills cut quickly and create holes large enough to land panfish, perch, and small game fish. Six-inch hand augers penetrate with moderate speed and forge holes large enough to accommodate most fish species. Larger eight-inch drills plug big holes, but they're strenuous to turn. Reserve 10- and 12-inch holes for the internal combustion engine.

An easy-starting, properly geared, gas-powered auger is the instrument of choice for the later two-thirds of the ice-fishing season. Two and three feet of ice are doable with standard drills; auger extensions will take you even deeper.

Any craftsman will tell you that even the finest tools are worthless in untrained hands. Operating a gas-powered auger isn't rocket science, but a little understanding is in order.

1. Push away as much snow from the intended area as possible.

2. Make sure the power head is full of properly mixed gas, and start it according to manufacturer's recommendation.

3. Firmly grip the handles, hold the auger straight up and down, and place feet slightly greater than shoulder-width apart.

4. Squeeze the throttle, and allow the auger's weight to apply the necessary down force. Quality Jiffy and StrikeMaster gas augers require little to no additional pressure.

5. Continue drilling until the auger breaks through the ice's underside, and release the throttle.

6. Give the throttle a short burst as you pull the drill up; the upward surge pulls ice chips from the hole.

7. Kick slush away from the hole, grab an ice skimmer, further clear the hole, and commence fishing. Jiffy's D-Ice'r ARMOR covered Chipper-Dipper is a good skimmer that features a handy chisel on top.

A firm two-handed grip and open stance promote safe and efficient drilling with a gas auger. Be careful to keep loose clothing (scarves and gloves) away from the moving parts of the auger. And always tote a hand auger and chisel in case your gas auger misbehaves or fuel sources exhaust.

trout fishery. The larger the lake, the more and bigger fish it likely holds. Classic formations (i.e., rock reefs, rock bars, islands, and steep rock breaks) provide protective cover, ambush points, and reference points for roving lakers. The last required element is an abundant and stable forage base. Nothing does a lake trout good like a healthy supply of ciscoes, whitefish, herring, smelt, or lake shiners.

Figure 8.1 shows the following:

a. Wedge-shaped narrows forged by two structures, such as an island and a shoreline point, create natural cruising lanes for nomadic lake trout. Make deep narrows the first place you investigate, or at the very least a "when all else fails" location.

b. Deep holes provide numerous "steps" to search while determining what specific depth lakers are using—lake trout can suspend at virtually any level within a deep column of water.

c. Ice fishermen are beginning to realize that lakers will roam expansive 30- to 50-foot deep flats. Flats situated between a pair or cluster of deep holes present the greatest possibilities.

d. Not necessarily do wintertime lake trout hover over a lake's deepest water, but you can bet that breaks and various structures near such chasms do hold fish—a lake's deepest hole provides a reference from whence to search.

e. Underwater bars have a corralling effect on all freshwater fish species—lake trout included. Activity should be concentrated on steep breaks and inside turns.

f. Hardwater lake trout anglers often overlook bays, but they should not. Bays often contain their own structure and deep water, and bays tend to host lakers early and late in the season.

g. Classic steep shorelines give anglers an opportunity to pinpoint wandering lakers. Junctions where steep shoreline breaks contact the basin, deep flats, or other formations warrant added attention.

h. Offshore humps give meandering lakers something to "bump into" and feed around. As expected, the bigger the hump the better, and ones peaking between 20 and 40 feet present more "usable" area across the top.

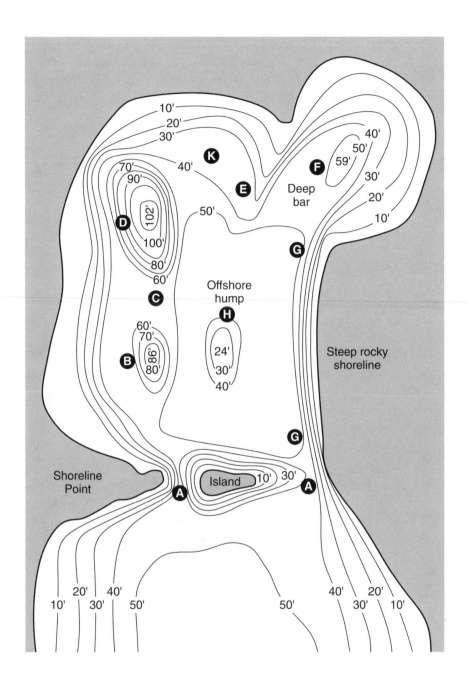

Figure 8.1 Trout can be found in some of these locations.

Most natural lake trout waters lie in the upper quadrant of northern border states, and throughout southern and middle Canada. Classic laker haunts are remote rock- and pine-trimmed lakes, which can be breathtaking in their beauty. Shield lakes are bodies of water that were forged a couple million years ago when the glaciers receded and deposited liquid into deep, rocky crags.

Only part of your task is complete once a lake is selected. The next step is to break the lake down, structurally. The first phase is locating the deepest water and nearest structure to it; a detailed topographical map is crucial. Lakers won't necessarily use the lake's deepest water but they'll keep it in their back pocket. Lake trout use an entire column of water, so don't be afraid of depth. Lakers are known to glide only 20 feet below the ice over 100 feet of water.

Classic structures such as offshore rock piles, islands, narrows, and steep shoreline bluffs are excellent starting points for locating hardwater lakers.

Lake trout like edges. Shoreline points, steep breaks, deep bars, islands, and rock reefs all furnish nomadic lakers somewhat of a boundary. Steep rocky points have the power to pen lakers while they traverse a shoreline. Nonprotruding, but steep, shoreline rocks also hold fish. Lakers commonly chase baitfish and pin them against rock banks.

Offshore rock piles and islands provide additional reference points for wintertime lakers. Sharply breaking banks of an island most certainly attract fish. Rocky humps are of special interest if they crest well below the surface, thus providing an abundance of useable water. Imagine an offshore hump having a 40-yard diameter on top, which peaks at 30 feet and is surrounded by 80 to 100 feet of water; the perfect blend of depth and structure. You could encounter active trout over the top, along the break, or hanging just beyond the pile.

Narrows are another can't-miss venue for pinpointing lakers. Spots where a deep bay funnels into the main lake or where two primary lake sections compress and join put the odds in your favor; the key here being depth. Lakers scarcely use four-, five-, or six-foot deep narrows, but an abruptly breaking 15-, 30-, or 45-foot deep narrows warrants intense investigation.

Often overlooked, deep flats and saddles also host winter lakers. A deep flat might range in depth from 20 to 80 feet, and as I've preached throughout the book, you'll want to find the edge and breaks coming off a flat. Sometimes a flat forms a workable gap between two distinct structural elements. Picture a 100-yard long, 40-foot deep flat situated between an 85-foot hole and a 120-foot hole. The flat itself and breaks leading down each gorge present prime circumstances.

How to Ice Winter Lake Trout

The Tools and Techniques. Say you've found an ideal rock bar extending past a shoreline point. The rock bar is narrow across the top, roughly 20 yards wide, but long, over 100 yards from base to tip. The bar's crown ranges from 20 to 30 feet in depth; one side tapers gradually to 40 feet while the other side plummets to 80 feet. What should you do?

The first thing you ought to notice is the seriousness of the depths we're dealing with. This isn't flag-fishing pike on a 10-foot weedline or jigging perch over shallow sand. Fishing in 80 feet of water is a whole different animal; heavy tackle is in order. Before I expound on lure selection, let's return to our hypothetical rock bar. In this scenario, lakers can roam anywhere within the 20- to 80-foot depth range. What specific depth they'll reside in depends on factors such as light intensity, time of day, barometric pressure, and the presence of baitfish.

Basically, the brighter the skies the deeper lake trout run. The presence of heavy snow cover and thick ice, though, permits lakers to range shallow. Looking at our rock bar, my inclination is to fish the steep break between 30 and 80 feet during daytime hours. Earlier, I established that lakers favor sheer edges, so the bar's slowly tapering backside plays second fiddle. Cut plenty of holes across the entire depth range and carefully watch your electronics for suspended fish.

Lake trout, like every species discussed in this book, increase feeding activity at dawn and dusk. They also tend to move shallower under low-light conditions. From sunup to a couple hours thereafter, and again for a few hours before the sun disappears, our bar's top, lengthwise breaks, and tip demand attention. Skate farther out if nothing happens over the rock bar or if the action wanes later in the day.

The effect water temperature has on fish diminishes as waters cool, stabilize, and reach equilibrium, but the silent power levied by barometric pressure transcends the frozen cap installed by Old Man Winter. Barometric pressure is basically atmospheric weight as it's felt on earth, and the amount of overall pressure rises and falls with weather patterns. Bright, clear skies typically accompany high pressure, while low clouds and moisture escort low pressure. How fish react to barometric pressure justifies an entire book's worth of content, but for this discussion, I'll keep things simple. In general, a high barometer encourages lake trout, and other species for that matter, to range deeper, be less aggressive, and concentrate feeding to the beginning and end of the day. Low pressure, a preferred condition, encourages increased overall activity and tendencies to run shallower. On our model rock bar, the application is obvious: low barometer—shallow top and breaks, high barometer—deeper 30- to 80-foot zone.

Let's swing back to the subject of lures. Deep water demands lure mass. As a rule, go to 1/2-ounce lures in less than 40 feet of water, 3/4-ounce lures in 40 to 80 feet of water, and 1 ounce or more when jigging beyond depths of 80 feet. With weight in mind, the next order of business is matching a style of lure to the conditions at hand. Consider overall depth, apparent fish aggressiveness, and whether you'll be using live bait, dead bait, or no bait at all.

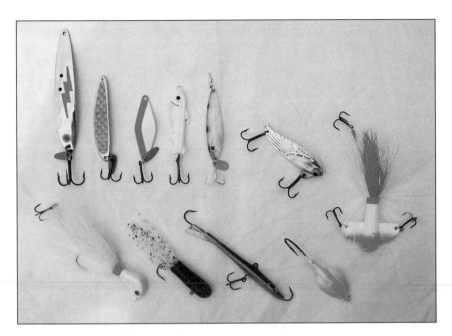

Moving clockwise from the upper left corner, you've got the definitive lake trout armory: Beginning with upsized vertical jigging spoons, here's the Bay de Noc Coho-Laker Taker, Bay de Noc Swedish Pimple, Bay de Noc Do-Jigger, System Tackle by Lindy Little Joe Deadly Dart, and Smasher from Ivan's Glo Tackle. Next is the Heddon Sonar, an outstanding blade bait, and the classic Northland Air-Plane Jig, a laker killer in deep water. System Tackle by Lindy Little Joe also gives us the Flyer, a less aggressive means for swimming live or dead bait. Rapala's vertical jigging lure can entice lakers at any depth. Large and heavy soft plastic tube jigs, sometimes referred to as gitzits, have become popular with lake trout anglers. Last, heavy bucktail jigs, like this Northland Sting'r Bucktail, effectively present live and dead bait.

Understand that unlike most freshwater species, which select from two or more forage categories, lake trout are fish eaters. Oh, possibly in a bind, lakers will partake in a bug hatch or scrape a few molting crayfish off the rocks, but these moments are too rare to affect your thinking. Whatever you drop down there has to look or smell like fish. Lake trout are primarily sight feeders, but their sense of smell doesn't lag far behind.

Lake trout lures fall into a few basic categories: vertical jigging spoons, swimming jigs, blade baits, and tube jigs. Spoons used on lakers are larger versions of the tried-and-true models that trick wall-eyes, perch, and bass, with the exception of a few models built chiefly for lakers. Bay de Noc Lure Co. out of Gladstone, Michigan, makes a few classic lake trout spoons. The Do-Jigger, Vingla, and Flutter-Laker-Coho Taker advance with unique and authentic wounded minnow dances. System Tackle by Lindy Little Joe comes to the table with the Deadly Dart. You can rig this minnow-looking bait horizontally or vertically, and Deadly Darts are available in sizes ranging up to one ounce. Shearwater Fishing Tackle Thumper and Smasher are effective alternatives if you're angling in 40 feet of water or less. The basic process for operating a vertical spoon is to begin on the bottom and jig your way up, pausing and quivering along the way. Vertical spoons are the reigning choice if lakers are lying close to the bottom.

Swimming jigs are the lures most closely associated with winter laker fishing. Their wide sweeping or circling action is ideal for attracting and triggering lakers in deep water. The heavily leaded and winged airplane jig sports chandelier-like treble hooks, leaving little opportunity for misses. Northland Tackle Air-Plane Jig is a solid representative of this genre. System Tackle by Lindy Little Joe Flyers, which come in sizes up to one ounce, are subtler single-hooked swimming

A heavy swimming jig, like this System Tackle by Lindy Little Joe Flyer, is a great all-around lake trout bait, especially when dressed with Berkley Power Bait, cut bait, a whole minnow, or a gut-trailed minnow head.

204

jigs that also spiral and enchant lakers. Slowly drop your swimming jig all the way to the bottom, permitting it to swirl and pause along the way. Once it reaches the lake floor, crank it up a few feet and methodically pump your rod tip up and down. The more line you have out (deeper), the wider its circling path.

Blade baits incorporate an appetizing action with an interesting fin-shaped profile. The two best examples are the Heddon Sonar and Reef Runner Cicada. A blade bait's erratic vibrating action results from its unique design, which places a bulbous lead body below a stamped, weblike fan. Ripping one aggressively through the water produces a wicked palpitation that entices active lakers and can cause inactive fish to react almost involuntarily. The weight-forward arrangement also bodes well for a subtler approach, in which you rhythmically pump and twitch the bait at a specified depth, then reel up or drop down 10 feet and begin again. The most applicable roles for blade baits are as a search lure or bait-free presentation for aggressive fish.

From the warm-water vaults come tube jigs. Open-water bass and panfish anglers have used soft plastic lures for decades, and the tantalizing tentacles and soft body of a lead-filled tube drive fish into a frenzy. Some years ago, a handful of trout fishermen took the same basic bait and applied it to winter laker fishing. Grab a one-half ounce or heavier tube-jig head and a large three- to five-inch tube body; special paintless and elongated tube-jig heads slide perfectly inside hollowed-tube bodies. A tube jig behaves much like a swimming jig (Airplane Jig, etc.) when pumped inside a deep column of water. The primary differences being that you can fish a tube jig at a much slower rate, and their circling patterns are mostly irregular, which is good.

The resulting effects of using heavy lures with lots of line are tangling and twisting. A quick and simple remedy is to implement a barrel swivel. Clip a one-foot section of line from your spool, tie the main line to one end of the swivel, and one end of the cut line to the swivel's other ring. Last, tie the remaining open end of line to your lure. The outcome is a lure that's less apt to tangle, and one that'll execute virtually twist free.

It's the sights and sounds that beckon lakers, but often it's the smell that ultimately prompts an attack. There's a myriad of available options for tipping the prescribed lures, and they fall into three basic classifications: live bait, dead bait (cut bait), and fake bait. Moments are few when live bait isn't the top choice, but certain circumstances sometimes limit its use. Live minnows are difficult to transport to remote lakes; handling live minnows on the ice is a pain; live bait is illegal on many designated trout waters. However, for entertainment purposes, let's suppose it's perfectly legal to use live bait where you're heading. Thriving minnows are best teamed with swimming jigs and tube jigs. Lip hook a shiner, chub, or small sucker on the forged rear hook of whichever lure you choose. A live minnow ads visual realism, natural motion, something soft to clamp down on, and tends to decelerate a falling lure.

Dead bait and cut bait are the most widely used dressings for jigging lakers. A deceased shiner, chub, or small sucker easily replaces live offerings when behind a tube jig or swimming jig, but that's just the beginning. Dead bait fishermen typically prefer ciscoes and smelt to bait shop variety minnows. Ciscoes (tullibee) and smelt are native to many trout lakes, thus making them especially attractive. Another upside of ciscoes and smelt is their ingrained pungency. They flat out stink, but in a good way.

Minnow heads make prime dressings for vertical spoons and blade baits. Thread a severed shiner, smelt, or cisco head onto one or two points of a vertical spoon's treble hook or the front treble on a blade bait. The added meat generates aroma and gives lakers something fleshy to grab. Another fashion for using dead bait is to cut strips of meat and skin from a large minnow or whitefish. Undulating and flashy, cut strips present a flavorful and eye-catching morsel. Grab a sharp fillet knife and slice several half-inch wide and one- to-three-inch long strips from a fish's belly. Belly meat offers a nice fleshy cut with plenty of rubbery skin to keep it on the hook. Also, cut strips make great streamers on the tails of tube jigs and swimming jigs.

Soft plastic grub bodies, particularly those formulated by Berkley, offer an alternative to cut bait. Take a two- or three-inch Berkley Power Grub and hook it vertically on a jigging spoon or blade bait; use soft plastics as a trailer on swimming jigs. I recommend minnow-imitating white and silver grubs, but don't hesitate to experiment with florescent colors.

Certain jigging sequences mirror certain lure types. I just discussed fundamental airplane jig technique; I have covered vertical spoon methods throughout and touched on tube-jig and blade-bait approaches. At this point, there are a couple of laker specific jigging tactics worth mentioning. For one, aggressive lakers respond best to lures that are constantly twitched and pumped. Second, an effective technique for triggering strikes with apprehensive lakers is employing short snaps (six inches to one foot) and subsequent free falls. Keep it moving because constant motion often spurs a reaction.

Setlines received little mention during the stream trout conversation, and they're only going to get modest exposure as a tool for lakers. However, when used effectively, tip-ups allow winter trout fishermen to explore various depths and structures while jigging nearby. In the northern pike chapter, I discussed tip-ups in detail, and nearly all the applications laid bare will translate to lakers. Depending on the size of lake trout you're after, downsizing bait and hook size may be required.

Specialized Gear

Getting Fixed Up With the Right Rod, Reel, and Line.   There's no other way to state it; fishing lake trout through the ice requires heavy-duty gear. The rods are barbarous, the reels are ironclad, and the line could harness a dinosaur. I've told you that rods, reels, and line meant for walleyes will suffice while perch fishing, and the same goes for panfish gear when fishing stream trout. Such is not true when speaking of lake trout equipment. The only anglers who might be able to head out for lake trout fishing without purchasing new stuff are those who are serious about their pike.

Length is important when determining what rod to use. As opposed to most species, 40 inches is median length for fishing lakers; 36 to 50 inches is a reasonable spectrum to work with. The supplementary length provides leverage for setting the hook in deep water. Rod blank composition is proportionately important. Fiberglass rods reign superior to graphite ones. Fiberglass delivers a smooth but decisive blow, and it also holds up well in extremely cold conditions. Many a junket has been ruined because somebody's graphite pole exploded during a stormy battle with a laker. Graphite stiffens and becomes less reliable when temperatures flirt with the zero mark. Who builds the ultimate fiberglass laker pole? My lake trout rods carry the Thorne Bros. (Fridley, Minnesota) and Red Barn Rods (Dodge Center, Minnesota) nameplates.

Picking the perfect reel requires less homework than choosing a rod. For my money, nothing beats an aluminum-cased, baitcast reel;

this, of course, means your rod has to be fitted for a baitcast reel. Baitcast reels are durable, little affected by extreme temperatures, and generally extend a smooth operating drag system. Abu Garcia 5500s and the larger 6500s are proven winter workhorses.

Next is outfitting your reel with the proper fishing line. The criterion here is finding something that's strong, doesn't stretch much, and aims to vanish in an ultraclear environment. Low-stretch nylon or copolymer lines (10- to 12-pound) meet the physical demands of lake trout while remaining nearly transparent. Upgrading into the 14- to 20-pound class shouldn't diminish success if you stick with lines such as Berkley XT and Silver Thread. The new breed of superlines, such as Berkley Fireline, provide exceptional toughness and strength, but if you're sitting outside in freezing temperatures, superlines tend to gather ice.

In closing this chapter, I want to reiterate the importance of ice-fishing electronics. An earlier chapter delved into the scope of electronics in ice fishing, but in no other circumstance are depth finders more important. Lake trout live in the deepest of deep, and they're also known to cover massive stretches of water in a day. A well-charged flasher reveals what depth you're in, what type of structure you're over, where the fish are, and most important, when a laker enters the strike zone.

A Final Thought

Trout may not be the most sought-after wintertime species, but their propensity for cold conditions certainly begs for attention. Opportunities abound now that stream-going species have been successfully planted in lakes and ponds. Naturally occurring lake trout provide even more occasions for hardwater fishermen to expand their ice-fishing horizons.

Chapter 9

Hardwater Exotics

THE BRANDING *EXOTIC* IS SOMEWHAT OF A MISNOMER. It implies that the subject matter is foreign or alien to a given range. For example, Eurasian milfoil is an exotic underwater plant when found in North American waters. For this case study, I attach exotic to freshwater fish that are native and can be caught during the hardwater period, but are seldom deemed primary winter targets.

You can divide hardwater exotics into two distinct groups. The first category includes temperate or warm-water species whose range extends well into ice-fishing country. These fish are largely associated with open-water fishing, and without question, they're far more active in milder conditions. Enter largemouth bass, smallmouth bass, white bass, and catfish.

The second classification embodies fish that favor cold water. Inherently, falling temperatures lower overall fish activity and metabolism, but not with these fish. When their blood turns icy and thick, it is mobilization time. Inversely, increasing water temperatures are to these cold-water critters what sunrise is to a vampire. Enter eelpout, whitefish, and tullibee.

Exotic is a relative term, considering that some winter anglers specifically target less than popular species. Here, hardwater angler Karl Kleman muscles up a largemouth bass from an outside weedline.

Largemouth Bass

Good Old Boys in an Icy World. A customary "Ooh Son!" exclaimed by legendary Florida angler Roland Martin reverberates across a lily pad field. His signature yelp is followed by the hoist of yet another massive black bass from the Lake Okechobee slop. On another lake, this one 1,000- miles north, a nameless ice fisherman pulls an impressive largemouth bass through an icy hole and yells into the barren whiteness. The first scenario, whether involving famous fishermen or not, has been commonplace for decades. The second illustration transpires with greater frequency with the passing of each ice-fishing season.

Northern anglers have come to embrace bass fishing. What was once considered a recreation principally enjoyed by sports enthusiasts living south of the Mason-Dixon Line has spread northward. The natural aging of lakes combined with intensive catch-and-release practices have fostered bass fisheries within the upper one-third of the United States that rival famed waters to the south. A natural by-product of the improved resource is an expansion in wintertime bass fishing.

Like muskies, another temperate species gaining patronage from ice fishermen, largemouth, or black bass, aren't custom made for cold-water environs. Their physiology is best suited for warm water and longer growing seasons, but bass, being highly adaptable, can prosper in any oxygenated water, regardless of temperature. Think of winter-time largemouths as a theoretical crossbreed between a sunfish and a northern pike. Biologically speaking, largemouth bass are the largest members of the sunfish family. Similar to panfish, the winter season also sees bass schooling or grouping in specific areas. Forage selection and habitat preference are what link hardwater bass to pike; both species prey on baitfish and panfish. Remaining weed growth makes a fine residence for both toothypike and bucketmouth bass.

Another largemouth bass trait, which parallels muskies, is their peak and off-peak schedule. Bass, like muskies, fatten up in the fall, readying for a wintry furlough. Waning metabolism and drive to pursue baitfish increasingly affect behavior during winter's course. The logical solution is to take advantage of the early ice period, which is essentially the end of the fall flurry. Anglers catch some of the year's biggest bass during ice fishing's first few weeks.

Again referencing muskies, select a bass fishing destination by sheer numbers. That is, because you're after a species of fish that is inauspicious to cold water, it's necessary to have a large population at your disposal; it's a numbers game. The best bodies of water feature large-mouth bass as the forerunning predator, or at least a major contender. Resources such as bait and tackle stores and fisheries can lead you to ideal venues.

Winter Largemouth Bass Location

Bass grow apathetic and cluster into tight communities beneath the ice as water temperatures plummet. Ultimately, what you've got is a fantastic opportunity to locate large numbers of fish in finite but criteria-specific zones. The leading locations to investigate are weedy or timber-filled bays, be they big or small, and found on lakes, reservoirs, or rivers. Such offshoots act as independent ecosystems of the main body of water, and wintertime bass find them appealing. The

The Griz ices yet another early winter bucketmouth. At first ice, the Griz focuses on weedy bays on lakes renowned for their largemouth bass. Put the odds in your favor by choosing a body of water containing high numbers of bass.

effectiveness of a particular bay depends on abundance of structure, cover, food, and overall depth. For instance, a heavily weeded or timbered bay hosts more bass than a more desolate version. Likewise, a bay offering mixed depth ranges and plenty of acreage beyond the outside weededge is far more inviting than a monodepth bowl.

Bays are of special interest at first ice and last ice. At first ice, before oxygenation becomes an issue, weeds are still up, shallow-water forage is plentiful, and bucketmouths find comfortable residency in only four, five, and six feet of water. As winter develops, bass settle into a bay's deeper reaches, the mouth area, and out into the main lake. At last ice, as bass begin staging outside spawning areas, bays again enter the fray; fertile, shallow bays are favored breeding grounds.

Let's look further into submerged weeds and how they relate to wintertime bass location. In essence, you can break the weed matter down to three primary components: inside edge and ultrashallow growth, middepth weed flats, and the outside weedline. Winter prompts an inside-out movement. First ice finds active bass patrolling the inside edge of lush, shallow weeds as well as hunkering amid standing vegetation over middepth flats. By midwinter, after most foliage has perished, largemouth bass slip out to remaining growth along the outside weededge, eventually pushing beyond the weedline in search of baitfish, offshore structure, and better oxygenated waters.

Obviously, this capsulated peek at the weed-bass relationship paints with broad strokes. Several environmental factors will modify this basic theory. For instance, on extremely clear and deep-water lakes, bass immediately cling to the outside weededge at first ice. Heightened sunlight penetration and skittishness to noise often keeps fish from inhabiting shallower weed zones. A bonus to locating active bass on such bodies of water is that the outside weededge remains intact throughout, or for most of the winter.

Inversely, shallow lakes with stained water maintain bass throughout the vegetated range. For example, imagine that a lake's outside weedline ceases at only eight feet of water. During the early ice period, you can expect to find bass working the entire region from eight feet right up to shore. The predicament with stained water is that thickening ice and building snow cover quickly erase submerged weeds, hence pressing bass into the basin. In short, shallow, stained-water lakes are reserved for first ice action, saving deeper, clearer venues for midwinter use. Stained and shallow waters reenter the picture at last ice. You can also find additional and relevant weed information in the walleye, northern pike, and panfish chapters.

In reservoirs and rivers, weeds, for the most part, are substituted with submerged timber. Wood provides protective cover, ambush points, and a feeding station. Sound familiar, kind of weedlike? The beauty of underwater wood is that, unlike greenery, wood doesn't wither and die when Old Man Winter hits the freeze button.

What distinguishes good wood from bad wood is a function of relative abundance. For example, an isolated clump of timber, standing or laying in shallow to middepths, will certainly attract largemouth bass. The less available wood is, the more attractive even a presumably insignificant patch becomes. A couple downed trees resting on an otherwise featureless sand flat is a worthy structural element. An opposite situation is where a shoreline or creek channel is fully lined with sunken brush and timber, which rambles on for great distances. It's time to draw distinctions. Consider the following:

- Where is the deepest timber?
- Are there any openings or cuts in the sunken forest?
- Is there a clear outside edge?
- Is there an inside edge?
- Is there a timber-covered hump or freestanding clump of trees nearby?
- Are there transitions from branches and brush to larger logs?

If the answer to any of these questions is yes, you've located a probable largemouth haunt.

A row of standing timber is to a reservoir or river what cattails and bulrushes are to a lake. Both timber and emergent vegetation provide a fixed cruising lane as well as a tuck-under garage for ambushing careless prey. Historically, shoreline cattails and bulrushes yield large-mouth bass during the early ice period, and offshore bulrush islands pick up the slack as winter progresses. Anytime cattails, bulrushes, or timber form a shoreline point, you've got something distinctive.

As slow as a midwinter bite can be, the late ice period has the capacity to churn out mega bass. Having said that, in many regions large-mouth bass season closes by mid- to late winter to protect prespawn fish—a noble cause. However, if you're able to legally track late ice bucketmouths, it's worth the effort. Huge bass swim back into or just outside favored spawning zones (i.e., shallow bays, shoreline timber, and weedy shorelines) and commence feeding. Please practice conservation by quickly releasing fish caught during this volatile period.

How to Ice Winter Largemouth Bass

The Tools and Techniques. Luckily for you, a comprehensive winter-time bass approach consists of elements already covered in the walleye and northern pike chapters. A mixture of jigging and tip-up strategies hooks just about any wintertime bass happened upon. During the cold-water months, as established, bass aren't on top of their game. Largemouths feed less frequently and prefer not to chase forage.

They're looking for an easy meal of small panfish or resident baitfish. Remember jigging? You know, that universally accepted method designed to imitate fleeing or injured baitfish? Ice fishing's leading technique enters the fold once again.

The bulk of wintertime bass fishing takes place in depths less than 20 feet, and usually under 15 feet. Combine this fact with a bass' physically oversized pie hole and propensity to react to flash and motion, and there's a demand for swimming jigs and wide-flashing spoons, both of which I characterized in the walleye chapter. A swimming jig and whole chub or shiner minnow is a menacing package. The dancing and spiraling motion of a Northland Mini-Air-Plane Jig or System Tackle by Lindy Little Joe Flyer is truly tantalizing. There's your horizontal approach; now you need a vertical option. The broad body of a Northland Fire-Eye Minnow or Luhr-Jensen Crippled Herring provide all the flash and profile a bucketmouth craves; tip each with a stocky shiner head. Whether conditions call for swimming jigs or wide-flash spoons, both regarded as aggressive presentations, choose metallic minnowlike finishes or bright sunfish imitations.

Consider using soft plastics and pork rind when dressing swimming jigs or vertical spoons. Warm-water bass anglers regularly pitch,

A jigging spoon teamed with a soft plastic tail can do wonders on wintertime bass. This Luhr-Jensen Crippled Herring and Berkley Power Grub are especially deadly.

toss, flip, and throw soft plastic lures, hard lures tipped with plastics, and hard lures dressed with pork rind. What about wintertime use? Thread on a colorful slice of Uncle Josh pork rind to a swimming jig, or take a two-inch twister-type grub body and hang it from a vertical jigging spoon. The Berkley Power Bait stuff works great.

Next, fuse your jigging tactic with a strategically placed field of tip-ups. A whole, live minnow and tip-up positioned away, but within range of jigging holes, is an effective approach for taking any game fish species, largemouth bass included.

The same Arctic Fisherman and HT Enterprises Polar Tip-Ups recommended throughout this book perform admirably on bucketmouths. Hook, line, and live bait selection are areas for specialization. The voluminous mouth of a black bass requires using bigger hooks than you'd tie on for walleyes and perch. Wide-gap or kahle-type hooks in sizes #4, #2, and #1 meet the demand. Spend the money and rely on quality products from VMC, Gamakatsu, Owner, and Mustad.

Nylon line is permissible as leader material because the relatively fine teeth of bass won't slice like the choppers on a pike or walleye. Fasten an 18- to 24-inch section of 8- to 14-pound test line to your tip-up line; barrel swivels provide fine connections.

Purchasing live bait for wintertime bass is simple: shiners, shiners, and more shiners. Dick "the Griz" Gryzwinski, a celebrated fishing guide, proved to me one afternoon that above all else, largemouth bass have a weakness for shiner minnows. We fished a bay on a particular Twin Cities lake and proceeded to catch and release between 15 and 20 largemouth bass without touching a single snaky northern. The Griz swore that, if we'd offered suckers rather than shiners, pike were inevitable. Now don't take this brief testimony as a guarantee that by using shiner minnows you'll only hook bass, but I can say most of my hardwater bass have fallen victim to shiner minnows; red-tail and rainbow chubs make plausible substitutes.

Smallmouth Bass

Bronzebacks Beneath the Ice.   If largemouth bass aren't a chosen species of ice fishermen, smallmouth bass receive even less attention. There is a handful of freshwater fish that ostensibly disappear when winter comes; smallies are one of them. However, as with largemouths, if you're sitting on a little honey hole, winter smallmouth bass are attainable.

Slack-water pockets beneath dams are classic holding areas for wintertime smallmouth bass. Current keeps ice conditions in flux, so pay close attention to where you're walking.

Population density is paramount to success. Don't waste your time targeting smallmouth bass on waters where their status is secondary, or worse, accidental. Choose a lake, reservoir, or river that abounds with bronzebacks, waters where competing species such as walleyes and northern pike play second fiddle. Again, bait stores, fisheries, agents, and resort owners, are excellent sources of information.

Winter Smallmouth Bass Location

A common thread among fish that prefer warm water to cold water is their inclination to dive deep as temperatures drop. A biological predisposition dramatically lowers the metabolism of smallmouth bass, and in an effort to subsist in comfortable and well-oxygenated waters, they must descend.

Even at first ice, the most reliable smallmouth haunts run deep. The key is finding deep water adjacent to classic smallmouth bass structure. Let's begin with rocks, a smallmouth bass' favorite structural element.

Rock Structures

The first places to explore are rocky shoreline points and connecting rocky bars. Whether you're fishing a lake, reservoir, or river, stony jettisons extending into deep water are prime candidates. Anticipate finding smallies sitting at the base of rocks, where boulders greet a deep flat or basin. Hugging close to the bottom, cold-water smallmouth bass prefer transition zones where rocks fade into sand or marl.

Offshore rocky reefs are next in line. Again, seek the base (transition). As usual, rock piles nearest other structure are even more appealing, other structure being points, bars, and so on. Here are a few additional rock-relating notions to consider: First, structures composed of large rocks seem to harbor more and larger bass. Second, smallies fancy steep rock ledges over gradually tapering formations. Last, there's apparently no such thing as too deep when smallmouth bass plunge for the winter months. It's possible to find hardwater bass lingering in 40, 50, 60 feet, or more, rocks or no rocks.

In lakes, rocks rank higher than timber, but in many river systems and reservoirs, rocky habitat is scarce. In such an event, track down the deepest wood available. Deep, submerged timber appears in the form of the flooded outside edge of a tree line, a wooded and submerged offshore island, or former creek channel inside a reservoir. Sunken wood provides cover, ambush points, and even a current break. As stated previously, focus on the transition, in this case where timber ends and touches the basin or main channel.

If your smallmouth destination is a river, the first place to seek is a man-made dam. Areas below dams routinely present deep slack-water areas, and there you'll encounter wintertime smallies. Once more, locate the deepest water, and do be careful of suspect ice conditions.

How to Ice Winter Smallmouth Bass

The Tools and Techniques.   Our previously detailed arsenal of walleye and largemouth bass gear and tackle certainly satisfies a smallmouth's demands. Regarding lure selection, choose from the swimming jig

218

and heavy-pounding spoon categories. Deep water or current requires using hefty lures that can efficiently reach the bottom and combat moving water.

Smallmouth bass are minnow eaters; additionally, they crave crayfish (crawdads). This information is undoubtedly a clue for picking colors and patterns. Consider tying on metallic models (minnow-looking) and crayfish patterns, something with splashes of orange, brown, and yellow. Rod, reel, line, and bait selection, as well as jigging patterns, are comparable to what a winter walleye fisherman has and does, so you should be in good shape.

White Bass

Nasty Little Predators. They look as harmless as a crappie lying in the palm of your hand, but don't be fooled. When schooled, white bass behave much like plundering piranhas. Have you ever witnessed a hoard of white bass massacre innocent gizzard shad? The telltale rippling explosion of fleeing baitfish is the signature of a white bass assault. This menacing behavior is associated with a warm-water atmosphere, but white bass do maintain some ferocity through the winter months.

White bass distribution flanks major river systems. Large rivers such as the Mississippi harbor substantial white bass populations; as well, its backwaters, adjacent lakes, and even nearby bodies of water (formerly connected or assimilated via flooding) potentially contain white bass.

Like most species, first ice and last ice provide the foremost windows to nab wintertime white bass. Plan to engage silvers on classic river and reservoir structure. Look for deep lazy-current river sections, immense points with deep-water access, a deep-river channel within a reservoir, narrows or bottlenecks between two large sections of water, slack-water pockets beneath dams, and various depths surrounding feeder creeks. Creek inlets and primary channels take center stage during last ice as white bass arrive in preparation to spawn.

White bass are notorious for using the entire column of water, regardless of overall depth. At midwinter, when silvers are the least active, it's common to find fish bellying up to the bottom in 20, 30, 40 feet of water, or more. Conversely, white bass inhabiting these same depths might cruise 10, 20, or 30 feet above the bottom during

219

Many river systems and scattered prairie-type lakes contain the wily white bass. When engaged, these communal carnivores unleash pure fury.

peak feeding periods. A flasher is paramount for locating white bass in deep water.

Presentation is a matter of applying a fundamental panfish strategy, aside from possibly upsizing lures a tad. White bass, chiefly minnow eaters, easily fall prey to small jigging spoons and swimming jigs tipped with crappie minnows or small fatheads. Summertime enthusiasts typically employ whites and silvers, and these carnivorous colors also apply to ice fishing.

Catfish

The Dog Days of Winter? Here we go again—another critter that's characterized as a summer-only catch. I've got news for you, wintertime catfish are alive, well, and looking to score a meal. It's unfair to say that winter provides the year's greatest catfishing opportunity, because it doesn't, but likewise, catfish aren't bears (you know, the hibernation thing). These fine whiskered friends forage throughout the winter season, albeit not as aggressively as they do under the stars on hot and humid July nights.

Like smallmouth bass, catfish move to deep, calm, and secluded dwellings. Like walleyes, catfish invigorate during low-light periods and seem to be at their best after the sun settles. Hardwater catfish anglers have the luxury of not agonizing about when they punch out from work, because that brief but magical interval at dusk merely marks the initiation of feeding time. You've got plenty of time to pick up bait, snacks, Uncle Eddie, and some cold beverages.

Winter Catfish Location

Catfish are one of North America's most widely distributed and environmentally adaptable creatures. In the upper states, catfish inhabit rivers, lakes, reservoirs, and even farm ponds. Point being, more than likely, there's a hardwater catfish experience waiting near your home.

River Habitats

The foremost winter catfish habitat consists of a river system that winds through a chain of lakes while cutting a distinct channel along the way. Such a setting grants catfish favorable river areas to patron during the summer and current-free holes in the lake to cluster in as temperatures fall.

Begin your catfish quest by navigating the river channel on a map. Identify any holes or pockets along the way and prioritize them in descending order from biggest and deepest on down. Next, look for holes, eddies, and bends along the river itself. These comparatively warm, deep, and typically soft-bottomed places are catfish magnets.

A third option is to locate slack-water holes beneath man-made dams. Often, the largest catfish a river has to offer loiter below dams. Be cautious of questionable ice conditions.

As ice thickens to seven or eight inches, ATVs join the battle. I do not guarantee any ice thickness to be safe, but only offer the framework from whence I operate.

Accolades go out to the fellow who engineered the first ATV (all-terrain vehicle); their presence has changed the face of ice fishing forever. If memory serves me, the original ATV was a Honda product, which offered three wheels of travel. Since that time Polaris, Yamaha, Kawasaki, Arctic Cat, and Ski-Doo have joined rivals at Honda in deluging the marketplace with more stable and sophisticated four-wheelers.

ATVs have taken on the role of ice fishing's workhorses. They're able to transport, pull, and push 99 percent of the equipment used on the ice. The 1 percent refers to giant permanent fish houses, which call for pickup truck torque. Speaking of torque, I'm going to pretend that you are interested in buying an ATV and have approached me for suggestions, pulling power included. The question and answer session might go something like this:

Q: What are a few fundamental features to look for in an ATV?

A: Automatic transmission, ample ground clearance, four-wheel drive, shaft or direct drive, quality suspension such as a MacPherson system, high capacity fuel tank, pulling power, storage, windshield, and equipment-carrying racks are all features to look for.

Q: Why is ground clearance a consideration?

A: Most four-wheel drive ATVs have minimal difficulty plowing through 6, 8, and even 10 inches of snow, but once the wintry blanket deepens and drifts form, units offering greater ground clearance perform better—11 inches is considered exceptional ground clearance.

Q: What is a reasonable amount of pulling power, and why is pulling power so important?

A: To answer your second question first, more pulling power means being able to drag more gear around. It's good to know

222

that if you linked up a couple flip-over houses and a carrying sled together your ATV could meet the task. As for a number, typical ATVs offer about 800 pounds of pulling capacity, and bigger units, such as a Polaris Sportsman 500 or Yamaha Kodiak 600, give in excess of 1,000 pounds.

Q: Most ATVs seem to come with front and rear racks, but what else can I do to dress up a unit for ice fishing?

A: First, throw in a windshield because there's nothing worse than a frostbitten nose and watering eyes; lakes are wide open and windswept. Next, companies such as Ryan's ATV Racks in Lindstrom, Minnesota, manufacture exceptional after-market ATV accessories. Check out their Hand-E-Hauler Racks with auger holder and portable fish house carrier. A set of chains gives even the strongest four-wheel drive a little oomph, and don't forget to install a trailer hitch that matches your intended portable fish house, trailer, or carrying sled.

Often, ice fishermen customize ATVs in their garages rather than at a dealership. This rugged Polaris ATV has been fitted with a homemade wood front rack and auger bracket, rear storage compartments, tire chains, and a windshield.

How to Ice Winter Catfish

The Tools and Techniques. The stereotypical catfish bait is both stationary and rancid. We've all seen shore-bound anglers launch hooks wadded with chicken livers, commercial stink baits, or dead minnows, then lay back on the riverbank and catch some Zs. Oddly enough, most of my lifetime catfish catches (open water) have come via crank baits and jigs, two dynamic presentations. Obviously, you can rule out crank baits and aggressive jigging methods for hardwater cats. Common sense says that by introducing cold water into the catfish equation, you should minimize movement, but I still open with a jigging approach.

For winter cats, employ what I call soft jigging. The process is essentially a slowed rendition of the traditional lift and fall sequence; avoid sharp jerks. Cold-water catfish locate food by smell, feel, and to some degree, sight. A gently rising and lowering jig or spoon provides enough movement, emits an enticing aroma when teamed with cut bait, and is easily hit.

As for lure types, traditional horizontally hung jig heads and lead swimming jigs do an outstanding job. Try reverse hooking a live fathead or shiner so the minnow faces away from the lure's head—a great presentation for daytime use. Once daylight fades, switch to dead bait. Reverse hook a cut minnow (slit the belly); odor emanating from expired bait is potent under darkness. Speaking of lightlessness, glow-in-the-dark jig heads come highly recommended.

Rod, reel, and line selection is kindred to your walleye arsenal, the heavier stuff. A sturdy but sensitive graphite or glass rod (24 inches plus), smooth delivering spinning or baitcast reel, and freshly spooled 8- to 12-pound test nylon or fluorocarbon line is in order. You can upgrade line strength while jigging in dark water or if big, flabby cats are present.

As expected, I endorse mixing in a few tip-ups while jigging. This is the juncture where warm-weather bank fishing and hardwater catfishing cross paths. Rig half your tip-ups with single-hook live minnows and the other with dead bait. The dead bait division also includes such favorites as chicken liver and commercial stink bait. Set live minnows no more than six inches from the bottom and dead bait either right on or just off the lake floor. Catfish are notorious for holding tight, but watch your electronics for suspended fish.

Whitefish and Tullibee

Stinky Yet Tasty.   There's a sizable group of fellows out there who view the cold-weather months as bucket-loading season, that's buckets of whitefish. These overblown minnow-looking critters roam the basins of large, deep, and generally clear waters, and once caught, unless released, whitefish are destined for the smoker.

I want to make a distinction between two species of whitefish, which are often mistaken for one another: the lake whitefish and tullibee (cisco). You can easily distinguish these two most commonly caught members of the whitefish family. You can recognize lake whitefish, the larger of the two, frequently reaching over three pounds, by a large snout that overhangs their mouths. Tullibee, a slimmer and typically smaller whitefish member, exhibit mouthparts that extend beyond its nostrils; tullibee are also more widespread.

Large whitefish are often bonus catches while pursuing deep-water walleyes, perch, and lake trout. These overgrown baitfish are best known for their battling skills and flavor after spending time over hickory chips.

Besides being prized by winter anglers, the greater role of white-fish is as a food source. Unequivocally, lakes and reservoirs sporting healthy populations of tullibee or whitefish raise the biggest wall-eyes, muskies, northern pike, and smallmouth bass. Whitefish gain favor from ice anglers because of their biological propensity to acti-vate in cold conditions; catches of lake whitefish and tullibee are rare from a boat.

Where does an ice fisherman find whitefish? Deep. Search for tullibee and whitefish over deep flats, deep bars, deep points and reefs, and the main basin. Like perch, whitefish are nomadic, but significant structural elements such as bars and reefs do offer useable reference points, and the idea of being too deep is seldom uttered on the ice.

Although whitefish get hooked all winter, their finest moments ar-rive during winter's final few weeks. This is when whitefish turn ag-gressive and crowd into deep holes. Often suspended, schools criss-cross the landscape pursuing small baitfish and willingly inhaling zooplankton along the way; their diet is similar to a crappie's.

Even their physically pe-tite mouths don't stand in the way when vora-cious tullibees encoun-ter a jigging spoon.

226

Deep-water panfish tactics, discussed previously, effectively put whitefish on the ice. Larger and heavier versions of the Fat Boy (System Tackle by Lindy Little Joe), Demon from Custom Jigs & Spins, and similar lures suffice. Once located, hardwater whitefish are less finicky than sunfish or crappies and readily accept a plethora of panfish-type lures.

Small vertical jigging spoons work well as search lures or when engaging large and hostile whitefish; 1/16-ounce and 1/8-ounce spoons in blue, silver, and white are traditional favorites. Tip each with maggots, wax worms, or a small minnow head—experiment.

Concerning technique, simply choose from your lexicon of panfish jigging methods; again, whitefish rarely deny tiny-baited lures. Having said that, neutral to inactive whitefish periodically verge upon lures, nose up to them, but don't strike. Flashers such as a Vexilar FL-8 indicate this action with red bars that instantaneously merge with your lure's established mark, but no impact. Whitefish like to chase. They habitually follow a swiftly raised lure; quivering it in place can stimulate a strike. If they chase but don't attack, quickly drop it down and pound again; repeat this process a few times. Sheer competitive nature will induce at least one fish to step up and smack it.

Eelpout

Dregs of the Underwater World. Only a mother could love them. Nature is a beautiful thing, but let's be serious, these are not. Eelpout, also known as burbot, lawyer, ling, and freshwater cod are commonly considered trash fish by winter anglers, but honestly, they deserve far greater respect. Buried beneath their outer hideousness is a strong fighter that carries tastier meat than you might think.

Eelpout were created for life beneath the ice. Like whitefish, eelpout flourish in cold water and ostensibly enter dormancy during the summer months. They're also middle of the night fish; these nocturnal beasts achieve peak feeding mode long after sunset.

Where do pout prosper? Big water. These bottom-hugging brutes thrive in large lakes featuring vast basins. The Great Lakes and Lake of the Woods maintain possibly the largest numbers of eelpout, in addition to some awfully big specimens. Serpentine 2- and 3-pound eelpout are accidentally hooked by walleye partisans, but with a little

Slimy skin and a tendency to wrap around an unwitting angler's arm compliment the heinous silhouette of an eelpout. All nastiness aside, eelpout are noble fighters and palatable to some.

effort, it's possible to track down 10-, 12-, and even 15-pound pout, which provide a true battle.

Specifically, on lakes containing both walleyes and eelpout, you'll find pout inhabiting classic walleye structure. Eelpout relate to bars, points, flats, and reefs. Offshore rock piles historically maintain the greatest populations, and eelpout are no strangers to exceedingly deep water. A lake's biggest eelpout tend to roam the deepest water.

Eelpout not only feed like walleyes, but also accept comparable offerings. Standard walleye jigging and setline techniques reign effective. Anglers aiming to specialize a trifle should opt for a glow lime-green jig head teamed with an oversized fathead or chub. Phosphorescent paint is enormously effective in the deep, dark lair of an eelpout.

Anytime a fish reaches such gluttonous proportions, it's something to behold. This large eelpout tipped the scales at over 16 pounds, and it was accompanied by a dozen other pout weighing over 10 pounds apiece.

A Final Thought

What I dub hardwater exotics are simply catchable, but less-pressured and recognized freshwater fish species. Hardwater exotics are divided into two categories: warm-water fish and cold-water fish. The warm-water crowd includes largemouth bass, smallmouth bass, white bass, and catfish. On the cooler side are whitefish, tullibee, and eelpout. All of these species play a role in our beloved winter sport.

Part III

Having Fun On Hardwater

Chapter 10

Fishing Competitions

I BELIEVE IT WAS COMEDIAN GEORGE CARLIN WHO PRO-
FESSED THAT, FOR AN ACTIVITY TO QUALIFY AS A SPORT, A
BALL NEEDED TO BE IN PLAY. Therefore, according to Carlin's
logic, baseball is a sport but fencing is not. Football is a sport
but fishing is not. Wait a minute, that's like saying that auto
racing isn't a sport—possibly not the best example because
many folks believe auto racing is just driving real fast.

The point I'm trying to convey is that, from an athletic standpoint, ice fishing is suspect. In fact, the fictitious but stereotypical ice fisherman carries a few extra inches around the
midriff, considers canned beer a food group, and rarely wan-
ders far from an overturned five-gallon bucket. From the onset, I've endeavored to dispel this cliche by drawing a mental
picture of the modern ice angler, who is hardly an athlete, but
certainly not a mindless couch potato.

Athletic competitions are the ultimate meter of one's com-
mand of a sport. Boxers train for weeks and even months for a
bout or prizefight. Baseball players shag grounders and take
BP (batting practice) preparing for every ball game. Fishermen

also have opportunity to prove their skills against others in tournaments and contests.

What's the difference between a fishing tournament and a contest? Typically, tournaments are open to a fixed number of anglers, and entry fees range quite high. Many tournaments are on an invitation-only basis. Contests offer open enrollments. Possibly the greatest distinction is that characteristically, tournaments feature an elite group of species-specific anglers, and contest participants are anglers possessing wide-ranging skills. It's also common for contest anglers to vie for winning catches in several species categories.

The most popular freshwater fish species find themselves the targets of both open-water tournaments and contests. Open-water largemouth bass and walleyes, for instance, are pursued at a professional level in which known fishermen contend for tremendous amounts of cash and prizes. Unfortunately for the serious and competitive ice fisherman, high-profile hardwater tournaments are scarce. However, what ice fishing lacks in tournaments it makes up for in contests.

Hardwater contests are common in the heart of ice-fishing country. Lions Clubs, VFWs, Jaycees, and other charitable organizations host ice-fishing competitions, and privately operated contests also exist. Contest sizes range from neighborhood affairs, where only a hundred people participate, to lavish media events drawing thousands of anglers.

The format for an ice-fishing competition includes a set number of holes predrilled within a designated section of a lake. Following a shotgun start, anglers have an established amount of time to fish these holes for categorized fish species. At the conclusion, cash and prizes are awarded for winning catches. Depending on the contest's magnitude, cash can mean a blazing $10,000 or a respectable $100. Prizes range from grocery gift certificates to trucks, boats, and snowmobiles.

Most fishermen approach winter competitions anticipating taking home some booty, but equal to their desire for material rewards is a pursuit of merriment. Groups, both large and small, indulge in the picnic-like atmosphere surrounding ice-fishing competitions.

An illustrative scene exhibits a family of anglers anxiously huddled over holes while bratwursts simmer on a nearby grill. Another cluster of fishermen, being old college buddies, exchange wisecracks while jigging and sipping hot adult beverages. Then you've got a couple hard-core contestants busy jumping from hole to hole—these folks are serious. Armed with the latest in electronics and gear, they hit the ice with full intention of collecting a check.

So what can a competitor do to increase his or her chances of reigning victorious? For openers, it's best to enter fishing contests hosted on lakes that you're familiar with; this is a significant advantage for obvious reasons. On strange waters, having a detailed lake map reveals classic structure such as humps, breaks, and bars, but first learn from contest organizers or local bait shops on what section of a lake they will hold the event. Apply this knowledge to a lake map, and chart potential fish structure. By arriving at the contest early, your odds of getting to prime locations before other entrants are greatly improved. Often anglers catch winning fish during the first hour of a timed event.

The generous format of many ice fishing contests makes just about everything that swims a potential winner. Cash and prizes are awarded for early entries, fish registered in certain numerical order, as well as winning weights.

Snowmobiles

Snowmobiles, or sleds, as they're commonly known, were designed for trekking across snow. A pair of steerable skis, driven by a forceful tanklike track, combine to propel the greatest form of winter travel.

Pretend you're preparing to shop for a snowmobile for ice fishing:

Q: Are all snowmobiles created equal? What are the essential features to look for?

A: There's a wide range of snowmobiles on the market both new and used. It pays to enter the market with established criteria, although you should certainly weigh any suggestions snowmobile dealers and other ice fishermen make. Fundamental features to look for are a long and wide track, high fuel capacity, reverse gear, hand or thumb warmers, mirrors, a high windshield, an engine in the 500cc or greater range with high and low gears, two-up seating, underseat storage, rear cargo rack, and a trailer hitch.

Q: Why a long and wide track?

A: Long tracks, such as the industry-leading 156 inches, provide a smooth-riding, yet powerful driving and pulling force. The gumption of a long track, with a wide track's stability, better accommodates two riders, such as in a two-up touring-type sled (20 inches is wide by today's standards). However, in extremely deep and powdery snow a short, narrow track yields a better burst. A track with one- to two-inch rubber lugs affords greater digging force, and metal studs, where legal, really get things done on ice.

Q: Why mirrors?

A: When you're pulling cargo, it's good to make sure your house is in order. Mirrors also lend a hand while running in reverse. Speaking of reverse gear, you'll be glad you have it when you relocate a permanent shelter or portable fish house and you want to back up and connect.

Q: What does having both high and low gears offer an ice fisherman?

A: High gear is the equivalent of normal range. It's for everyday riding and light pulling. Low gear gives you four-wheel drive capabilities for getting unstuck and dragging serious loads.

Q: Are there any specific makes and models to favor?

A: Polaris, Arctic Cat, Ski-Doo, and Yamaha all build fantastic sleds. Big touring sleds, which all four manufacturers market, are fantastic ice-fishing machines; they're comfortable to ride, powerful, spacious, and offer ample storage. Work, or utility, sleds, such as the Ski-Doo Skandic series, make rugged ice-fishing tools, but they're certainly not the leading choice for recreational riding. All things considered, a 500cc touring sled with a long and wide track is the best all-around design. Larger, heavier sleds can be difficult to move in freezing slush or exceptionally deep snow.

Groups of anglers use Bombardiers and customized trucks with tracks to travel to remote fishing locations. These spacious and comfortable vehicles are commonplace on big waters such as Lake of the Woods.

Fishing with an organized group of pals or family members further increases your advantage. Before taking to the water, arrange to split cash awards among members, and discuss buyout possibilities if you receive product prizes. Once fishing, spread out to various locations inside the contest boundaries and have members rig for different fish species, because you never know what will be biting strong on event day.

Targeting big fish is another edge. Although formats vary from event to event, you can't go wrong hooking a beefy northern pike, walleye, trout, or eelpout. Either top honors or other favorable placement befall an angler who weighs in the largest fish overall. Aiming for big fish often means going with large lures or bulky minnows. Big fish tend to range deep, so choose deep breaks or structure adjacent to deep water.

Additionally, it's important to address the consequences of angling pressure. With hundreds and possibly thousands of human feet pounding above, you can guess that fish will be out of their element. Excessive commotion drives fish deeper and away from the hullabaloo.

The sight of thousands of hopeful anglers jigging and partying at a single frozen location is truly astounding.

Avoid heavily fished areas within the contest perimeter even if that means finding unorthodox zones. Attack prime structure early and move away if surrounded by other participants.

Ice-fishing contests provide a pressure-free environment to test your ice-fishing skills while spending time with family and friends. There's nothing wrong with aspirations of entering the winner's circle, but with only nominal entry fees on the line, ice-fishing competitions are chiefly intended for jollity.

A Final Thought

There are basic differences between fishing tournaments and contests. Tournaments are as follows:

- They are usually open to a fixed number of anglers.
- They have higher entry fees than contests.
- They are sometimes held on an invitation-only basis.
- They feature an elite group of species-specific anglers.

Contests are as follows:

- They offer open enrollments.
- They include participants possessing wide-ranging skills.

Chapter 11

Catch and Release, and Sometimes Cooking

IT MAY SEEM ODD TO FIND RECIPES IN A CHAPTER FUNDAMENTALLY DEVOTED TO CONSERVATION, BUT TAKING A FEW FISH EVERY NOW AND THEN ISN'T SINFUL. In fact, battered fish fillets are well-deserved rewards for the time, energy, and money you exhaust pursuing hardwater catches.

Having said that, conservation and ethics are no longer fringe characteristics a select group of fishermen exhibit. The number of anglers who now favor releasing quarry demonstrates the conservation element of ice fishing. Angler-sponsored catch-and-release practices are increasingly responsible for salvaging and improving countless fisheries.

Ethics encompasses not only how winter anglers treat game, but also how they handle themselves on the ice. Over the decades, ice fishermen became stereotyped as beer-swilling savages that cared more about achieving a good buzz than the state of the environment. Supporting the typecast, many of these folks left piles of cigarette butts, scattered cans, and discarded fishing line on the ice. Fortunately, the modern ice fisherman is more inclined to pick up someone else's mess than leave one, and the number of litterbugs who fish has dwindled.

Fish released through the ice have a higher rate of survival than any other time of the year. Why? Cold water's inherent mellowing capability lowers overall stress on fish. Here's what you can do to bolster successful releases:

1. Quickly get fish back into the water.

2. Handle fish as little as possible; overhandling removes their protective skin coating.

3. Do not attempt to pry out deeply hooked lures; instead, cut the line as close to the lure as possible and release the fish. A fish's body chemistry will dissolve the hook point and free the lure.

Feel no sorrow for these guys. The outwardly desolate and frigid backdrop is actually the frozen surface of Lake of the Woods. On this balmy winter afternoon a trio of anglers iced more than 60 walleyes and sauger.

4. In deep water, reel fish up slowly, allowing them to adjust to changes in pressurization. Don't plan on releasing many fish, especially small ones, that you pulled through more than 30 feet of water. Favor shallower venues if you're killing small fish in deep water.

5. Following an extended battle, exhausted fish benefit from being oxygenated in the hole before release. Clutch the fish above the tail and gently pump it up and down in the water. The pulsing motion opens its gill flaps and promotes respiration. Continue the procedure until the fish swims away under its own power.

Government agencies also have a hand in promoting fish populations. Fish-stocking programs and management through regulations are the primary means used by fishery agencies and departments of natural resources. From the stocking side, walleyes, northern pike, muskies, and trout have been successfully placed in waters formerly void of such species. Perch, panfish, and largemouth bass are rarely stocked because of their ability to reproduce naturally. Additionally, certain species are stocked into lakes where they're native, thus augmenting populations and offsetting angler harvest.

State and provincial agencies introduce slots, minimums, and special catch-and-release-only designations to further safeguard fisheries. Protective slots mean that you must immediately release fish measuring between two specified lengths. On the flip side, some imposed slots only permit the harvest of fish measuring between specified lengths. Both sets of regulations are carefully crafted to preserve fish that experts deem critical for proliferation. Minimums are typically in place to protect stocked fish and young fish from overharvest. Young fish tend to school tightly and be highly susceptible to angler pressure; therefore their prosperity needs insurance to bring them to breeding age. Catch-and-release-only waters are geared toward generating trophy-class fish and meeting the desires of true sport fishermen.

The following recipes are excerpts from the acclaimed game cookbook, *"Bobber" Anne's Fish-Fowl-Game Recipe Book* from the Gapen Co. The tackle-box-sized cookbook is brimming with everything from basic shore lunch recipes to elaborate culinary masterpieces.*

---

*Recipes reprinted, by permission, from Orth, A. 1994. *Bobber Anne's Recipe Book* is available for $12.95 (plus $3 shipping) at The Gapen Co., 17910 87th Street, Becker, MN, 55308; 612-263-3538.

243

Oven Crispy Panfish

1-1/2 lb. panfish fillets
1 egg
1 tbsp. milk
1/2 tsp. Tabasco sauce

1/2 tsp. salt
1 c. cornflake crumbs
1/4 c. melted butter

Beat together the egg, milk, Tabasco, and salt. Dip panfish fillets into egg mixture; roll in the cornflake crumbs until well coated. Place on greased baking sheet and drizzle with the melted butter. Bake at 375 degrees for 20 minutes or until fish is done. Serve with fresh lemon wedges.

Wood Fire Steamed Trout

2, 3, or 4 trout, 1/2 to 1 lb., cleaned whole
Salt and pepper
Juice of 1 lemon
1/2 c. melted butter
Barbecue sauce (bottled, if available)
6 green willow sticks 1/2 to 1 inch thick, 2 feet long (bark on)
12 birch or hardwood sticks, 1 to 4 inches diameter
2 green logs, 4 feet long, 8 inches in diameter
1 qt. water

Place green logs 16 inches apart and build a fire between them from hardwood. Allow the fire to burn down to red coals; stirring sticks together will help. Place larger willow sticks across logs at 2-inch spacing; then place smaller willow sticks the opposite way at same distance apart. Put butter, salt, and pepper on the gutted and gilled fish, inside and out. Set fish on side (skin on) on small stick platform above coals. Pour small amount of water on fire to create steam. Drip lemon juice and barbecue sauce over cooking fish. Allow to cook a few minutes; turn and repeat water, juice, and sauce. Turn the fish four times, dripping ingredients each time. If fire cools, add short hardwood pieces. It takes about 20 minutes to cook trout. You can cook fish in aluminum foil, if available, for similar results.

Beer Battered Walleye Fillets

1-1/2 lb. thin walleye fillets
Beer batter
Salt and pepper
Cooking oil
1/4 c. lemon juice
Flour seasoned with salt and pepper

Cut fillets into 1- to 1-1/4-inch strips and toss into lemon juice with salt and pepper added. Let mixture stand in the refrigerator for one-half hour. Drain fillets, dredge with seasoned flour, and dip into beer batter. Quickly deep fry in hot oil at 360 degrees for about two minutes. Drain on paper towel and hold in warm oven until all fillets are done.

Mix the following together to make beer batter.

1-1/2 c. stale beer	1/2 c. flour
1 egg, beaten	1/2 c. biscuit mix
Dash of salt	Pepper to taste

A Final Thought

For the most part, catch and release is a preferred practice on the ice. Supplemental stocking and harvest restrictions go further to preserve fish populations. Occasionally, though, you may want to taste the victory, and that's okay, too.

Index

Index

Index

About the Author

Noel Vick is the publisher and editor of *Fish & Game Finder,* a popular outdoor magazine whose companion web site (www.fishandgame.com) is one of the largest outdoor-related sites in North America. He has been running the magazine since 1991 and since that time has propelled the monthly publication to regional prominence. An avid writer who specializes in freshwater fishing in Midwestern states, he has been fishing since he "was able to clutch a fishing pole."

In *Fishing on Ice*, Vick was assisted by contributing writers who are also experts with rod and reel, as well as in their knowledge of what lies beneath the ice. Vick is married and lives in Isanti, Minnesota.

Fly fishing tips from veteran Art Lee

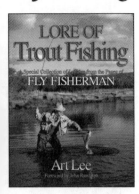

Lore of Trout Fishing puts Art Lee's most valuable lessons, from essays in *Fly Fisherman* magazine, into one comprehensive volume. You'll find detailed information on choosing flies, selecting fishing locations, presenting flies to fish, and countless other tips. The book also contains nearly 200 photographs and illustrations; including an eight-page, full-color insert showing the intricate details of Lee's favorite flies.

Item PLEE0790
ISBN 0-88011-790-7
$26.95 ($39.95 Canadian)

Let Art Lee teach you one of fly fishing's best kept secrets—the Riffling Hitch. Lee explains the art and science of this little-known technique that you can use to land more fish every time you're on the water. Combined with detailed instruction and 73 full-color illustrations and photographs, *Tying and Fishing the Riffling Hitch* is a readable, useful guide—an essential book for any serious angler.

Item PLEE0782
ISBN 0-88011-782-6
$21.95 ($29.95 Canadian)

Whether you're new to fly fishing or you're a veteran angler, *Fishing Dry Flies for Trout on Rivers and Streams* is a must-read. Art Lee, recognized as one of the best fly fishing writers in America, weaves top-notch instruction with insight and wisdom gleaned from a lifetime on the water. This book explains both the essentials and the nuances of fly fishing, fly presentation, casting, and fly tying, and amply covers the often-neglected subject of landing trout.

Item PLEE0777
ISBN 0-88011-777-X
$24.95 ($36.95 Canadian)

To place your order, U.S. customers call toll free:

1-800-747-4457

Customers outside the U.S.:
Place your order using the appropriate
telephone number/address shown in the front of this book.

HUMAN KINETICS
The Premier Publisher for Sports & Fitness
P.O. Box 5076, Champaign, IL 61825-5076

www.humankinetics.com
Prices are subject to change.

2335

9/99

OUTDOOR PURSUITS SERIES

The books in the highly acclaimed Outdoor Pursuits Series emphasize safety, environmental responsibility, and — most of all — the fun of outdoor activity! All of the books feature full-color photos; knowledgeable, well-known authors; excellent instruction on a specific activity; and valuable experiential information.

Canoeing
Item PGUL0443 • ISBN 0-87322-443-4 • $14.95 ($21.95 Canada)

Hiking and Backpacking
Item PSEA0506 • ISBN 0-87322-506-6 • $12.95 ($17.95 Canada)

Kayaking
Item PFOR0688 • ISBN 0-87322-688-7 • $14.95 ($21.95 Canada)

Mountain Biking
Item PDAV0452 • ISBN 0-87322-452-3 • $12.95 ($17.95 Canada)

Orienteering
Item PREN0885 • ISBN 0-87322-885-5 • $14.95 ($20.95 Canada)

Rock Climbing
Item PWAT0814 • ISBN 0-87322-814-6 • $13.95 ($19.95 Canada)

Snowboarding
Item PREI0677 • ISBN 0-87322-677-1 • $13.95 ($19.50 Canada)

Snowshoeing
Item PEDW0767 • ISBN 0-87322-767-0 • $13.95 ($19.50 Canada)

Walking
Item PRUD0668 • ISBN 0-87322-668-2 • $13.95 ($19.95 Canada)

Windsurfing
Item PWIN0760 • ISBN 0-87322-760-3 • $13.95 ($19.50 Canada)

To place your order, U.S. customers call toll free:

1-800-747-4457

Customers outside the U.S.:
Place your order using the appropriate
telephone number/address shown in the front of this book.

HUMAN KINETICS
The Premier Publisher for Sports & Fitness
P.O. Box 5076, Champaign, IL 61825-5076

www.humankinetics.com
Prices are subject to change.